AF280404

Christian Maurer and Hubert J. Siller
(Editors)

ISCONTOUR 2025

Tourism Research Perspectives

Proceedings of the International Student Conference in
Tourism Research

Verlag: BoD · Books on Demand GmbH,

Überseering 33, 22297 Hamburg, bod@bod.de

Druck: Libri Plureos GmbH, Friedensallee 273,

22763 Hamburg

ISBN: 978-3-8192-0831-7

Preface & Acknowledgements

The **12th International Student Conference in Tourism Research** (ISCONTOUR) was successfully held at the campus of the IMC Krems University of Applied Sciences, Austria, from May 12-13, 2025.

The annual ISCONTOUR was collaboratively founded in 2013 by Christian Maurer, Professor at IMC University of Applied Sciences Krems, Austria, and Roman Egger, Professor at Salzburg University of Applied Sciences, Austria. In 2019 the MCI The Entrepreneurial School Innsbruck became the new cooperation partner of IMC University of Applied Sciences Krems.

The aim of ISCONTOUR is to provide international students and graduates of Bachelor, Master and PhD Programmes with a platform where they can present their tourism related research papers based on their approved Bachelor theses, Master theses or work-in-progress PhD theses. In particular, ISCONTOUR strives to encourage students and graduates to engage in academic research and foster the knowledge transfer between academic education institutions and practitioners from the tourism industry.

In total 22 full research papers by 30 authors from 6 countries were submitted to ISCONTOUR 2025. Each submission went through a blind review process with three members of the ISCONTOUR 2025 Research Programme Committee assigned as reviewers. The authors then received the comments of the reviewers and had to revise the papers accordingly. Only papers of authors who adhered to this process were accepted for the conference. As a result, 17 full research papers were accepted for presentation at the conference and are included in these proceedings; unfortunately, four authors withdrew their submissions on short-notice.

The research papers cover a wide variety of topics, ranging from consumer behaviour, tourist experience, marketing, information and communication technologies, destination management, and sustainable tourism management. This does not only indicate the variety of the tourism industry, but also how relevant and impactful applied research projects conducted by students and graduates can be for the further developments in tourism in particular and the society in general. We hope these proceedings will serve as a valuable source of information on applied tourism research for students, scholars and practitioners.

Above all, we want to thank all authors who submitted their papers for the conference. We further appreciate the considerable time invested by all members of the ISCONTOUR 2025 Research Programme Committee who ensured the high quality of the submissions. We are also grateful for the support we receive from the management board, rectorate and colleagues of both the IMC University of Applied Sciences Krems as well as the MCI Innsbruck.

We are also indebted to the conference keynote speakers Roman Egger (CEO of SmartVisions) and Anita Zehrer MCI The Entrepreneurial School Innsbruck) and to the research workshop presenters Anita Zehrer, Cornelia Dlabaja, Mattia Rainoldi, and Markus Eitle.

We hope that ISCONTOUR will continue to establish an international community that motivates more students and graduates to engage in applied research and submit papers to ISCONTOUR 2026.

Christian Maurer & Hubert J. Siller

ISCONTOUR 2025 Conference Chairs

Krems, May 2025

Research Programme Review Committee

ADAMER-König Eva, Joanneum University of Applied Sciences Bad Gleichenberg, Austria

AUBKE Florian, University of Applied Sciences for Management & Communication Vienna, Austria

BAGGIO Rodolfo, Bocconi University Milan, Italy

BINDER Daniel, Joanneum University of Applied Sciences Bad Gleichenberg, Austria

BUHALIS Dimitrios, Bournemouth University, Great Britain

DEL CHIAPPA, Giacomo, University of Sassari, Italy

EBSTER Claus, University of Vienna, Austria

EITLE Markus, IMC University of Applied Sciences Krems, Austria

ENNEN Jens, IMC University of Applied Sciences Krems, Austria

FEDELI Giancarlo, IMC University of Applied Sciences Krems, Austria

GRETZEL Ulrike, University of Southern California, USA

GROTH Aleksander, MCI Innsbruck, Austria

HAGE Roger, IMC University of Applied Sciences Krems, Austria

HUANG Rong, Plymouth University, Great Britain

KASTNER Margit, Vienna University of Economics and Business, Austria

KENNELLY James, Skidmore College, USA

KRUGER Martinette, Tourism Research in Economic Environs and Society, South Africa

LASSNIG Markus, Salzburg Research, Austria

LIEBRICH Andreas, Lucerne University of Applied Sciences and Arts, Switzerland

MAURER Christian, IMC University of Applied Sciences Krems, Austria

MATTEUCCI Xavier, Modul University Vienna, Austria

MCCOLE Dan, Michigan State University, USA

MURPHY Jamie, University of Eastern Finland, Finland

PESONEN Juho, University of Eastern Finland, Finland

PIKKEMAAT Birgit, Institute for Innovative Tourism, Austria

POSCH Arthur, IMC University of Applied Sciences Krems, Austria

PÜHRETMAIR Franz, Kompetenznetzwerk IT zur Förderung der Integration von Menschen mit Behinderungen, Austria

ROMERO ANIA Alberto, Rey Juan Carlos University, Spain

SCHACHNER Max, IMC University of Applied Sciences, Austria

SCHOENBERG Alina, IMC University of Applied Sciences Krems, Austria

SIGALA Marianna, Sheffield Hallam University, Great Britain

STANGL Brigitte, University of Surrey, Great Britain

STECKENBAUER Georg Christian, Deggendorf Institute of Technology, Germany

TISCHLER Stephanie, IMC University of Applied Sciences Krems, Austria

VOLCHEK Katerina, Deggendorf Institute of Technology, Germany

WAIGUNY Martin, IMC University of Applied Sciences Krems, Austria

WEGERER Philipp, MCI Management Center Innsbruck, Austria

ZEHRER Anita, MCI Management Center Innsbruck, Austria

Table of Contents

Examining the Digital Marketing Barriers for Sri Lankan Travel agents through the lens of RACE model

Udanee Samarasinghe
University of Plymouth, United Kingdom
daneesach123@gmail.com

Abstract

Sri Lanka's tourism industry has faced significant setbacks, but digital marketing offers a promising opportunity for SME resilience in the travel sector. This study addresses a research gap by applying the RACE model to identify digital marketing adoption barriers among SME travel agents in Sri Lanka. This research uniquely uses the RACE framework to identify digital marketing barriers faced by SME travel agents in Sri Lanka at each stage of the customer journey. Unlike previous studies that use technological adoption models, this customer-centric approach is unprecedented in existing literature, offering fresh insights and valuable guidance for enhancing digital marketing strategies in the travel industry. Through 25 in-depth interviews, thematic analysis revealed six barriers at the Reach stage, four at the Act stage, and one each at the Convert and Engage stages. This study provides crucial insights for policymakers and industry stakeholders to develop targeted support and training programs, enhancing digital marketing adoption and resilience among SMEs in Sri Lanka's tourism sector.

Keywords: Digital Marketing adoption, SME, travel agents, barriers, RACE model

1. INTRODUCTION

The importance of digitalization is evident in its ability to enhance global visibility. According to the Sri Lanka Tourism Development Authority (SLTDA, 2023), online engagement through digital platforms has led to a 30% increase in international tourist inquiries. Additionally, digital marketing strengthens crisis management by allowing businesses to maintain communication with potential visitors during periods of uncertainty. A study by Huynh et al. (2025) highlights that effective digitalization efforts have increased tourist confidence by 25% in developing regions. Furthermore, integrating digital marketing strategies supports sustainable tourism by promoting eco-friendly travel options and reducing reliance on physical marketing materials, contributing to a more sustainable business model. By offering dependable, real-time communication, digitalization boosts crisis management, helps sustainable tourism, increases globally visibility, improves visitor experience, and empowers local companies (Huynh, Stangl, & Thi Tran, 2025).

The ability of digitization to increase global awareness makes it clear how important it is. The Sri Lanka Tourism Development Authority (SLTDA, 2023) reports that inquiries from foreign tourists have increased by 30% because of online engagement through digital media. Additionally, by enabling companies to stay in touch with prospective customers during uncertain times, digital marketing improves crisis management. According to research by Huynh et al. (2025), successful digitization initiatives have raised tourist confidence in developing nations by 25%. Additionally, by encouraging eco-friendly travel options and lowering dependency on physical marketing materials, including digital marketing methods promotes sustainable tourism and helps create a more sustainable company model.

Understanding the barriers to SME travel agents' adoption of digital marketing is crucial given the growing digitalization of consumer behavior and the revolutionary potential of digital technology in the travel industry (Sharma, Sharma, & Chaudhary, 2020). Travel agents can increase customer relationships, streamline operations, and reach a worldwide audience by utilizing digital marketing techniques including social media marketing, SEO, and content marketing. SMEs in the tourism sector around the world, including Sri Lanka, continue to adopt digital marketing at a low rate despite its many benefits. Limited capital, a lack of understanding reluctance to adapt, and poor infrastructure are some of the main barriers (Abou-Shouk, Lim, & Megicks, 2013; Jones, Borgman, & Ulusoy, 2015; Martins, Salazar, & Inversini, 2015).

The significance of digitization and the challenges associated with its adoption are both highlighted in studies conducted by the Sri Lanka

Tourism Development Authority (SLTDA) (SLTDA, 2023). However, little research has been done on the current digital marketing strategies used by Sri Lankan SME travel firms, thus it is crucial to recognize and successfully handle these issues. Prior research has thoroughly examined the adoption of digital marketing, as well as its perceived advantages and barriers (Abou-Shouk et al., 2012; Chiappa, 2013). Research that has already been done has mostly focused on the wider effects of digital marketing strategies on technological adoption, organizational performance, and the shift from traditional marketing methods to digital platforms (Sharma, Sharma, & Chaudhary, 2020). Researchers have examined topics such how travel agents use the internet, the digital skills needed in the travel industry, and the general advantages of digitization. Understanding how digital marketing is applied at different points in the customer journey, from initial engagement to interactions after a purchase, is still lacking, but (Chiappa, 2013; Abou-Shouk et al., 2012).

The Diffusion of Innovation (DOI), the Unified Theory of Acceptance and Use of Technology (UTAUT), and the Technology Acceptance Model (TAM) are examples of traditional models of technology adoption that provide useful information on the acceptance of technology in general (Venkatesh et al., 2003; Williams et al., 2009). However, these models tend to overlook more general organizational and external factors like trust, perceived risk, and competitive pressures in favor of concentrating exclusively on individual perceptions of technology, stressing perceived usefulness and simplicity of use (Davis, 1989; Venkatesh et al., 2003). Furthermore, TAM and UTAUT are less appropriate for comprehending SME travel agents' adoption of digital marketing since they are primarily employed to analyze customer adoption rather than supply-side perspectives (Dwivedi et al., 2021).

The AIDA (Attention, Interest, Desire, Action) model and other marketing-specific frameworks, on the other hand, concentrate on customer engagement but do not offer a comprehensive view of the continuous nature of digital marketing. A more thorough and flexible framework for this research is provided by the RACE (Reach, Act, Convert, Engage) model, which emphasizes consumer interactions at each step of the marketing funnel (Chaffey et al., 2016). In contrast to conventional adoption models, RACE emphasizes digital interaction across the customer journey while integrating organizational dynamics and external influences. This study attempts to offer a detailed knowledge of how SME travel agents may optimize digital marketing tactics to improve customer engagement and get beyond adoption obstacles by using the RACE model.

This study advances both theoretical and practical knowledge regarding the use of digital marketing by small and medium-sized travel firms. By offering a customer-focused framework that combines supply-side viewpoints with digital interaction dynamics, it theoretically expands on the body of previous literature. The study is also compatible with other studies that look at digitization initiatives in developing nations and how they affect tourism management, like Huynh et al. (2025). Empirically, the study offers insightful information about Sri Lanka's SME tourist industry, a region that is going through major change.

The findings are essential for creating practical strategies that promote the use of digital marketing, assist the expansion and long-term viability of small and medium-sized travel agencies, and help in the overall recovery of Sri Lanka's travel sector. The following research question is the focus of this study, which is based on the information above: What are the barriers that Sri Lankan SME travel agents face when implementing to use digital marketing? By answering this question, the study hopes to pinpoint the elements that support or impede the adoption of digital marketing and offer strategies specific to Sri Lanka's SME Travel sector.

2. LITERATURE REVIEW

Traditional marketing strategies are becoming less effective as the tourism industry shifts to digital interactions (Sharma, Sharma, and Chaudhary, 2020). Businesses must adopt digital marketing to be competitive as more and more tourists use online platforms to research destinations, compare deals, and make reservations. Through convenience and customisation, digital marketing supports local companies, promotes sustainable tourism, and improves the visitor experience (Huynh, Stangl, & Thi Tran, 2025). As demonstrated by the Vietnamese Mekong Delta case, destination marketing companies in developing nations have effectively used digital tools to expand their reach, enhance service quality, and adjust to customer expectations. These examples provide important insights for comparable regions like Sri Lanka.

Despite the potential for expansion and resilience, digital marketing technologies like social media, SEO, and content marketing are still not widely used by small and medium-sized travel agencies, especially in developing nations (Buhalis, 2003; Chaffey & Ellis-Chadwick, 2019). By using inexpensive, focused promotional techniques, small-business travel brokers may be able to compete with larger companies. However, several interconnected issues, such as low levels of digital literacy, budgetary limitations, reluctance to adapt, and insufficient IT infrastructure, hinder their capacity to do so (Alford & Page, 2015; Mehrtens, Cragg, & Mills, 2001). Travel agents' capacity to successfully execute and oversee digital marketing is restricted by a substantial skills gap that has been made worse by a lack of digital literacy and training programs (Molinillo & Japutra, 2017). Numerous theoretical frameworks have been employed to comprehend and tackle these issues. Though fundamental to comprehending technology adoption, conventional models such as the Unified Theory of Acceptance and Use of Technology (UTAUT) and the Technology Acceptance Model (TAM) have drawbacks when it comes to digital marketing for SMEs. These models ignore organizational dynamics, environmental constraints, and the comprehensive range of customer contact necessary for digital marketing, instead concentrating on individual evaluations of usability (Davis,1989; Venkatesh et al.,2003). Among these, Smith and Chaffey's (2008) RACE (Reach, Act, Convert, Engage) framework is especially well-suited for understanding digital marketing in the travel industry. It offers a methodical, customer-focused perspective that fits nicely with the ever-changing landscape of online consumer behavior. It enables a detailed examination of the ways in which travel agencies engage with clients, from raising awareness to building enduring connections, by encompassing every phase of the digital marketing funnel. Building on the findings of Huynh et al. (2025), this study acknowledges that both internal (organizational preparation, resources) and external (consumer engagement, infrastructure) factors must be taken into account for a thorough understanding of digital marketing adoption. This dual focus is made possible by the RACE model, which makes it particularly pertinent for SMEs in developing nations like Sri Lanka.

This study makes a significant contribution to our understanding of the barriers faced by small and medium-sized travel agents in Sri Lanka by utilizing the RACE model. This study offers a comprehensive viewpoint that considers both organizational barriers and consumer interaction tactics, in contrast to earlier research that mostly focuses on larger organizations or uses generic technology adoption models. It responds to the pressing demand for workable, context-sensitive solutions that enable digital transformation in tourism SMEs and fills a significant gap in the literature. To sum up, the RACE model provides a thorough, flexible framework that effectively conveys the complexities of digital marketing adoption in the travel industry. By developing a more comprehensive, customer-focused understanding of digital marketing, this study advances theory. It also advances practice by offering strategic insights that enable Sri Lankan SME travel agents to surmount obstacles, make effective use of digital tools, and strengthen their position in a competitive global market.

3. METHODOLOGY

Qualitative research was chosen because these questions focus on the "how" of digital marketing adoption. It is well known in the social sciences for revealing underlying mechanisms and processes (Denzin, 2007). This study conducted 25 in-depth interviews with Sri Lankan SME travel agencies to understand their experiences and viewpoints on digital marketing. Qualitative interviews provide deep insights into opportunities and problems unique to the context, enhancing the understanding of tourism research (Clarke and Braun, 2017).

4. RESULTS

This section provides an analysis of the barriers faced by small and medium-sized travel agents in Sri Lanka during the Reach, Act, Convert, and Engage stages of digital marketing adoption.

4.1 Reach Stage

In the Reach stage barriers identified are technological, Human Resources, Financial and Social Media barriers.

4.1.1 Technological Barriers

21 out of 25 interviewees identified barriers relating to technology as the main barrier to Sri Lankan SME travel agencies' digital marketing use, particularly during the "reach" stage, due to infrastructure constraints and rapid technology development.

Interviewee IN01 noted, *"Big companies are focusing on different things. So most of the barriers were related to infrastructure development."* This interview quote highlights the emphasis difference, as larger companies typically allocate resources to more wide areas, resulting in insufficient online infrastructure that restricts the effectiveness of SMEs' digital marketing.

IN04 emphasized the challenge of staying updated with technological advancements, explaining, *"The technology is changing, that is a barrier. Time to time technology is changing. It might be hard to sort of keep up with the latest trends and tools…I've seen a lot of people doing new trend, new tools, SEO tools, new digital marketing tools."*

Similarly, IN06 expressed the difficulties posed by the dynamic nature of technology, stating, *"One of the biggest barriers that we are facing when it comes to digital, it's changing every day.*

A robust online infrastructure is crucial for targeted and effective digital marketing, as highlighted in literature on tourism and digital marketing from 2005 to 2023 (Nuseir and Aljumah, 2020; Xiang and Gretzel, 2010; Buhalis and Law, 2008). Countries like UAE benefit from robust digital ecosystems, enabling advanced digital marketing, while Sri Lankan SMEs face challenges due to inadequate infrastructure and limited access to advanced tools (Nuseir and Aljumah, 2020; SLTDA, 2021).

For Sri Lankan SMEs, keeping up with the quickly evolving digital trends is a major technological barrier since new platforms are often appearing, making it difficult to stay current. IN04 brought to light the challenge of incorporating dynamic platforms such as TikTok, which are crucial for digital relevance but challenging to successfully implement. This difficulty can be observed in existing research, which demonstrates that continuous adaptation is necessary due to the rapid development of digital marketing technologies (Leung et al., 2013; Huang et al., 2017). Similar to other Asian nations, Sri Lankan businesses have difficulty with the rapid pace of digital innovations and the efficacy of digital marketing (Hays, Page and Buhalis, 2013; Choe, Kim and Fesenmaier, 2017; Gunawardena, 2017).

4.1.2 Human Resource Barriers

Sri Lankan SME travel agents face challenges in adopting digital marketing due to human resource constraints, skill gaps, and inadequate third-party support. IN02 noted a significant resistance among employees, particularly those who are used to traditional methods, to adopting digital tools like AI, fearing it might replace jobs (Gretzel, 2018; Rusu, Balasuriya, and Bah, 2020).

The lack of inhouse talent in the travel industry is a significant barrier to creating high-quality, engaging content, which often requires skills such as graphic design and video editing (Xiang, Magnini and Fesenmaier, 2015) According to IN10, IN17 Sri Lanka faces a significant digital marketing knowledge gap, with many agents underutilizing user-generated content and visual storytelling in the travel industry. While some agents are proficient in advanced tools like Google Analytics and SEO, most rely on basic social media posting.

Lastly, third-party marketers' lack of understanding makes digital marketing even more difficult.IN22 noted that "*I have had discussions with different digital marketing companies, but they don't have any clue about the online domain. They just do normal digital marketing* *campaigns. So those are not basically relevant to the online travel domain''.*This lack of specialized knowledge among third-party marketers underscores the need for tailored digital marketing expertise within the tourism domain (Carlisle, Ivanov, and Dijkmans, 2021).

4.1.3 Financial Barriers

Financial barriers rank as the third largest obstacle to Sri Lankan SMEs' adoption of digital marketing. These problems are made worse by the nation's foreign exchange crisis, as SMEs find it challenging to finance necessary software, technology, training, and advertising campaigns due to exchange rate volatility (Arora and Sarker, 2022). For example, IN02 emphasized the effects of the US dollar issue by saying, "*We are currently paying between Rs. 200 and Rs. 325 per dollar. Who in Sri Lanka has these kinds of dollars*? This circumstance is consistent with the results of the 2023 Digital Outlook Report, which highlighted how Sri Lanka's currency decline and financial instability prevent companies from launching large-scale digital advertising, like those on Google AdWords, YouTube. High costs of creating quality content, such as videos and advertisements, often hinder small businesses from maximizing their digital marketing efforts. They often look for stock footage and minimal-cost solutions, which may not be as effective in capturing audience attention (Tiago and Veríssimo ,2014). Financial constraints pose a significant challenge in measuring ROI, as employees often lack the necessary knowledge and tools to assess digital marketing performance. This lack of expertise results in underinvestment in platforms with high engagement potential, such as TikTok. SMEs often struggle with ROI measurement due to limited expertise and resources, affecting their ability to make informed budgeting decisions. The cost of maintaining a digital presence adds to the financial burden. In Sri Lanka's economic context, where capital access is constrained and borrowing costs are high, sustaining a digital strategy is particularly challenging.

4.1.4 Social Media barriers

Social media barriers represent a significant challenge for Sri Lankan SMEs in the tourism sector, as evidenced by interview responses. These challenges can be broadly categorized into emotional and psychological barriers, competitive imitation, targeting issues, and the reliability of social media leads.

One prominent barrier relates to competitive imitation, where the transparent nature of social media allows competitors to easily replicate new campaigns. Interviewee IN02 mentioned, *"If you're dealing with Instagram and Facebook, especially in showcasing the products, the other competitors also get to know what we are doing...people like to copy what others are doing."* This competitive imitation dilutes the uniqueness of marketing strategies, impacting brand differentiation. Research by Bharadwaj et al. (2013) supports this observation, noting that while transparency can drive sector wide improvements, it also introduces instability, making it difficult to sustain a unique market position. Targeting difficulties also emerged as a crucial issue, with SMEs struggling to reach their desired audience effectively on social media. As IN04 explained, *"Targeting is one of the barriers...we don't see that we can target the correct clientele."* This issue is especially challenging on platforms like Facebook, where the quality and accuracy of leads have proven unreliable.

Emotional and psychological barriers further complicate digital communication efforts. IN14 pointed out, *"The emotional barriers, individual beliefs, attitudes, and values have a strong influence on how they process information. We don't get vocal inflections, tone of voice, or body language."* The absence of non-verbal cues can lead to misinterpretations which affect the effectiveness of social media messaging. Lastly, the reliability of social media leads is inconsistent across platforms, with Instagram often outperforming Facebook in generating quality leads. This disparity suggests a need for tailored strategies for each platform. Felix et al. (2017) support this view, noting that platform-specific approaches can be critical for achieving success in social media marketing.

4.2 Act Stage

IN14 : *"So many big people... a lot of competition. So you have to spend like 60 or \$70 per day to advertise."* ....*SEO is not free. People think it's free, right? But it's not free.......Our ad is not only showing for them the other one as well... wasting my time and our cost is also money."*

IN12 :*"It's difficult to win their trust within the social media without directly meeting them."*

The competitive online marketplace in Sri Lanka requires constant innovation and strategic investment in digital marketing to build recognition and credibility. To maximize effect and optimize spending, more accurate and data-driven strategies are needed. Inefficient targeting and resource waste are issues, and misconceptions about SEO's costs emphasize the need for precise and data-driven marketing strategies to overcome these barriers.

4.3 Convert Stage

The study identifies the lack of dedicated digital marketing specialists as a significant barrier faced by SME travel agents in Sri Lanka during the convert stage of digital marketing adoption. Out of 25, only four agents (IN1, IN2, IN7, IN14) actively utilize digital marketing during the conversion stage, while the remaining agents do not employ digital marketing strategies. The barriers identified in the study highlight the need for more dedicated digital marketing specialists.

IN 14: " you know there are no proper staff to conduct the marketing activities during the convert stage, some people think the activities are similar in reach and convert stage both".

Digital marketing strategies in the conversion stage differ significantly from those in the reach stage, requiring specialized knowledge that many SME travel agents in Sri Lanka lack. While the reach stage focuses on broad audience engagement through social media and content marketing, the conversion stage demands expertise in personalized email marketing, retargeting ads, and conversion rate optimization.

4.4 Engage Stage

To identify the barriers faced by SME travel agents in Sri Lanka during engage stage of Digital Marketing Adoption one question raised which was "Can you identify any barriers or barriers you have encountered when implementation digital marketing initiatives es to enhance customer engagement? ". From responses to this question one barrier which is lack of responses was identified. Table 04 presents the theme of barriers in the engage stage of digital marketing adoption.

If customers are not responding to communications, there may be problems with how engagement activities are understood and implemented. The interview response highlights significant barriers in customer engagement, particularly the low response rate to the messages.

IN05: *"Most of the times we don't get any response to the messages we sent; customers are not responsive much."*

5. DISCUSSION

When SME travel agents in Sri Lanka use digital marketing, several significant obstacles appear at the Reach stage. SMEs seem to be most active at this stage of their digital marketing activities, which include building awareness and drawing in tourists. Two important insights are shown by the large range of barriers found at this point. First, SME travel agencies understand the strategic significance of the Reach phase they know that being visible digitally is essential to attracting clients and starting the marketing process. Second, the number and intensity of the obstacles indicate that SMEs are trying to create a digital presence but are having difficulty doing so successfully. Specific issues include low brand awareness, restricted funds, insufficient marketing tools, and a lack of digital abilities. The limitations highlight the Reach stage's basic function as well as the critical need for these enterprises to have access to reasonably priced digital technologies and help for capacity-building.

SMEs have increasingly subtle but no less substantial challenges when they progress into the Act stage, which entails promoting interactions like website visits, social media involvement, or content consumption. Even while they are less common, these obstacles such as fierce online competition, costly advertising expenses, and inadequate content strategies can reduce exposure and consumer interest. SMEs who have already succeeded in gaining some digital presence but find it difficult to keep up and differentiate themselves in a competitive online market are typically impacted by these issues.

Lack of technical and strategic skills is one kind of barrier that is revealed by the Convert stage, which focuses on converting online encounters into bookings or purchases. Many small-business travel agencies lack the skills necessary to create appealing landing pages, put in place efficient calls to action, or examine consumer behavior to maximize conversion. Even a good Reach or Act strategy might not result in tangible business consequences if this information is lacking.

Last but not least, the Engage stage which aims to cultivate enduring relationships with clients and increase loyalty is frequently the one that gets overlooked. The absence of customer relationship management (CRM) systems, uneven post-purchase contact, and low response rates to client inquiries are the main problems here. These results imply that although Sri Lankan SMEs are beginning to embrace digital marketing, especially during the Reach phase, they need focused assistance at every point of the customer experience. These barriers can be overcome with the aid of organized training, easier access to digital infrastructure, and reasonably priced marketing tools.

The RACE framework offers a helpful road map for enhancing SME travel agents' adoption of digital marketing by highlighting specific barriers and solutions at each step.

6. IMPLICATIONS OF THE STUDY

It has been found that many barriers are seen in the reach stage because Sri Lankan SME travel agents primarily use digital marketing in this first phase, with only few SME travel agents are utilize digital marketing during other stages. SME travel agents may make sure that resources are distributed efficiently to support each step by comprehending and reacting to consumer behaviours at the entire four stages rather than focusing on only the first stage of the customer journey. A comprehensive strategy like RACE model would improve the possibility of generating conversions and maintaining long term client connections while also helps in the removal of the barriers faced at the reach stage.

The study also provides a more detailed understanding of how digital adoption barriers impact the customer journey, from initial engagement to post-purchase relationship management, contributing to the literature on digital transformation in tourism by incorporating the RACE model (Buhalis and Law, 2008; Gretzel, 2018).

REFERENCES

Abou-Shouk, M., Lim, W.M. and Megicks, P. (2012). Internet Adoption by Travel Agents: a Case of Egypt. International Journal of Tourism Research, 15(3), pp.298–312. doi: https://doi.org/10.1002/jtr.1876.

Alford, P. and Page, S.J. (2015). Marketing technology for adoption by small business. The Service Industries Journal, 35(11-12), pp.655–669. https://doi.org/10.1080/02642069.2015.1062884

Arora, R.U. and Sarker, T. (2022). Financing for Sustainable Development Goals (SDGs) in the Era of COVID-19 and beyond. The European Journal of Development Research, 35(1), pp.1–19. doi: https://doi.org/10.1057/s41287-022-00571-9

Asia Pacific Institute of Digital Marketing (2023). Digital Outlook Sri Lanka. [online] Available at: https://apidm.asia/resources/digital-outlook-srilanka/

Bharadwaj, Anandhi and El Sawy, Omar A. and Pavlou, Paul A. and Venkatraman, N. Venkat, Digital Business Strategy: Toward a Next Generation of Insights (June 1, 2013). MIS Quarterly (2013), 37 (2), 471-482, Available at SSRN: https://ssrn.com/abstract=2742300

Carlisle, S., Ivanov, S. and Dijkmans, C. (2021). The digital skills divide: evidence from the European tourism industry. Journal of Tourism Futures, [online] 9(2), pp.240–266. doi: https://doi.org/10.1108/jtf-07-2020-0114.

Central Bank of Sri Lanka (2019). Annual Report 2019 | Central Bank of Sri Lanka. [online] www.cbsl.gov.lk. Available at: https://www.cbsl.gov.lk/en/publications/economic-and-financial-reports/annual-reports/annual-report-2019.

Central Bank of Sri Lanka (2022). Annual Report 2022 | Central Bank of Sri Lanka. [online] www.cbsl.gov.lk. Available at: https://www.cbsl.gov.lk/en/publications/economic-and-financial-reports/annual-reports/annual-report-2022

Chaffey, D. and Ellis-Chadwick, F. (2019). Digital Marketing. [online] www.pearson.com. Available at: https://www.pearson.com/en-gb/subject-catalog/p/digital-marketing/P200000003911/9781292241623.

Chaffey, D. and Ellis-Chadwick, F. (2022). Digital Marketing. 8th ed. S.L.: Pearson Education Limited.

Chiappa, G.D. (2013). Internet versus travel agencies. Journal of Vacation Marketing, 19(1), pp.55–66. doi: https://doi.org/10.1177/1356766712466613.

Christou, E. (2016). Social Media in Travel, Tourism and Hospitality. doi: https://doi.org/10.4324/9781315609515.

Clarke, V. and Braun, V. (2017). Thematic analysis. The Journal of Positive Psychology, [online] 12(3), pp.297–298. doi:https://doi.org/10.1080/17439760.2016.1262613.

Denzin, N.K. and Lincoln, Y. (2007). Collecting and Interpreting Qualitative Materials. Third Edition. [online] ERIC. SAGE Publications. Available at: https://eric.ed.gov/?id=ED500410.

Dimitrios Buhalis. Buhalis, D., 2003,ETourism: Information Technology for Strategic Tourism Management,Pearson (Financial Times/Prentice Hall), London ISBN 0582357403.

Dimungu Hewage Nilusha Erangi and Inna Stecenko (2023). Digital Transformation In Sri Lanka: Evaluating Progress And Addressing Challenges. Green Blue and Digital Economy Journal, [online] 5(2), pp.1–11. doi: https://doi.org/10.30525/2661-5169/2024-2-1.

Durrani, Z., Zia, Asbah., Ali, T. Y. and Shahid, M. N. (2023). Impact of Digital Marketing on the Tourism Industry Business Profitability of UAE through the role of Effectiveness. IUBJournal of Social Sciences, 5(2), 117–131.

Felix, R., Rauschnabel, P.A. and Hinsch, C. (2017). Elements of Strategic Social Media marketing: a Holistic Framework. Journal of Business Research, [online] 70(1), pp.118–126. doi: https://doi.org/10.1016/j.jbusres.2016.05.001

Gretzel, U. and Yoo, K.H. (2008). Use and Impact of Online Travel Reviews. Information and Communication Technologies in Tourism 2008, [online] pp.35–46. doi: https://doi.org/10.1007/978-3-211-77280-5_4

Gunawardene, N. (2017). Digital Transformation In Sri Lanka: Opportunities And Challenges In Pursuit Of Liberal Policies. [online] Available at: https://www.rticommission.lk/web/images/pdf/DigitalTransformationi nSriLankareport-FINAL-30Nov2017.pdf.

Hays, S., Page, S.J. and Buhalis, D. (2013). Social media as a destination marketing tool: its use by national tourism organisations. Current Issues in Tourism, 16(3), pp.211–239.

Huang, C.D., Goo, J., Nam, K. and Yoo, C.W. (2017). Smart tourism technologies in travel planning: The role of exploration and exploitation. Information and Management, [online] 54(6), pp.757–770. doi: https://doi.org/10.1016/j.im.2016.11.010

Huynh, D.V., Stangl, B. and Tran, D.T. (2023). Digitalization of information provided by destination marketing organizations in developing regions: the case of Vietnamese Mekong Delta. European Journal of Innovation Management. doi:https://doi.org/10.1108/ejim-06-2022-0334.

Iskender, A., Sirakaya-Turk, E., Cardenas, D. and Harrill, R. (2022). COVID or VOID: A systematic literature review of technology adoption and acceptance in hospitality and tourism since the breakout of COVID-19. Tourism and Hospitality Research, p.146735842211336. doi: ender.

Leung, D., Law, R., van Hoof, H. and Buhalis, D. (2013). Social Media in Tourism and Hospitality: a Literature Review. Journal of Travel and Tourism Marketing, [online] 30(1-2), pp.3–22. doi:https://doi.org/10.1080/10548408.2013.750919.

Martins, C., Salazar, A. and Inversini, A. (2015). The Internet Impact on Travel Purchases: Insights from Portugal. Tourism Analysis, 20(2), pp.251–258. doi: https://doi.org/10.3727/108354215x14265319207632

Mehrtens, J., Cragg, P.B. and Mills, A.M. (2001). A model of Internet adoption by SMEs. Information and Management, 39(3), pp.165–176. doi: https://doi.org/10.1016/s0378-7206(01)00086-6.

M. Nuseir and A. Aljumah (2020). The Role of Digital Marketing in Business Performance with the Moderating Effect of Environment Factors among SMEs of UAE. [online] Available at: https://www.semanticscholar.org/paper/The-Role-of-Digital-Marketing-in-Business-with-the-Nuseir-Aljumah/eb5bd1b7527cb22d86f3e40aafc0b719b0def5ca.

Molinillo, S. and Japutra, A. (2017). Organizational adoption of digital information and technology: a theoretical review. The Bottom Line, 30(1), pp.33–46. doi: https://doi.org/10.1108/bl-01-2017-0002

Rusu, L., Balasuriya, P.B.L. and Bah, O. (2020). Cultural Barriers in Digital Transformation in a Public Organization: A Case Study of a Sri-Lankan Organization. Information Systems, pp.640–656. doi: https://doi.org/10.1007/978-3-030-63396-7_43

Sharma, A., Sharma, S. and Chaudhary, M. (2020). Are small travel agencies ready for digital marketing? Views of travel agency managers. Tourism Management, [online] 79(1), p.104078. doi: https://doi.org/10.1016/j.tourman.2020.104078 .

SLTDA. (2022). SLTDA | Sri Lanka Tourism Development Authority. [online] Available at: https://www.sltda.gov.lk/en/annual-report.

Smith, P. and Chaffey, D. (2008). eMarketing eXcellence. Routledge. doi: https://doi.org/10.4324/9780080878966

Suhaib Aamir, Nuray Atsan and Mohammad Saud Khan (2023). Going digital with multisided platforms: Assessing the innovation adoption process from the perspectives of travel agents. doi: https://doi.org/10.1177/14673584231186535

Tiago, M.T.P.M.B. and Veríssimo, J.M.C. (2014). Digital Marketing and Social media: Why bother? Business Horizons, [online] 57(6), pp.703–708. doi:https://doi.org/10.1016/j.bushor.2014.07.002.

Venkatesh, V., Morris, M.G., Davis, G.B. and Davis, F.D. (2003). User Acceptance of Information technology: toward a Unified View. MIS Quarterly, [online] 27(3), pp.425–478. doi: https://doi.org/10.2307/30036540

Xiang, Z. and Gretzel, U. (2010). Role of Social Media in Online Travel Information Search. Tourism Management, 31(2), pp.179–188. doi: https://doi.org/10.1016/j.tourman.2009.02.016

Xiang, Z., Magnini, V.P. and Fesenmaier, D.R. (2015). Information technology and consumer behavior in travel and tourism: Insights from travel planning using the internet. Journal of Retailing and Consumer Services, 22, pp.244–249. doi: https://doi.org/10.1016/j.jretconser.2014.08.005

The Impact of the Covid-19 Pandemic on Travel Insurance Purchases and Factors Affecting Consumers' Choice of Purchase Channels

Thuy Nguyen Thi Hong,
tnguyenthihong.imte-m2023@fh-salzburg.ac.at

Aisha Jagne, ajagne.imte-m2023@fh-salzburg.ac.at

Halimat Shadia Abati, habati.imte-m2023@fh-salzburg.ac.at

Kejdi Cela, kcela.imte-m2023@fh-salzburg.ac.at

Salzburg University of Applied Sciences, Austria

Abstract

Travel insurance is mentioned as a risk-reduction strategy for travellers, particularly during the pandemic. Therefore, this study aims to evaluate the performance of travel insurance under the effect of the Covid-19 pandemic and investigate the factors influencing purchase decisions. The study also examines participants' preferences for different purchase channels, including traditional and digital channels. This study employed a quantitative approach, collecting primary data from 125 participants through an online survey. IBM SPSS Statistics version 29-2022 was selected for data analysis. The results indicate that (1) even though the Covid-19 pandemic had a significant impact on the purchase of travel insurance during and post-pandemic, its effect on the intention to purchase travel insurance is negligible. (2) Traditional channels, such as insurance providers with personal contact or official insurance companies' websites, remain primary selections due to their authority, credibility, reliability, and human interaction. Conversely, convenience, flexibility, and speed are key motivations for respondents selecting digital channels. These findings highlight the necessity for travel insurance providers to enhance their distribution strategy and optimise their existing channels to align with travellers' expectations.

Keywords: travel insurance; pandemic; COVID-19; distribution channels

1. INTRODUCTION

In recent years, the tourism industry has witnessed significant transformations, influenced by globalisation, technological advancements, and unforeseen global events, such as the COVID-19 pandemic. The pandemic has led to unprecedented increases in risks and uncertainty, posing significant challenges to society (Chen et al., 2023). As travellers are more aware of a variety of risks and uncertainties, such as medical emergencies or flight cancellations, travel insurance has become an essential risk reduction strategy (Leggat et al., 1999).

Demographic factors such as age, income, and education significantly impact in shaping insurance purchasing decisions (Lo et al., 2011). Simultaneously, the digital transformation has significantly shifted the travel industry as well as consumer behaviour, leading to increasing preference for online transactions over traditional channels (World Economic Forum, 2021; Longo, 2024). Nevertheless, there are limited studies exploring the pandemic's influence on travel insurance purchase decisions as well as purchase methods.

This research aims to address the following research questions:

1. What effects has the COVID-19 pandemic had on intentions of purchasing travel insurance?
2. What factors affect travellers' preference when selecting between traditional and digital distribution channels?

By addressing these questions, this research aims to gain deeper insights into the impact of the COVID-19 pandemic on individuals' travel insurance purchasing decisions and examine key factors influencing preferences for traditional versus digital purchasing methods.

Research indicates a marked increase in travel insurance uptake as travellers seek to mitigate the risks associated with potential disruptions caused by the pandemic. A recent study found that the COVID-19 pandemic significantly increased the adoption of travel insurance. Reports indicate that travel insurance premiums rose by approximately 20% to 30%, reflecting heightened consumer awareness and increased demand for coverage during periods of uncertainty (Lim, 2023). Other findings suggest that the COVID-19 pandemic has reshaped travellers' risk perceptions, leading to a higher focus on health and safety. Consequently, travel insurance has become an essential component of travel planning. (Fitriadi et al., 2022; Tan & Caponecchia, 2021). Additionally, the pandemic has catalysed a shift in consumer behaviour, with many individuals prioritising travel insurance to mitigate risks associated with unforeseen events, such as trip cancellations or health emergencies (Mamun et al., 2022; Qian, 2021). This trend is particularly evident among demographics that previously exhibited lower insurance uptake, indicating a broader recognition of the importance of travel insurance in the current climate (Loxton et al., 2020).

Consumer purchasing behaviour for travel insurance through traditional and digital distribution channels varies significantly across different age groups and education levels. However, existing literature suggests that these differences may not be as pronounced as one might expect. For instance, Lo et al. (2011) found that younger travellers (aged 25 or below) and older travellers (aged 65 and above) are generally less likely to purchase travel insurance compared to middle-aged groups. It indicates potential uniformity in purchase behaviours across age demographics rather than a distinct divergence based on the distribution channel used. This suggests that age may influence overall purchasing tendencies, but it does not necessarily dictate the selection of distribution channels.

Ulbinaite et al. (2013) suggested that different factors, such as financial, social, psychological, and emotional, heavily influence decisions about insurance coverage purchases. Supporting this line, Yang et al. (2023) highlight that many travellers prioritise pricing over service details when purchasing travel insurance, which implies that the decision-making process is more influenced by financial factors than the distribution channel itself. This trend is aligned with findings from Sarman et al. (2019), who also confirmed that higher education levels are associated with an increased likelihood of purchasing travel insurance, but the distribution channel through which it is obtained remains insignificantly related to this variable.

Furthermore, Choe et al. (2022) suggest that willingness to pay for travel insurance is influenced by health-related risk perception and sociodemographic factors, such as age and education. Their findings indicate that age follows a U-shaped relationship, while education has a positive correlation with willingness to pay. However, the choice of distribution channel does not play a significant role in this dynamic. In addition, the study by Mamun et al. (2022) suggests that attitudes and perceived behavioural controls are significant predictors of travel insurance purchases, indicating that psychological factors may overshadow the influence of distribution channels. This is further reinforced by the work of Yang et al. (2021), which indicates that a substantial portion of travellers lack adequate knowledge about travel insurance, suggesting that education and awareness may be more influential than the distribution channel. Moreover, the literature indicates that the digitisation of travel insurance purchases does not necessarily lead to a significant change in behaviour across different age groups. For instance, while younger consumers may be more inclined to use digital channels, their overall purchasing behaviour remains consistent across age groups, as indicated by the findings of Lim, who discusses the impact of digital tools on insurance purchases but does not find a significant divergence in behaviour based on age or education (Lim, 2023). Studies have shown that the effectiveness of traditional distribution channels, such as travel agencies, remains significant due to their personalised services that can appeal to all age groups, including younger consumers (Aslanzadeh & Keating, 2014). Additionally, the research by Zalech indicates that socio-demographic features, including age, significantly affect risk perception and willingness to purchase TI, implying that younger individuals may not be as inclined towards digital channels as presumed (Zalech, 2020). Moreover, while digital channels are growing, traditional channels still hold substantial influence, particularly among older demographics who may prefer personal interactions and established trust with agents (Aslanzadeh & Keating, 2014). This is supported by findings from

Chen et al. (2023), which highlight that traditional distribution methods continue to be effective, even in the face of increasing digitalisation Furthermore, Yang emphasises that price sensitivity often outweighs the appeal of digital convenience, suggesting that young travellers may prioritise cost over the medium of purchase. Chloe et al.'s (2022) findings further this. They demonstrate that risk perception and past experiences significantly influence the willingness to pay for travel insurance, more than their age-related preference for digital channels.

On the other hand, the assertion that higher-educated individuals are more likely to purchase travel insurance through digital channels compared to their lower-educated counterparts is contested by various studies. Research indicates that despite the increasing prevalence of digital channels, many consumers, including those with higher education, still prefer traditional distribution methods due to the perceived reliability and personal interaction offered by agents (Gronflaten, 2009). Additionally, the complexity of insurance products often necessitates guidance, which may lead individuals of varying educational backgrounds to prefer traditional channels over digital ones (Amaro & Duarte, 2016). Research indicates that recommendations from friends and family can significantly affect consumers' attitudes towards insurance products, highlighting the importance of social influence over educational background in shaping purchasing behaviours (Sun et al., 2023; Sebastian et al., 2018). Furthermore, social factors, including peer effects, can lead to conformity in purchasing decisions, suggesting that individuals may follow the choices of their social circles regardless of their educational attainment (Yang et al., 2021). This indicates that, while education may influence awareness and understanding of insurance products, social influences can be equally impactful in determining purchasing behaviour across different educational levels.

2. METHODOLOGY

2.1 Questionnaire design

This study used a quantitative approach to investigate travellers' knowledge and experiences with travel insurance in general, particularly the distribution channels. The questionnaire was designed to separate participants into two groups: group one, those who had travel insurance purchase history in the past, and group two, those who had not purchased travel insurance before. The questionnaire was designed using the online server SoSci Survey, selecting English as the primary language and offering German as an option. A pretest version was sent to 10 respondents of different nationalities to ensure that the questions were clearly stated and understandable before the final version was officially distributed.

2.2 Sample and data collection

The researchers employed the simple random sampling technique through online distribution channels, including email and popular social media platforms such as Facebook, Instagram, and WhatsApp. The process of data collection started on 18th October 2024 and continued for one month, concluding on 18th November 2024. By the end of the process, 161 individuals participated in the survey, but only 125 participants completed it, comprising 84 in English and 41 in German. IBM SPSS Statistics, version 29-2022, was used to analyse the results.

3. RESULTS

3.1 Sample description

Of these 161 respondents, 125 successfully completed the survey.
Table 1 describes the demographic data for the participants.

Table 1. Sample demographic characteristics, own calculation (n=125)

	Frequency	Percent (%)
Gender		
Female	74	60.8
Male	46	36.8
Non-binary	2	1.6
Prefer not to respond	1	0.8
Age groups		
15 – 19	1	0.8
20 – 29	68	54.4
30 – 39	35	28.0
40 – 49	9	7.2
50 – 59	10	8.0
60 – 64	2	1.6
Education level		
Still in school	3	2.4
Compulsory school or equivalent	1	0.8
High school/ College or equivalent	22	17.6
Vocational school or equivalent	8	6.4
University or equivalent	91	72.8

3.2 Results

Among the initial 125 individuals, the majority (96%, n=120) reported that they were familiar with travel insurance, ranging from somewhat familiar to extremely familiar. Notably, 54.4% of respondents (n=68) demonstrated extreme familiarity with it. Over half of the respondents (62.4%, n=78) had previously acquired travel insurance, whereas 37.6% (n=47) indicated no prior experience with such purchases. Regarding the types of trips or trip purposes, international trips were, as anticipated, the most prevalent occasions for opting for travel insurance (93.6%, n=73). Sarman et al. (2020) reported a comparable result in their study, revealing that travellers consider international trips more risky than domestic ones. The data revealed a notable increase in travel insurance purchases observed following the Covid-19 pandemic, with 78.2% of respondents reporting that they acquired travel insurance compared to 59.0% prior to the pandemic and 35.9% during the pandemic. This result supported the study by Lim (2023). It can also be explained when Covid-19-related travel restrictions were lifted (WTO, 2023) or there are some countries (e.g., Singapore, Thailand) that required mandatory travel insurance covering Covid-19 treatment (Glušac, 2021; Ministry of Foreign Affairs, Singapore, 2022; Ministry of Foreign Affairs, Kingdom of Thailand, 2021).

Second group participants (n=47) reported that they didn't buy travel insurance they don't find it necessary (40.4%) and/or are covered by their home country's health insurance (38.3%)

1. A Chi-Square test was conducted in response to question

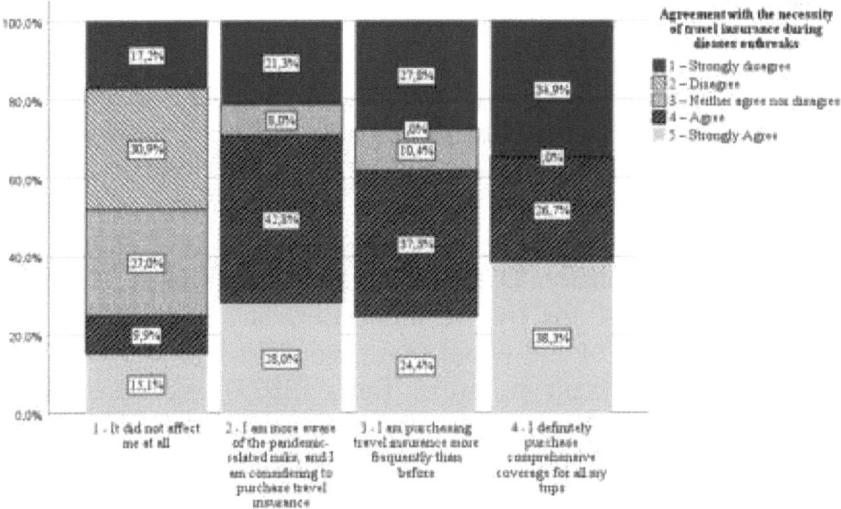

Fig. 1: Cross tabulation, agreement with necessity of travel insurance and change in purchase intentions due to the pandemic, own calculation (n=125)

1. Our hypothesis is the more people agree on the importance of travel insurance for disease outbreaks, the more they change purchase intentions. The two variables used include "how strongly people agreed

that travel insurance was needed during disease outbreaks like the Covid-19 pandemic" (1-5 scale; strongly disagree to strongly agree) and "the shift in travel insurance purchase intention due to the pandemic" (1-4 scale; not affected at all to definitely purchase for all my trips). 70.4% of participants agreed and strongly agreed that travel insurance is important for disease outbreaks. However, more than 50% of participants reported that the pandemic did not affect their purchase intentions at all. The test was significant (p=0.013, <0.05); however, the linear correlation between the two variables is modest. The correlation test resulted significantly (p=0.014, <0.05), highlighting a relevant interaction between two variables, but did not align with the expected direction (Fig.1), and the effect was small (Kendall's Tau-B: 0.194). Therefore, the hypothesis can't be accepted. Despite an increase in travel insurance purchases post-pandemic, there is insufficient evidence to prove that the Covid-19 pandemic has significantly altered travel insurance purchase intentions.

In address question 2, the age and education level variables were analysed. This variable has both MEAN and MODE of 5, MEDIAN of 4.46 with a standard deviation of 0.972. This indicates that the distribution is left-skewed towards high education levels (university or equivalent) and the education levels have a narrow variation among respondents. Additionally, 83.2% of respondents are under 40, so it is difficult to generalise the true relationship (Choe et al., 2022). The uneven distribution of the population, including age and education level, makes it difficult to prove Dai's (2023) argument, which mentions the connection between these variables and purchase intentions. Figures 2 and 3 illustrate the distribution of population.

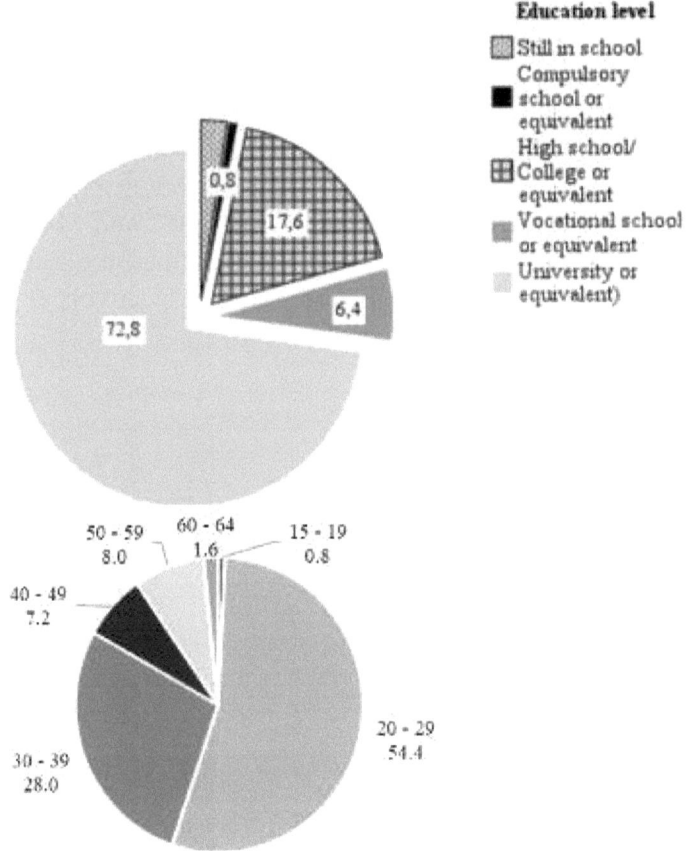

Fig. 2 & 3: Education level and age groups of population, own calculation (n=125)

Despite the inability to explore the relationship between demographic characteristics and travellers' insurance preferences, this study examined consumers' preferences between traditional and digital purchase methods of travel insurance. We asked participants which information source and purchase methods they trust the most. The variables for the most reliable information sources and purchase channels for travel insurance were derived from Nicoletti (2021), Bainbridge (2020), and Nowotarska-Romaniak (2016), which were categorised into two types: direct contact and online contact. The statistics revealed that "insurance companies (direct contact)" (47.4%) were the most trusted information source of information among respondents when seeking information. Interestingly, options of "social media platforms (e.g., Facebook, Twitter, Instagram)" and "online travel agencies (e.g., Booking.com, Expedia.com)" gained the lowest levels of trust among respondents, at 0% and 3.8%, respectively (Fig. 4)

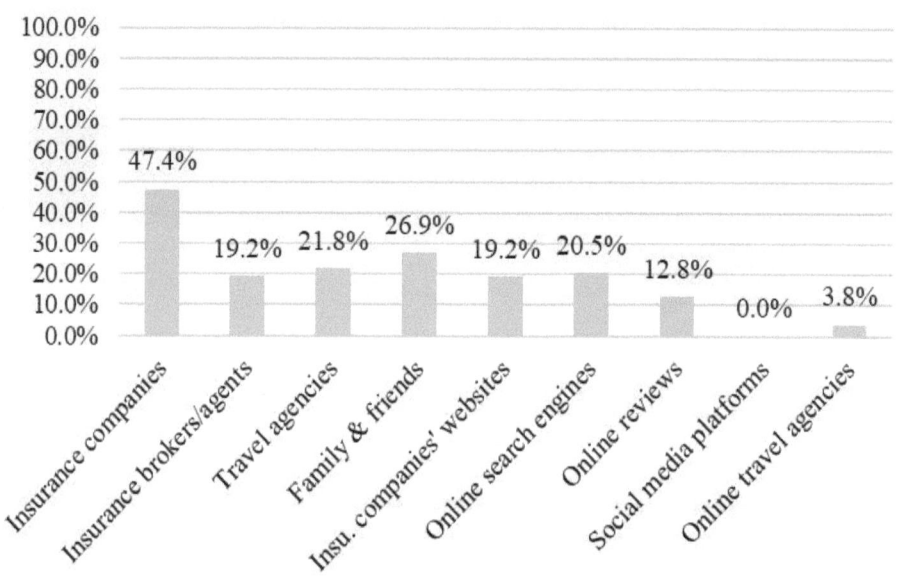

Fig. 4: The most trusted information sources for searching travel insurance information from participants with purchase history, own calculation (n=78)

A comparable trend in responses was observed regarding the most reliable channels for purchasing travel insurance, with 55.1% of respondents expressing a preference for direct purchases from insurance companies. In contrast, participants regarded "social media platforms" (2.6%) and "mobile apps" (3.8%) as the least trustworthy options. This result suggests that although digital channels may provide insurers with cost advantages (Wang, 2016), they do not contribute substantially to customers' perceptions of trustworthiness. The second group of participants showed a similar trend, preferring "insurance companies" when they plan to purchase travel insurance. The primary distinctions from the first group were the "travel agencies" and "online travel agencies" channels, which ranked as the second and third most trusted channels, respectively. Figure 5 describes the detailed results.

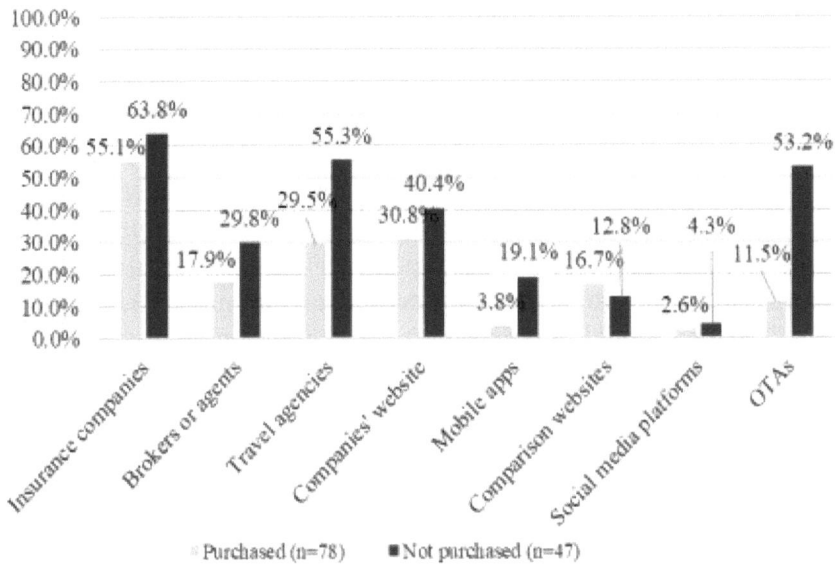

Fig. 5: The most trusted channels for travel insurance purchase, own calculation (with purchase history, n=78; no purchase history, n=47)

An open-ended question was asked to elicit a more comprehensive understanding of the respondents' selections. Key drivers for their preferences are first, insurance providers are perceived as authorised and legitimate and provide guaranteed coverage, thereby creating a sense of safety, security, and peace of mind for respondents.

Participants frequently cited "safety, security, and peace of mind" as their primary motivations. Moreover, these channels are considered credible, reliable, and trustworthy because they provide non-suspicious and accurate information. Additionally, participants find it advantageous and accessible to purchase directly, as they benefit from quality customer service, long-term relationships, and interpersonal interaction for all their questions. Similar findings were conducted by Szymańska & Klapkiv (2019), indicating that "trust in the agent and loyalty to the insurer" are the main factors for not purchasing via the Internet. Furthermore, they repeatedly mentioned cost aspects like cost-effectiveness and "affordable price" as reasons to purchase directly from insurance companies. This finding supports the study by Yang et al. (2023).

In alignment with the research conducted by Singh et al. (2020), the responses for digital channels indicated that convenience, ease of use, speed, and flexibility were the primary factors influencing participants' selection. Nevertheless, these digital channels appear to be secondary to direct channels to some respondents, as they involve "intermediate steps" or additional "commission fees" for third parties, apart from insurance companies' websites. Notably, there is a key opinion, supported by Singh et al. (2020), that digital channels, such as insurance aggregators and comparison websites, are more objective, making travellers more comfortable and not hustling when purchasing. Figure 6 illustrates key drivers for travellers' preferences.

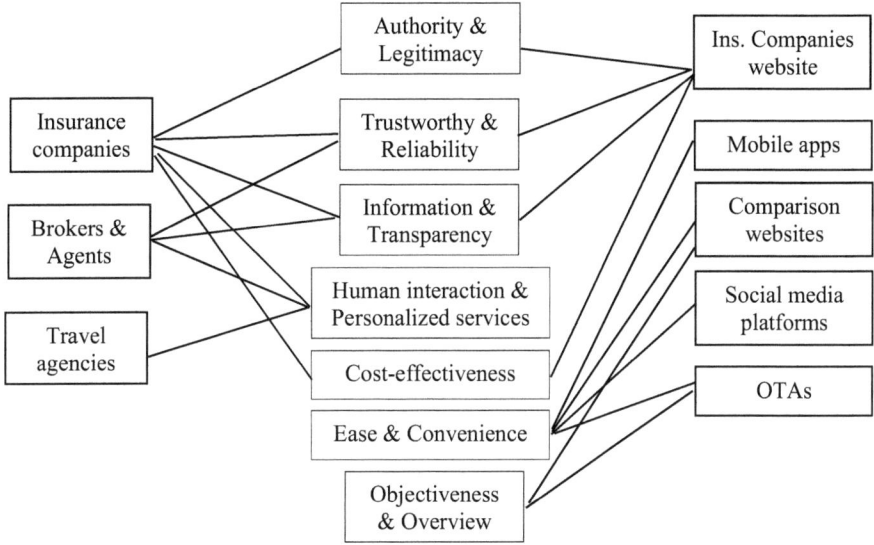

Fig. 6: Key drivers for consumers' preferences when selecting travel
insurance purchase channels, own demonstration

4. DISCUSSION AND LIMITATION

4.1 Discussion

This study revealed an increase in travel insurance purchases under the influence of the COVID-19 pandemic (Lim, 2023), but there is no significant evidence of its effect on travellers' purchase intentions in the future (Fitriadi et al., 2022; Tan & Caponecchia, 2021)

Due to their validity, dependability, and personalised services that offers security and legitimacy, direct channels, such as insurance companies and agents, remain the most popular and trusted way to buy travel insurance. These findings were reinforced by those of Chen et al. (2023). It emphasises the importance of travel insurance companies building credibility and trustworthiness through both traditional and digital distribution channels.

Despite the convenience and accessibility of online platforms, social media, and mobile applications, they are viewed suspiciously due to a lack of trustworthiness, which prevents their widespread adoption (Amaro & Duarte, 2016). Consumers prefer comparative websites owing to their impartiality and objectiveness. This result highlights the importance of social effects when consumers trust other consumers' opinions and reality experiences more than marketing and advertising do (Yang et al., 2021).

For trust-dependent products, younger, more educated consumers also surprisingly favour direct channels, demonstrating that product complexity and trust are more crucial factors than their preferences in determining channel choices.

4.2 Limitation

As with any research project, this study is subject to limitations. First, the study was limited by the sample size, which was not sufficiently large to accurately represent the population. Time constraints and limited access to appropriate respondents with a history of travel insurance purchases also contribute to this limitation.

The second limitation of this study was convenience and random sample collection through social media distribution networks. The sample contains an overrepresentation of the young and university-level population (83.2% of the respondents were under 40 and 72.8% of them had a university education level). Therefore, we were unable to examine the true correlation between these sociodemographic factors and travel insurance purchase preferences (Lo et al., 2011; Choe et al., 2022).

Another limitation of this study is that it relies on social media distribution networks. Individuals with less technical expertise were unable to participate in this survey. Furthermore, self-reported data might contain biases such as inaccurate recollection or overestimation of familiarity. For future research, a larger and broader sample that represents the diverse demographics of the population would contribute to the study's results. Despite the limitations, the findings of this study provide useful insights to approach customers and enhance distribution channels for insurance companies

5. CONCLUSION

This research demonstrates a rise in the demand for travel insurance due to the COVID-19 pandemic. Furthermore, traditional distribution channels, such as purchasing directly from insurance firms and travel agents, are still preferred because of their perceived dependability, trustworthiness, and personal services, despite the increasing use of digital channels. The study indicated that trust and product complexity had a greater influence on channel selection than demographic factors, such as age and education, which did not always correspond with digital preferences. These findings highlight the need for travel insurance providers to refine their distribution strategies and improve their existing channels to meet travellers' expectations.

REFERENCES

Amaro, S., & Duarte, P. (2016). Travellers' intention to purchase travel online: Integrating trust and risk to the theory of planned behaviour. *Anatolia, 27*(3), pp. 389-400.

Aslanzadeh, M., & Keating, B. (2014). Inter-channel effects in multichannel travel services. *Cornell Hospitality Quarterly, 55*(3), pp. 265-276.

Bainbridge, R., 2020. The evolution of travel insurance distribution channels. *International Travel & Health Insurance Journal*, (239), pp. 30–34.

Chen, A., Chen, Y., Murphy, F., Wei, X., & Xu, X. (2023). How does the insurer's mobile application sales strategy perform? Journal of Risk and Insurance, 90(2), pp. 487-519.

Chen, S., Lin, Z., Wang, X., & Xu, X. (2023). Pandemic and insurance purchase: How do people respond to unprecedented risk and uncertainty? China Economic Review, 79(15), 101946.

Choe, Y., Kim, H., & Choi, Y. (2022). Willingness to pay for travel insurance as a risk reduction behaviour: Health-related risk perception after the outbreak of COVID-19. Service Business, 16(3), pp. 445-467.

Dai, Y. (2023). The factors drive people buy travel insurance. In Proceedings of the 2nd International Academic Conference on Blockchain, Information Technology and Smart Finance (ICBIS 2023). Atlantis Press. pp. 217-227.

Fitriadi, B., Hurriyati, R., & Widjajanta, B. (2022). The impact of COVID-19 pandemic on consumer behaviour in tourism sector. Advances in Economics, Business and Management Research.

Glušac, D. (2021, June). The role of travel health insurance in tourism development: Challenges and perspectives. Tourism International Scientific Conference Vrnjačka Banja - TISC, 6(1), pp. 145-161.

Gronflaten, O. (2009). Consumer attitudes towards online insurance purchases. International Journal of Bank Marketing, 27(3), pp. 202-221.

Leggat, P.A., Carne, J., Kedjarune, U., (1999) Travel insurance and health. Journal of Travel Medicine, 6(4), pp. 243-248.

Lim, S. (2023). Predicting travel insurance purchases in an insurance firm through machine learning methods after COVID-19. Journal of Informatics and Web Engineering, 2(2), pp. 43-58.

Lo, A., Cheung, C., & Law, R. (2011). Hong Kong residents' adoption of risk reduction strategies in leisure travel. Journal of Travel & Tourism Marketing, 28(3), pp. 240-260.

Longo, J. (2024). The data-driven future: How technology is impacting customer buying habits and market research. Forbes.

Loxton, M., Truskett, R., Scarf, B., Sindone, L., Baldry, G., & Zhao, Y. (2020). Consumer behaviour during crises: Preliminary research on how coronavirus has manifested consumer panic buying, herd mentality, changing discretionary spending and the role of the media in influencing behaviour. Journal of Risk and Financial Management, 13(8), 166.

Mamun, A., Rahman, M., Yang, Q., Jannat, T., Salameh, A., & Fazal, S. (2022). Predicting the willingness and purchase of travel insurance during the COVID-19 pandemic. Frontiers in Public Health, 10.

Ministry of Foreign Affairs. (2022). COVID-19 – General Information for Travellers to Singapore and the UK.

Ministry of Foreign Affairs, Kingdom of Thailand. (2021). Thailand Pass FAQs.

Nicoletti, B., 2021. Place or Channels in Insurance 4.0. In: B. Nicoletti, ed. Insurance 4.0: Benefits and Challenges of Digital Transformation. Cham: Springer International Publishing. pp. 147–172.

Nowotarska-Romaniak, B. (2016). Preferences and motives of consumer behaviour in the process of purchasing travel insurance. Ekonomiczne Problemy Turystyki, 36, pp. 133-139.

Qian, X. (2021). The impact of COVID-19 pandemic on insurance demand: The case of China. The European Journal of Health Economics, 22(7), pp. 1017-1024.

Sarman, I., Curtale, R. and Hajibaba, H., 2020. Drivers of travel insurance Purchase. Journal of Travel Research, 59(3), pp. 545–558.

Sebastian, T., Yammiyavar, P., & Jones, S. (2018). Brand selection in planned purchasing: An analysis of Asian user behaviour. IAFOR Journal of Psychology & the Behavioural Sciences, 4(2), pp. 3-14.

Singh, R.K., Singh, A., & Chavan, S. (2020). Distribution Channels in Life and General Insurance: A Conceptual Analysis, pp. 590-609.

Sun, D., Chen, W., & Dou, X. (2023). Formation mechanism of residents' intention to purchase commercial health insurance: The moderating effect of environmental pollution perception. Journal of Public Health, 32(6), pp. 917-930.

Szymańska, A., & Klapkiv, J. (2019, September). Impact of the e-commerce on distribution channels of insurance services. Proceedings of the 10th International Conference on Applied Economics. Olsztyn: Institute of y Research, pp. 171-178.

Tan, D., & Caponecchia, C. (2021). Covid-19 and the public perception of travel insurance. Annals of Tourism Research, 90, pp. 103-106.

Ulbinaite, A., Kucinskiene, M., & Le Moullec, Y. (2013). Determinants of Insurance Purchase Decision Making in Lithuania. Inzinerine Ekonomika, 24(2), pp. 144-159.

Wang, H.-C., 2016. E-commerce and Distribution of Insurance Products: A Few Suggestions for an Appropriate Regulatory Infrastructure. In: The

'Dematerialized' Insurance: Distance Selling and Cyber Risks from an International Perspective. pp. 39–58.

World Economic Forum. (2021). We're all shopping more online as consumer behaviour shifts.

World Tourism Organization (2023), *The End of COVID-19-related Travel Restrictions – Summary of findings from the COVID-19-related Travel Restriction reports*, UNWTO, Madrid.

Yang, C., Lu, C., Chiang, C., Chang, H., Yao, C., & Huang, K. (2023). Traveler's knowledge, attitude, and practice about travel health insurance: A community-based questionnaire study. *PLOS ONE, 18*(2), e0281199.

Yang, C., Lu, C., Chiang, C., Chang, H., Yao, C. & Huang, K. (2021). Knowledge, attitude, and awareness of health insurance in travel during the COVID-19 pandemic. Research Square.

Yang, K., Zhujun, K., Zhijie, C., Sun, X., & Tang, W. (2021). Social learning? Conformity? Or comparison? — An empirical study on the impact of peer effects on Chinese seniors' intention to purchase travel insurance. *Tourism Management Perspectives, 38*, 100809.

Zalech, M. (2020). Socio-demographic features and risk perception as determinants of taking out travel insurance. *Tourism Analysis*.

A Virtual Museum - The Case of Bringing Equestrian Heritage to the Digital Age In Lower Bavaria

Valizadeh, Taha, TH Deggendorf, Germany
taha.valizadeh@stud.th-deg.de

Trujillo Rodríguez Diana-L TH Deggendorf, Germany
diana.trujillo-rodriguez@stud.th-deg.de

Bashynskyi Roman, TH Deggendorf, Germany
roman.bashynskyi@stud.th-deg.de

Hoang Vy, TH Deggendorf, Germany
vy.hoang@stud.th-deg.de

Ghabouli Shahroudi Bahareh, TH Deggendorf, Germany
bahareh.ghabouli-shahroudi@stud.th-deg.de

Abstract

Digital innovations are reshaping tourism experiences, particularly through the integration of user experience design (UXD), web design, storytelling, and virtual reality (VR). This study explores the development of a virtual museum dedicated to horses in Lower Bavaria, applying UXD principles to enhance engagement, accessibility, and cultural immersion. The paper discusses how web design fosters immersive interactions, storytelling enriches visitor experiences, and VR enables remote exploration, catering to modern tourist needs. The study also highlights the role of service blueprinting in structuring user journeys and refining digital interfaces. Findings indicate that a UX-centered approach significantly enhances user satisfaction and engagement in digital tourism platforms. By integrating intuitive navigation, interactive storytelling, and multilingual accessibility, the virtual museum effectively promotes Lower Bavaria's equestrian heritage. This research underscores the potential of virtual museums as sustainable and inclusive tourism solutions, providing a model for future digital cultural heritage initiatives.

Keywords: Virtual Museum, Lower Bavaria, Rotaller Horses, VR Technology, User Design Process, Service Blueprint, Digital Heritage, Prototype Testing

1. INTRODUCTION

The integration of digital innovations in tourism has significantly improve user experience design (UXD), especially in the context of virtual museums (Trunfio et al., 2021; Heidari et al., 2024). Web design, storytelling and virtual reality (VR) have reshaped modern tourism experiences by fostering engagement, accessibility and interactivity (Heidari et al., 2024; Chronis, 2012; Yung & Khoo-Lattimore, 2017). Effective tourism websites are primary sources of information that influence visitors' decision-making and reinforce emotional connections (Heidari et al., 2024; Li et al., 2024). Storytelling plays a key role in personalising visitor experiences and evolving through social networks and interactive media (Chronis, 2012; Mossberg, 2008; Bassano et al., 2019). VR further enhances cultural heritage preservation and offers opportunities for remote exploration, making tourism more inclusive and immersive (Yung & Khoo-Lattimore, 2017; Trunfio, Della Lucia, Campana, & Magnelli, 2021). These digital advances in storytelling align with UXD principles, creating personalised and engaging experiences for visitors.

Virtual reality has revolutionised the tourism sector by offering simulated experiences that allow users to explore destinations without physical limitations (Yung & Khoo-Lattimore, 2017). VR applications facilitate the preservation of cultural heritage, promote the inclusion of people with physical disabilities and contribute to sustainable tourism by minimising environmental impact (Calisto & Sarkar, 2024). Despite difficulties related to cost and sensory limitations, VR remains a promising tool for improving user engagement on tourism platforms (Rauscher, Humpe and Brehm, 2020). Virtual museums, in particular, have leveraged VR and augmented reality (AR) technologies to create immersive environments that transcend geographical barriers and enhance visitors' learning experiences (Trunfio et al., 2021). These platforms respond to the needs of tourists by integrating educational content, interactive storytelling and gamification techniques (Morse et al., 2021). The strategic application of UXD principles ensures that virtual museums remain accessible, engaging and culturally enriching. The study emerged in response to the lack of accessible information on the equestrian heritage of Lower Bavaria, particularly the Rottaler horse, which limited the region's tourism potential.

The aim of this research is to explore the capabilities of the VR technologies to create a virtual museum dedicated to horses in Lower Bavaria. By applying design thinking methodologies, the study conceptualised a virtual museum to enhance user engagement through intuitive web interfaces, immersive storytelling and VR integration. The research targets a diverse audience of millennials and Generation Z with equine cultural interests. The development of a user-centred virtual museum is in line with digital tourism trends, ensuring an accessible and interactive experience for visitors.

Initial interviews with students at the Deggendorf Institute of Technology helped identify gaps in awareness and accessibility, shaping the problem definition. The prototype was tested with users, refining navigation, content accessibility, and multilingual support to enhance engagement and inclusivity.

2. LITERATURE REVIEW

2.1 Web Design in Tourism Attractions

Web design has been revolutionising the tourism industry, particularly in the development of virtual museums, by improving accessibility and engagement. Destination management organisations (DMOs) are increasingly using web design strategies to influence tourists' decision-making processes (Kim & Fesenmaier, 2008). Effective web design goes far beyond aesthetics by addressing visitors' motivations and providing immersive digital experiences (Heidari et al., 2024). Websites with high-quality visual and interactive elements have a meaningful impact on user engagement, making destinations more appealing and fostering emotional connections (Heidari et al., 2024). In addition, social evidence such as reviews and visitor testimonials increase credibility and encourage potential tourists to explore new places (Heidari et al., 2024).

Advanced web platform integration has further transformed digital tourism experiences. Cloud-based web applications make it easier to visualise and interact with large 3D datasets, enabling real-time data sharing and enhanced collaboration (Li et al., 2024). These platforms are widely used in architecture, archaeology and heritage conservation, offering a digital alternative to physical site visits. Leveraging cloud computing minimises local computing costs while enabling efficient data management, ensuring that virtual museums and tourism platforms remain dynamic and accessible (Li et al., 2024). The application of web-based 3D data management goes beyond tourism and influences other sectors, such as engineering and urban planning.

The theory of colour plays a crucial role in web design, as it shapes user perceptions and emotional responses. The arrangement of colours in web interfaces influences usability and engagement, with colour schemes ranging from monochromatic to tetradic harmonies (Machí Hervàs, 2024). The psychology of colour influences visitor interaction with tourism websites, as different colours can evoke specific emotions that guide user behaviour. An understanding of the target audience is essential when selecting colours to effectively convey the desired message. A well-designed tourism website strategically uses colour to enhance the storytelling and foster greater visitor engagement, eventually improving conversion rates (Machí Hervàs, 2024).

Digitalisation of tourism services has considerably increased the efficiency of travel planning and information management. Tourism online systems offer streamlined alternatives to traditional paper-based systems, improving data security and accessibility (Nadda et al., 2020). The ability to book entire trips online, from selecting a destination to arranging accommodation, has reshaped consumer travel behaviour (Yuan, Tseng, & Ho, 2018). Information and communication technologies (ICTs) have further empowered consumers by providing comprehensive data and diverse choices, allowing travellers to make informed decisions regarding quality, prices and services (Gupta & Utkarsh, 2014). Tourism websites, as primary sources of information, play a key role in marketing and customer acquisition.

Innovative web design techniques, such as personalisation and multimedia integration, have improved the user experience in digital tourism. High-definition images and attractive content help to retain visitors, while personalised recommendations increase satisfaction and interaction (Carvalho et al., 2010). The application of design thinking methods in the development of tourism websites has improved user engagement by prioritising both usability and interactivity (Sutrensno & Singgalen, 2023). As smart tourism technologies advance, the concerns around security and data privacy remain critical as tourists seek secure digital platforms to plan their trips (Pai et al., 2020). Future developments in tourism website design must address these concerns while leveraging technological advances to improve engagement and accessibility (Pai et al., 2020).

2.2 Storytelling in Tourism

Storytelling has long been a central mechanism of cultural expression and communication. As one of humanity's first tools for knowledge transfer, storytelling facilitates the preservation of traditions and the explanation of natural events (Gottschall, 2012; Hou, 2024). Boyd (2009) highlights that storytelling helps individuals interpret the world and build relationships by sharing emotions and experiences. From oral traditions to cave paintings, the evolution of storytelling underlines its role in cultural continuity. With the advent of written language, stories were no longer restricted to temporal and spatial boundaries, allowing societies to document their histories and transmit knowledge from one generation to the next (Heller, 2005). Today, digital storytelling reflects this evolution, moving from ancient walls to social media platforms, while maintaining its essential role in human connection (Hou, 2024).

The persuasive nature of storytelling also makes people susceptible to being manipulated, as persuasive narratives can shape public perception and influence opinions (Gottschall, 2012). Regardless of this risk, storytelling remains central to communication, as it involves the emotional and cognitive functions of the brain, enhancing empathy and understanding. The moral dimension of storytelling assures that societies continue to use narratives to strengthen ethical frameworks and shared values (Boyd, 2009). The ability of storytelling to shape reality, whether through literature, media or digital platforms, underscores its enduring influence on human thought and interaction.

In tourism, storytelling has become a critical element in shaping experiences and destinations. By combining historical authenticity with modern engagement techniques, tourism narratives can create immersive experiences that attract visitors and enhance their connection to places (Mossberg, 2008). Chronis (2012) explains that iconic tourism relies on cultural imaginaries, shared narratives that shape visitors' perceptions and engagement. Places like Gettysburg exemplify how storytelling enhances tourism by endowing destinations with collective meaning and emotional resonance. Co-creating stories between visitors and the tourism industry promotes a sense of participation and makes tourism experiences more personal and memorable (Chronis, 2012).

Creating engaging tourism experiences requires both an engaging environment and a break from everyday routine (Chronis, Arnould and Hampton, 2012). Facilitating characters, such as tour guides, play a crucial role in bridging the ordinary and the extraordinary, guiding visitors through immersive storytelling that transforms their experiences. The active participation and interactive storytelling allows tourists to shape personal interpretations, leading to memorable and emotional connections with destinations (Chronis, Arnould and Hampton, 2012). These moments of emotion and amazement contribute to creating long-lasting impressions that increase the attractiveness of destinations.

In the digital era, storytelling in tourism has evolved with the integration of technology. Digital platforms and social media make narrative dissemination easier, allowing tourists to interact with stories before, during and after their visits (Bassano et al., 2019). The shift towards digital storytelling presents both opportunities and challenges, requiring tourism professionals to leverage technology effectively to create compelling and authentic narratives. As storytelling remains a driving force in shaping tourism experiences, its continuous adaptation to digital media will define future trends in destination marketing and visitor engagement (Bassano et al., 2019).

2.3 Virtual Reality in Tourism

Virtual Reality (VR) emerged in the 1970s and is defined as a computer-based technology that simulates a three-dimensional environment, utilizing sensors to facilitate user interaction through visual and auditory stimuli (Oxford University Press, n.d.). This technology can either replicate or extend beyond physical reality which was initially developed for the gaming industry, VR has since been widely adopted across various sectors, including tourism.

VR has been increasingly recognized as a transformative technology in the tourism sector. Not only does it facilitate stakeholders in building immersive destination experiences, enhancing marketing effectiveness, and contributing to cultural heritage preservation, but also simultaneously mitigates traveller information uncertainty within desired destinations and influences travel decision-making (Yung & Khoo-Lattimore, 2017).

This tool has the potential to create alternative experiences that can be highly beneficial for heritage preservation (Guttentag, 2010). Besides, VR is providing a way for museums and heritage sites to offer immersive educational experiences that go beyond physical limitations (Rauscher, Humpe, & Brehm, 2020). In terms of customer experience, Neuhofer, Buhalis, and Ladkin (2015) examined the role of information and communication technologies (ICTs) as drivers of transformation in tourist experiences. A crucial aspect in assessing the effectiveness of VR in simulating authentic travel experiences is the concept of "presence," which refers to the psychological sensation of being physically immersed in a virtual environment regarding three aspects (1) immersion and enjoyment, (2) destination preference and (3) behavioral intention (Tussyadiah et al., 2018). VR also promotes inclusion by enabling travel for people with physical disabilities or economic limitations and contributes to sustainable tourism initiatives by reducing carbon footprint and over-tourism in popular destinations (Calisto & Sarkar, 2024).

Despite its advantages, VR in tourism faces several challenges that make widespread adoption difficult. VR alternatives may be susceptible to unauthorized copying by competitors, who could offer them for free or at a reduced price. As a result, VR applications like Petra, for example, theoretically have the potential to benefit VR developers globally (Guttentag, 2010). Technological and economic barriers, such as high hardware and infrastructure costs, limit accessibility (Rauscher et al., 2020). Furthermore, Rauscher et al. (2020) note that perceptions of VR's utility vary, with some users seeing it as an inadequate substitute for real-world travel, particularly for active holiday experiences that involve direct engagement with the natural and cultural environment.

The role of VR in sustainable tourism development is particularly promising. By offering virtual alternatives to physical travel, VR can help mitigate the problems associated with over-tourism, protecting fragile destinations while still offering enriching experiences (Rauscher et al., 2020). Furthermore, VR can make remote or dangerous destinations accessible, ensuring that cultural and natural heritage sites remain available to the global public without compromising their conservation. As the technology evolves, its integration with other digital innovations will continue to shape the future of tourism, balancing accessibility, sustainability and immersive experiences (Calisto and Sarkar, 2024).

The acceptance of VR tourism by individuals is influenced by their experience motivations (Neuhofer, Buhalis, & Ladkin, 2015). While tourism primarily serves recreational purposes, travellers may also be driven by other factors, such as the desire to escape daily life, seek novelty, experience excitement, or engage in social interactions. VR is able to provide mental rather than physical escapism, and offers novelty and excitement but cannot fully replicate real-life experiences (Guttentag, 2010). Future research should explore the integration of advanced technologies such as Artificial Intelligence (AI) and 5G networks to enhance the realism and interactivity of VR experiences (Calisto and Sarkar, 2024). In addition, the inclusion of multisensory elements such as touch and smell could address current limitations, increasing immersion and making virtual travel a more attractive alternative (Calisto and Sarkar, 2024).

2.4 Virtual Museums Offers Innovations and Tourist Needs

Virtual museums have significantly transformed the cultural heritage sector by leveraging digital technologies such as virtual reality (VR) and augmented reality (AR) to provide immersive and interactive experiences (Trunfio, Della Lucia, Campana, & Magnelli, 2021). These platforms go beyond traditional museum spaces, providing access to cultural heritage without geographical or temporal limitations (Trunfio, Della Lucia, Campana, & Magnelli, 2021).

Originally conceived as static websites, virtual museums have evolved into dynamic environments enhanced with multimedia content, such as 3D reconstructions and guided video tours (Shehade & Stylianou-Lambert, 2020). The development of VR and AR technologies has allowed museums to offer interactive and sensory experiences, bridging the gap between physical and virtual spaces (Wu, Jiang, Liang, & Ni, 2022).

The integration of mixed reality (MR) improves the visitor experience by merging AR and VR elements, enabling users to interact with physical artefacts while interacting with digital overlays (Trunfio et al.,

2021). These technologies allow for personalised museum experiences, as seen in institutions such as the Ara Pacis Museum, which offers multilingual and interactive tours, ensuring accessibility to diverse audiences (Trunfio, Campana and Magnelli, 2019). Furthermore, according to Morse, Lallemand, Wieneke, & Koenig, 2021 virtual museums are employing storytelling techniques to engage visitors; for example, using applications to transport users into reconstructed historical environments, offering an enriched cultural narrative.

Tourists' engagement with virtual museums is driven by four main needs: educational value, accessibility, entertainment and cultural connection (Flavián, Ibáñez-Sánchez & Orús, 2019; Wu et al., 2022). The immersive attributes of VR and AR redefine traditional museum visits, transforming them into interactive and entertaining journeys (Shehade & Stylianou-Lambert, 2020). Virtual museums strategically balance intellectual stimulation with entertainment by incorporating gamification techniques such as the Art Remix app, which encourages creative exploration of digital artefacts (Morse et al., 2021). Furthermore, VR storytelling transforms passive viewing into active participation, ensuring that visitors deeply engage with cultural storytelling while enjoying an immersive and enjoyable experience (Trunfio et al., 2019).

Virtual museums are at the forefront of cultural innovation, bridging the gap between historic preservation and modern technological advances (Flavián, Ibáñez-Sánchez and Orús, 2019; Morse et al., 2021). Through the integration of digital tools, personalised experiences and interactive narratives, these institutions effectively respond to the diverse expectations of contemporary tourists (Flavián et al., 2019; Morse et al., 2021). Their evolution highlights a more strategic response to changing visitor needs, combining intellectual engagement with cultural resonance (Shehade & Stylianou-Lambert, 2020; Wu et al., 2022). As such platforms are further developed, future research should explore their long-term impact, cross-cultural applicability and sustainability (Shehade & Stylianou-Lambert, 2020; Wu et al., 2022).

Virtual museums therefore represent a crucial advance in cultural heritage, ensuring accessibility, preservation and engagement of historical narratives in the digital age (Flavián, Ibáñez-Sánchez & Orús, 2019).

3. METHODOLOGY

Horses are a noticeable part of the Bavarian travel region identity. However, the information about them is scarce, especially in online sources. As s result, the travel potential of the region among equestrian tourists is not realised.

Design thinking is a series of human-centred ongoing interactions to innovate a product (service) which can address a specific need of a group of people by possible technology. "it is a discipline that uses the designer's sensibility and methods to match people's needs with what is technologically feasible and what a viable business strategy can convert into customer value and market opportunity." (Brown, 2008, p. 86). There are several proposed stages for DT by different authors and organization. However, most of the researches agree that design should be an iterative and non-linear process (e.g. Boldrini, 2022, Rösch et al., 2023). To developing a solution for our subject we followed design thinking stages as suggested by Boldrini (2022).

1. Empathizing is about understanding the problem and trying to look at the issue from the viewpoint of people who we are trying to solve their problem. To design a virtual horse museum in Lower Bavaria, the empathy phase must begin with understanding the specific interests and expectations of the target audience, which may include equestrian enthusiasts, historians, tourists, and local communities with cultural connections to equestrian traditions. Interviews were conducted with students at the Deggendorf Institute of Technology for being potential users that could provide information on their levels of knowledge, motivations and preferred interaction modes within a virtual space (Barbieri, Bruno and Muzzupappa, 2017). Additionally, participatory design techniques were implemented in these interviews, in which users

actively contributed to the conceptualisation of the virtual space, playing a crucial role in ensuring that the project fits both the educational and emotional expectations of the customers (Zidianakis et al., 2021).

2. Define: Clearly articulate the problem to be solved based on the insights gathered during the empathize stage. This stage primarily involves the synthetization of research through developing a clearly defined problem statement which will lead to ideation (Brown, 2008). To tackle the challenges identified, we engaged in brainstorming sessions to explore various ideas.

3. Ideate: Generate a wide range of potential solutions, thinking creatively and outside the box.

It consists in generating a broad range of ideas to address the defined problem. This phase encourages creative thinking and the exploration of diverse solutions (Brown, 2008).

4. Prototype: Create tangible representations of the most promising solutions to test and refine. Service blueprint tool has been used to distinguished components of our product and the relation of the components to each other. Service blueprint is a visual tool that maps out all steps of a service process, helping businesses design, analyze, and optimize their operations. It ensures efficiency by standardizing service delivery while allowing flexibility to adapt to customer needs. This method helps identify fail points, manage customer expectations, and improve coordination among employees. It is especially useful in complex services, where multiple touchpoints influence customer experience.

5. Test: Gather feedback on the prototypes from users, iterate on the design, and repeat the process until a desirable solution is reached.

The "Testing stage" is a critical component of the design thinking process, allowing designers to evaluate prototypes by observing real users' interactions and gathering feedback to inform iterative improvements (Brown, 2008). In our project, we conducted usability testing on the digital sketches of the Horses Virtual Museum web design to assess its effectiveness and user experience. We selected random participants from the Deggendorf Institute of Technology who represented our target audience of millennials and Generation Z. An invitation was sent to schedule remote interviews, during which participants tested the prototype while recording their screens for analysis. The digital sketches were forwarded to the participants during the first section of the video call which would be in an attempt to emulate the aspects of communicating with a live webpage. Participants provided feedback on the accessibility of information, intuitiveness of the interface, and interest level.

Participants went through the virtual museum's six sections, each designed with a storytelling approach: (1) History of Horses, (2) Rottaler Horse, (3) Locals and Horses, (4) Horse Training Process, (5) Races in the Region and (6) Horses in Art. They were asked to explore the website's sections, interact with features like 360-degree views and audio guides, and evaluate usability through navigation tasks and the loading screen animation. The interface was tested on various devices, including laptops, PCs, mobile phones, and tablets, under both high and low bandwidth conditions to assess performance.
By integrating market orientation, formal service design, and a strong service climate, businesses can enhance customer satisfaction and operational effectiveness. (Kostopoulos, Gounaris, & Boukis, 2012)

DT Phase	Research Activity	Outcome

1. Empathize	Semi-structured interviews with potential users (students at Deggendorf Institute of Technology) Participatory design sessions to collect user expectations and insights	Identified user needs, barriers to engagement, and expectations for an equestrian virtual museum
2. Define	Thematic analysis of interview responses Development of a clear problem statement based on key findings	Framed the core problem: Lack of awareness and digital access to Lower Bavaria's equestrian heritage
3. Ideate	Design workshops Sketching & wireframing Brainstorming and ranking key website features	Conceptualized the Virtual Museum, defining its six thematic stables, storytelling elements, and navigation structure
4. Prototype	Service Blueprinting to map out user interaction and service flow Initial	Created the first interactive prototype with a structured visitor journey

	wireframes and low-fidelity sketches	
5. Test	Usability testing with target users Screen recordings & post-test interviews	Collected feedback on usability, navigation clarity, and content accessibility, leading to iterative improvements

Table 1 - The research methodology, linking each Design Thinking phase to specific research activities and outcomes

Six participants were selected for the study based on usability research indicating that small sample sizes can effectively identify the majority of usability issues. Faulkner (2003) found that testing with five to ten users can uncover most usability problems, with diminishing returns beyond this range. This means that a small but well-selected sample can effectively identify major navigation, accessibility, and content clarity issues without unnecessary redundancy.

The participants were diverse in digital literacy and interest in equestrian tourism, ensuring that our findings captured a broad range of potential user experiences. By using six participants in both the Empathize (interviews) and Test (usability testing) phases, the study was able to collect sufficient qualitative insights to refine the virtual museum's design while maintaining an efficient and focused research process.

4. FINDINGS

4.1 Empathise

The conducted interviews and participatory design techniques revealed the barriers to accessibility, engagement challenges and interaction preferences. Specifically, the participants highlighted that there is no dedicated channel exists for guests to obtain this information Many visitors were unaware of the presence of the stables and horses in the area and were surprised to find them. Furthermore, there are no online resources, even in English, that provide details about the Rottaler horses in Lower Bavaria, which makes it difficult for international visitors to find out about them. Consequently, the equestrian events are still mainly known to a niche audience that follows the sport as a habit. These insights were translated into design requirements for the virtual museum (Zidianakis et al., 2021; Siegel & Dray, 2019).

4.2 Define and Ideate

After evaluating multiple concepts, we have proposed a Virtual Museum of Horses in Lower Bavaria. It is ideated as an innovative online platform designed to provide an engaging and educational experience about the history, culture, and significance of horses in the region. This web-based museum offers an immersive environment that, in the future, may also become accessible via virtual reality (VR) technology. By integrating digital tools with a structured narrative, the museum aims to enhance visitors' understanding of horses from historical, cultural, and practical perspectives.

We selected the development of a web page for a virtual museum dedicated to horses in Lower Bavaria. This solution was chosen for its ability to provide an accessible platform for visitors to engage with lower Bavaria equine heritage, aiming at offering a comprehensive insight into the cultural heritage of horses in lower Bavaria. By providing detailed information and immersive experiences, the museum enhances visitor preparedness and awareness of lower Bavaria equine traditions, strengthening its tourism appeal and destination's tourist offerings.

A service blueprint (Fig 1) was designed to provide a detailed visualisation of the service delivery process of our virtual museum (Bitner et al., 2008). The blueprint allowed us to map out the user journey, frontstage and backstage interactions, supporting processes and physical evidence This ensured a seamless, cohesive user experience.

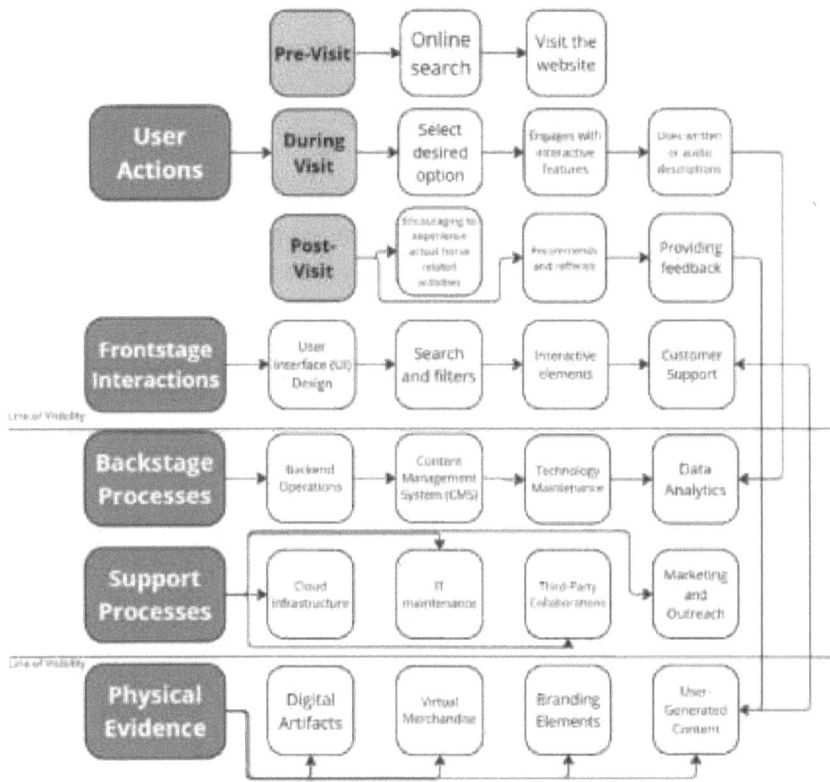

Figure 1 - Proposed Service Blueprint for potential customers of virtual museum about horses in Lower Bavaria

4.3 Prototype

Following the selection of the virtual museum web page concept, we employed digital sketching as a method to visualize and refine our ideas. Sketching serves as a fundamental tool in the design process, allowing designers to externalize thoughts and iterate on concepts quickly (Hoffmann, 2020). This approach facilitated the exploration of various layouts and user interfaces which ensured that the final design would be user-friendly and engaging.

Upon entering the website, visitors first encounter a loading page, which serves as an introduction to the digital experience. Following this, users are given the option to choose between a high-speed version optimized for broadband connections and a low-bandwidth version, ensuring accessibility for users with limited internet connectivity. After making their selection, visitors proceed to another loading page before reaching the main exhibition space.

The website designed minimalistic with 4 functional buttons in each page to avoid confusing visitors because each virtual content of each room has many details. The function keys are the key of going back to the previous page, help, exit and audio.

The virtual museum is structured into six thematic virtual stables, each dedicated to a distinct subject related to horses. Within each stable, the museum presents content through a well-structured narrative format, guided by an audio tour that is accompanied by subtitles if selected. Each stable provides a general storyline, introducing visitors to the overarching theme, while individual exhibits within the stable offer detailed explanations about specific elements. Each stable includes interactive components, allowing visitors to click on certain objects to access additional information on separate pages dedicated to those elements. This approach enables a dynamic and engaging learning experience rather than a static display of information.

The museum's content is divided into six primary sections, each represented by a virtual stable:

The History of Horses

This section explores the domestication of horses and their role in human civilization. It discusses how different societies utilized horses for various purposes, including transportation, agriculture, warfare, and recreation. Visitors can learn about the evolutionary adaptations of horses and how selective breeding influenced their characteristics over time.

Bavaria and Horses

This stable focuses on the historical significance of horses in Bavaria, tracing their role in local traditions and daily life. It examines the cultural heritage associated with horses in the region, including folklore, festivals, and traditional occupations. Additionally, the stable highlights various local equestrian communities and organizations that contribute to the preservation of equine culture in Bavaria.

The Rottaler Horse

This section is dedicated to the Rottaler horse, a rare and endangered breed native to Bavaria. It provides an in-depth look at the unique characteristics of the breed, its historical importance, and the conservation efforts undertaken to protect it. Visitors can explore ongoing breeding programs and initiatives aimed at ensuring the survival of this important equine lineage.

The Training Process

This stable delves into the methods of horse training and management, covering topics such as breeding, raising, and conditioning horses. It includes information on training techniques, essential accessories, and horse care practices. Interactive elements allow visitors to learn about various riding disciplines and equestrian sports, as well as the ethical considerations involved in horse training.

Equestrian Races in the Region

This section highlights horse racing traditions in Lower Bavaria, showcasing the historical and contemporary significance of equestrian competitions. It presents information about popular regional races, their rules, and the impact of these events on local communities.

Horses in Art
The final stable explores the representation of horses in various art forms, including paintings, sculptures, literature, and folklore. It examines how horses have been depicted throughout history, from ancient cave paintings to modern artistic interpretations. This section also discusses the symbolic and aesthetic significance of horses in different artistic traditions and how they have inspired artists across time periods.

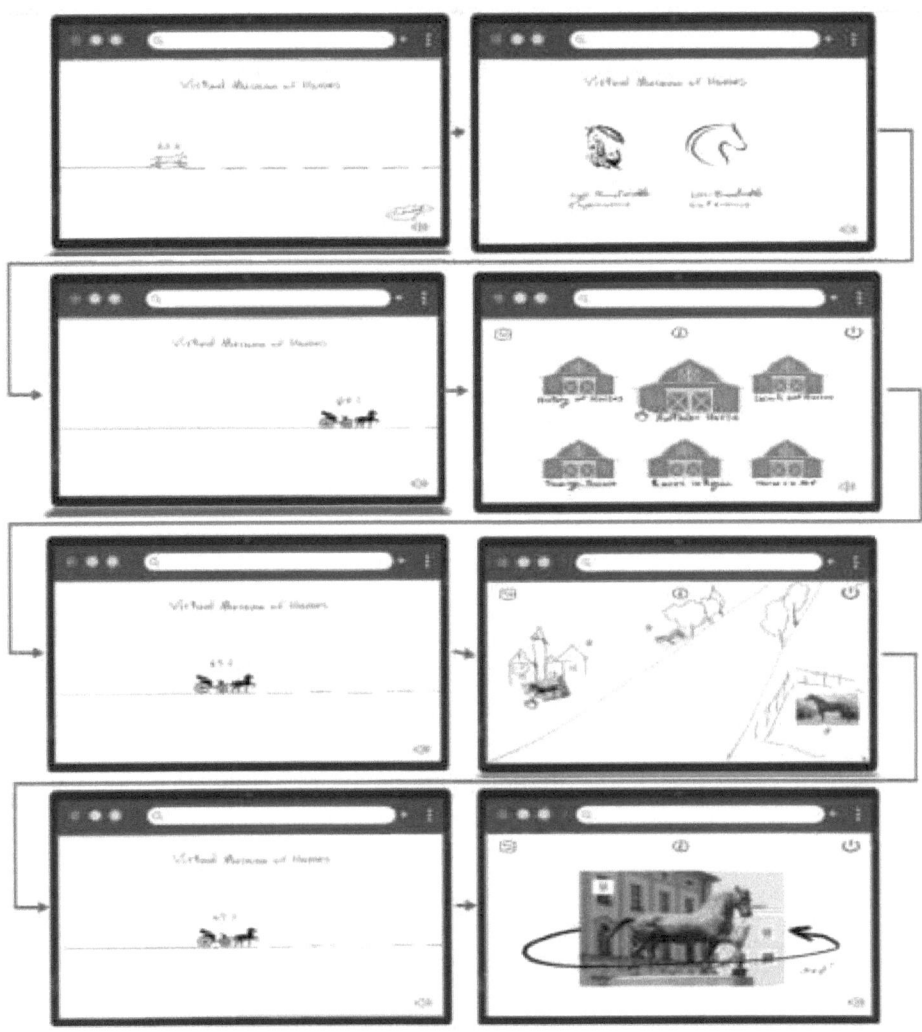

Figure 2 - Prototype - Virtual Museum Lower Bavaria

4.4 Testing

The evaluation focused on several key aspects, which were identified as key issues earlier. Table 1 summarises the key findings of the evaluation:

Navigation	Assessing the ease with which users could move between sections and find information.
Content Accessibility	Examining how easily users can access and comprehend the information presented.
Interactivity	Evaluating the effectiveness of interactive elements, such as 360-degree views and audio guides.
Performance	Observing the website's functionality across different devices and bandwidth conditions.

Table 1 - Evaluation focused on several key aspects

The usability testing revealed several key aspects of the user experience. Participants generally found the website engaging, particularly appreciating the storytelling approach used in the sections of the virtual museum. The integration of interactive elements such as 360-degree views and audio guides contributed to a more immersive experience, aligning with literature on digital tourism that highlights the role of multimedia in enhancing engagement (Heidari et al., 2024). However, certain aspects of navigation and clarity needed improvement. For instance, user feedback emphasized the importance of an easy-access menu bar, allowing for seamless movement between sections. This suggestion aligns with best practices in web design, where clear and intuitive navigation is crucial for user retention (Kim & Fesenmaier, 2008).

Participants' feedback highlighted the importance of intuitive navigation, clear labelling of buttons (e.g., return to the previous page, information icons, and home page access), and the effectiveness of the loading screen animation in providing visual feedback during loading times. These insights will guide the iterative refinement of the virtual museum's design to enhance user experience. It was further noted that some pages lacked clear directional routes, leading to occasional confusion regarding the next steps. Furthermore, users suggested that the site could benefit from customization features, such as a personalized experience mode that allows visitors to save their progress and revisit specific sections easily.

Tourists, particularly non-German speakers, often struggle with understanding local cultural offerings, making language a significant barrier to participation. One significant recommendation was the inclusion of a language selection button to cater to a diverse audience. As virtual museums serve both local and international visitors, multilingual support is essential in ensuring inclusivity and wider reach. This insight is consistent with previous research on virtual museums, which stresses the need for personalized and accessible content to engage a global audience (Flavián, Ibáñez-Sánchez & Orús, 2019). Another accessibility consideration involved optimizing the interface for visually impaired users. Participants suggested implementing screen reader compatibility and alternative text descriptions for images to ensure a more inclusive experience.

Participants also gave their feedback regarding the clarity of certain elements. For instance, some found it unclear whether the "High and Low" options referred to different levels of immersion (e.g., VR vs. non-VR) or differences in the depth of storytelling. Ensuring that these options are explicitly labeled and explained within the interface would help mitigate confusion. Additionally, some users questioned how different pages were connected and whether progress through the museum followed a structured path. This highlights the importance of providing clear visual indicators of progression, such as a breadcrumb trail or a dynamic progress tracker, to help users understand where they are in the virtual journey.

In addition, feedback suggested a need for more engaging textual content. While the storytelling approach was well received, some users recommended incorporating more interactive storytelling techniques, such as quizzes or decision-based exploration paths, to further involve the audience and enhance learning retention.

While the interactive elements were well-received, users expressed a need for better integration of audio features with text-based alternatives for accessibility. For example, if the audio button narrates a story, a corresponding text description should be available for users who are hearing-impaired or prefer reading. The significance of offering alternative interaction methods aligns with literature on inclusive digital experiences, where accessibility features improve engagement and user satisfaction (Nadda et al., 2020). Additionally, there is a strong preference for implementing virtual reality (VR) capabilities, as some users expected more immersive experiences, such as guided VR tour elements that allow users to interact with 3D-rendered horses.

5. DISCUSSION

The virtual horse museum prototype incorporates key UXD principles such as simplified navigation, interactive storytelling and personalised user experiences. The digital platform features a structured narrative divided into themed virtual stables, each offering a unique exploration of horse-related topics. Accessibility considerations, such as multilingual support and content adaptable to different user preferences, have been integrated into the design. The iterative development process follows the phases of design thinking, ensuring continuous refinement based on user feedback (Boldrini, 2022). By aligning with contemporary UXD frameworks, the virtual museum serves as a model for digital tourism experiences that prioritise user engagement, accessibility and cultural immersion (Trunfio et al., 2021; Heidari et al., 2024).

The findings align with broader trends in digital tourism, where immersive storytelling and personalization play a central role in enhancing visitor engagement (Chronis, Arnould, & Hampton, 2012). Traditional museums and guided tours can have physical limitations, but an online museum expands accessibility while minimizing environmental impact. The museum not only promotes lower Bavaria cultural assets but also enhances regional tourism appeal, encouraging visitors to explore the area physically after experiencing it digitally. Currently, information about equestrian events, history, and cultural narratives is fragmented across various sources, making it difficult for travelers to find informative insights. Consolidating this information into a single interactive platform, the virtual museum bridges the gap between local tourism providers and visitors, creating a more enjoyable and user-friendly experience.

The methodological approach of design thinking has been essential in developing the virtual museum by emphasizing user needs, iterative prototyping, and continuous improvement. Future research should explore partnerships with local tourism boards, equestrian associations, and cultural institutions to expand the scope and impact of the museum. The Virtual Horses Museum can serve as a model for the integration of technology and cultural heritage in digital tourism. Moving forward, continuous adaptation and technological advancements will be key to ensuring the museum's sustainability and continued impact in the evolving landscape of digital tourism.

The study shows that digital technologies enhance the cultural experience. This is consistent with research by Styliani et al. (2009) and Liestøl (2014), who emphasize that virtual museums make hard-to-reach places accessible. Falk and Dierking (2013) also support the idea that interactive experiences create a deeper connection to culture. Smith (2006), however, warns that digital experiences can simplify content. Our study confirms that well-designed multimedia content can mitigate this risk.

Flavián et al. (2019) emphasize that digital museums should offer accessible and personalized content. Our results show that language barriers and a lack of support for the visually impaired are problematic. Multilingual offerings and screen readers are essential future improvements.

Implementing virtual reality (VR) in virtual museums presents additional technical challenges.

VR requires high computing power, especially for complex, detailed environments that are intended to provide a realistic experience. This means users need powerful devices such as gaming PCs or modern VR headsets. Also, the study focused primarily on the user experience and learning effect. Economic issues were not examined, such as the costs and long-term benefits of the virtual museum for tourism in the region. Future studies could explore this in more detail.

6. CONCLUSION

To sum up, the Virtual Horses Museum has demonstrated how digital platforms can transform regional tourism by enhancing accessibility, engagement, and cultural preservation. Through the implementation of an interactive virtual museum, this project has provided an innovative solution for promoting lower Bavaria equestrian heritage while addressing key challenges such as fragmented information, accessibility barriers, and limited tourist engagement. Using technologies, the virtual museum offers immersive storytelling, personalized navigation, and interactive features, improving the overall visitor experience. The incorporation of elements such as 360-degree views, multilingual support, and audio guides enhances accessibility and fosters a more inclusive digital environment. These features contribute to a more informed and engaged audience, ensuring that both local and international visitors can explore and appreciate the region's rich cultural assets.

This project has also demonstrated how digital tourism can bridge the gap between physical and virtual experiences, allowing users to interact with cultural heritage before, during, and after their visit. The virtual museum minimizes environmental impact by offering sustainable alternatives to traditional tourism while increasing global awareness of Lower Bavaria's historical and cultural significance.

The limitations persist, particularly in the areas of user engagement and technological integration. The usability testing phase identified navigation challenges, clarity issues, and the need for additional customization options. Future iterations of the museum should focus on implementing expanded VR capabilities, and real-time event updates to further enhance interactivity and user experience. Additionally, there is a need for further testing and improvements to refine the platform and ensure its long-term success.

REFERENCES

Barbieri, L., Bruno, F., & Muzzupappa, M. (2017). Virtual museum system evaluation through user studies. Journal of Cultural Heritage, 26, 101–108. https://doi.org/10.1016/j.culher.2017.02.005

Bassano, C., Barile, S., Piciocchi, P., Spohrer, J. C., Iandolo, F., & Fisk, R. (2019). Storytelling about places: Tourism marketing in the digital age. Cities, 87, 10–20. https://doi.org/10.1016/j.cities.2018.12.025

Bitner, M. J., Ostrom, A. L., & Morgan, F. N. (2008). Service blueprinting: A practical technique for service innovation. California Management Review, 50(3), 66-94.

Boldrini, N. (2022). Design Thinking: Definition, Application, and Benefits for Businesses. THE FUTURES & FORESIGHT TEAM. https://tech4future.info/en/design-thinking/

Boyd, B. (2009). On the origin of stories: Evolution, cognition, and fiction. Harvard University Press.

Bray, A., & Tangney, B. (2017). Technology usage in mathematics education research–A systematic review of recent trends. Computers & Education, 114, 255–273.

Brown, T. (2008). Design thinking. Harvard Business Review, 86(6), 84-92.

Calisto, M. L., & Sarkar, S. (2024). A systematic review of virtual reality in tourism and hospitality. International Journal of Hospitality Management.

Carvalho, A., Cunha, C. R., & Morais, P. (2010). A framework to support the tourist's information needs based on a ubiquitous approach. Business Transformation through Innovation and Knowledge Management, 14th IBIMA Conference Proceedings, 2470–2479.

Chronis, A. (2012). Between place and story: Gettysburg as tourism imaginary. Annals of Tourism Research, 39(4), 1797–1816.

Chronis, A., Arnould, E. J., & Hampton, R. D. (2012). Gettysburg re-imagined: The role of narrative imagination in consumption experience. Consumption Markets & Culture. https://doi.org/10.1080/10253866.2011.652823

Cross, N. (2023). Design thinking: What just happened? Design Studies, 86. https://doi.org/10.1016/j.destud.2023.101187

Flavián, C., Ibáñez-Sánchez, S., & Orús, C. (2019). The impact of virtual, augmented, and mixed reality technologies on the customer experience. Journal of Business Research, 100, 547–560. https://doi.org/10.1016/j.jbusres.2018.10.050

Faulkner, L. (2003). Beyond the five-user assumption: Benefits of increased sample sizes in usability testing. Behavior Research Methods, Instruments, & Computers, 35(3), 379–383. DOI: 10.3758/BF03195514

Gottschall, J. (2012). The storytelling animal: How stories make us human. Houghton Mifflin Harcourt.

Gupta, D. D., & Utkarsh. (2014). Information technology & tourism: Assessing the website effectiveness of top ten tourist-attracting nations. Inf Technol Tourism.

Guttentag, D. A. (2010). Virtual reality: Applications and implications for tourism. Tourism Management, 31(5), 637–651. https://doi.org/10.1016/j.tourman.2009.07.003

Heidari, M., Hosseininezhad, M. F., & Emami, H. (2024). Leveraging neuromarketing and neuroscientific approaches into persuasive tourism web design and its usability. Journal of Tourism Research.

Heller, S. (2005). The evolution of storytelling: From cave art to digital narratives. Princeton Architectural Press.

Hoffmann, A. R. (2020). Sketching as design thinking. Routledge.

Hou, D. (2024). Origin and development: History of storytelling. Dean & Francis, 1(9). https://doi.org/10.61173/xkvvf133

Katja Tschimmel. (2012). Design Thinking as an effective Toolkit for Innovation. https://doi.org/10.13140/2.1.2570.3361

Kim, H., & Fesenmaier, D. R. (2008). Persuasive design of destination websites: An analysis of first impression. Journal of Travel Research.

Kostopoulos, G., Gounaris, S., & Boukis, A. (2012). Service blueprinting effectiveness: Drivers of success. Managing Service Quality, 22(6), 580-591. https://doi.org/10.1108/09604521211287552

Leonard, D., & Rayport, J. F. (1997). Spark Innovation Through Empathic Design. Harvard Business Review, 75(6), 102–113.

Li, F., Spettu, F., Achille, C., Vassena, G., & Fassi, F. (2024). The role of web platforms in balancing sustainable conservation and development in large archaeological sites. ISPRS Archives.

Machí Hervàs, E. (2024). Design and development of a website for promoting local tourism in the Ribera Alta region. Universitat Politècnica de València.

Mossberg, L. (2008). Extraordinary experiences through storytelling. Scandinavian Journal of Hospitality and Tourism, 8(3), 195–210. https://doi.org/10.1080/15022250802532443

Morse, C., Lallemand, C., Wieneke, L., & Koenig, V. (2021). Virtual masterpieces: Innovation through public co-creation for digital museum collections. International Journal of the Inclusive Museum, 15(1), 65–83. https://doi.org/10.18848/1835-2014/CGP/v15i01/65-83

Nadda, V., Chaudhary, H. S., & Arnott, I. (2020). Cloud computing in tourism. Digital Marketing Strategies for Tourism, Hospitality, and Airline Industries. Neuhofer, B., Buhalis, D., & Ladkin, A. (2015).

Neuhofer, B., Buhalis, D., & Ladkin, A. (2015). Technology as a catalyst of change: Enablers and barriers of the tourist experience and their consequences. In I. Tussyadiah & A. Inversini (Eds.), Information and Communication Technologies in Tourism 2015 (pp. 789–802). Springer. https://doi.org/10.1007/978-3-319-14343-9_57

Oxford University Press. (n.d.). Virtual reality. Oxford English Dictionary. Retrieved March 18, 2025, fromhttps://www.oed.com/dictionary/virtual-reality_n?tl=true#:~:text=The%20earliest%20known%20use%20of,virtual%20adj.%2C%20reality%20n

Pai, C.-K., Kang, S., Liu, Y., & Zheng, Y. (2020). An examination of revisit intention based on perceived smart tourism technology experience. Sustainability, 13(2), 1007.

Rauscher, M., Humpe, A., & Brehm, L. (2020). Virtual reality in tourism: Is it 'real' enough? Academica Turistica.

Rösch, N., Tiberius, V., & Kraus, S. (2023). Design thinking for innovation: Context factors, process, and outcomes. European Journal of Innovation Management, 26(7), 160–176. https://doi.org/10.1108/EJIM-03-2022-0164

Shehade, M., & Stylianou-Lambert, T. (2020). Virtual reality in museums: Exploring the experiences of museum professionals. Applied Sciences, 10(11), 4031. https://doi.org/10.3390/app10114031

Siegel, D., & Dray, S. (2019). The Long and Winding Road: The Evolution of Human-Centered Design. Journal of Usability Studies, 14(2), 77–105.

Sutrensno, S., & Singgalen, Y. A. (2023). Digital innovation design of tourism destination marketing websites. Journal of Information Systems and Informatics, 5(2), 428–439.

Trunfio, M., Campana, S., & Magnelli, A. (2019). Measuring the impact of functional and experiential mixed reality elements on a museum visit. Current Issues in Tourism. https://doi.org/10.1080/13683500.2019.1703914

Trunfio, M., Della Lucia, M., Campana, S., & Magnelli, A. (2021). Innovating the cultural heritage museum service model through virtual reality and augmented. reality: The effects on the overall visitor experience and satisfaction. Journal of Heritage Tourism. https://doi.org/10.1080/1743873X.2020.1850742

Tussyadiah, I. P., Wang, D., Jung, T. H., & Tom Dieck, M. C. (2018). Virtual reality, presence, and attitude change: Empirical evidence from tourism marketing .Tourism Management, 66, 140–154. https://doi.org/10.1016/j.tourman.2017.12.003

Wu, Y., Jiang, Q., Liang, H., & Ni, S. (2022). What drives users to adopt a digital museum? A case of virtual exhibition hall of National Costume Museum. SAGE Open, 12(1), 1–17. https://doi.org/10.1177/21582440221082105

Yuan, Y., Tseng, Y.-H., & Ho, C.-I. (2018). Tourism information technology research trends. Journal of Travel Research.

Yung, R., & Khoo-Lattimore, C. (2017). New realities: A systematic literature review on virtual reality and augmented reality in tourism research. Current Issues in Tourism.

Zidianakis, E., Partarakis, N., Ntoa, S., Dimopoulos, A., Kopidaki, S., Ntagianta, A., Ntafotis, E., Xhako, A., Pervolarakis, Z., Kontaki, E., Zidianaki, I., Michelakis, A., Foukarakis, M., & Stephanidis, C. (2021).

The Invisible Museum: A user-centric platform for creating virtual 3D exhibitions with VR support. Electronics, 10(363). https://doi.org/10.3390/electronics10030363

Preserving Paradise: Framework to Develop Sustainable Tourism in San Vicente, Palawan, Philippines

Joseph Henessey Gorriceta, Technische Hochschule Deggendorf – European Campus Rottal-Inn, Henessey.Gorriceta@gmail.com

Abstract

This study examines the intersection of tourism and sustainability in San Vicente, Palawan, Philippines, a municipality designated as a Tourism Enterprise Zone (TEZ). It evaluates the current state of tourism development and its alignment with sustainability principles, highlighting opportunities and challenges unique to San Vicente's context. The research incorporates global sustainable tourism development models to propose a tailored framework addressing the municipality's specific needs.

The methodology combines stakeholder engagement through surveys and semi-structured interviews, offering nuanced perspectives on tourism practices, growth opportunities and key challenges. Data analysis through Thematic Analysis and SWOT Analysis revealed critical themes and strategic insights shaping San Vicente's tourism landscape.

These findings informed the creation of the San Vicente Sustainable Tourism Pyramid (SVSTP), a bespoke framework designed to preserve San Vicente's natural and cultural assets while fostering steady, sustainable growth. The SVSTP provides actionable guidelines to balance economic development with environmental and social stewardship, ensuring the municipality remains a thriving yet sustainable destination for future generations.

Keywords: Sustainable tourism, San Vicente, tourism enterprise zone, sustainable development framework, Palawan.

1. INTRODUCTION

Tourism is a critical contributor to the global economy, yet it faces unprecedented challenges due to climate change and environmental degradation. By 2070, over one-third of the global population could be living in areas with uninhabitable climate conditions if current carbon emissions remain unchecked (Xu et al., 2020). Such projections have significant implications for tourism, including disappearing island destinations, degraded natural and cultural attractions, and operational challenges due to altered peak seasons and increased costs for resilient infrastructure (Belias et al., 2022; Wall and Badke, 1994). These risks underscore the urgency of embedding sustainability into tourism development to ensure the long-term viability of destinations and communities.

The Philippines, with its rich biodiversity and over 7,000 islands, exemplifies the challenges and opportunities of sustainable tourism development. While initiatives like the Department of Tourism's emphasis on sustainable practices are commendable, the country's current ranking of 158 out of 180 on the Environmental Performance Index and 94 out of 99 in the 2020 Sustainable Travel Index indicate significant room for improvement (Environmental Performance Index, 2022; Euromonitor International, 2021).

San Vicente, Palawan, emerges as a promising case study for sustainable tourism. Designated as a Flagship Tourism Enterprise Zone (TEZ) under the Tourism Act of 2009, San Vicente aims to balance economic growth, environmental preservation and community empowerment (Republic of the Philippines, 2009). Home to the longest white sand beach in the Philippines and endowed with vast mangroves, mountain ranges and rich marine ecosystems, the municipality's masterplan emphasises infrastructure development across tourism clusters such as eco-tourism and agri-tourism. However, it lacks a comprehensive framework addressing the interconnections between social, environmental and economic sustainability (Palafox Associates, n.d.).

This research seeks to bridge this gap by proposing a sustainable tourism framework tailored to San Vicente's unique context. Guided by the following research questions, this study aims to explore and implement global best practices to secure the municipality's long-term sustainability:

      1.   What constitutes a framework for sustainable tourism, and what are its key components and principles?

      2.   What sustainable tourism framework would be most relevant to San Vicente's socio-economic and ecological context?

      3.   How can insights from this study inform policy and practice in San Vicente and similar destinations?

Positioned as a micro-pilot study, this research focuses on a specific and localised geographic scope within San Vicente. The limited scale, involving a modest sample size for data collection, aims to provide preliminary insights and serve as a foundational step toward a broader, more comprehensive research agenda for sustainable tourism development in the municipality.

2. LITERATURE REVIEW

2.1 Concept of Sustainability

The modern concept of sustainability emerged in the 20th century amidst growing concerns about environmental degradation, resource depletion and socio-economic inequality (Caradonna, 2014; Morse, 2015). Meadows et al. (1972) catalysed this shift with The Limits to Growth, which highlighted the unsustainable trajectory of unchecked economic expansion due to finite resources and its interactions with population growth, agriculture, industrialization and pollution. This work ignited international dialogues on the need for a balanced approach to development. In 1987, the Brundtland Commission introduced a widely recognised definition of sustainable development: "meeting the needs of the present without compromising the ability of future generations to meet their own needs" (World Commission on Environment and Development, 1987). This definition underscores the interconnectedness of environmental, social and economic dimensions, forming the basis of the triple bottom line framework introduced by

Elkington (1994). This model remains a cornerstone for sustainability, guiding businesses and governments in adopting practices that balance these three pillars.

2.2 United Nations Sustainable Development Goals (SDGs)

The 2015 adoption of the United Nations Sustainable Development Goals (SDGs) marked a critical milestone in global sustainability efforts. The SDGs, consisting of 17 goals, aim to address a range of challenges, including poverty, inequality, environmental degradation and climate change, with an overarching vision of fostering a sustainable and equitable future (United Nations, 2015). These goals were a response to the shortcomings of the Millennium Development Goals (MDGs), which failed to adequately address environmental sustainability and the root causes of global challenges (Sachs, 2012).

Key SDGs relevant to sustainable tourism include Goal 13 (Climate Action), Goal 8 (Decent Work and Economic Growth), and Goal 12 (Responsible Consumption and Production). While the SDGs have spurred positive changes globally, challenges such as persistent inequalities, climate change and the impacts of the COVID-19 pandemic have hindered their full realisation (Meyer, 2020; United Nations, 2020). These challenges underscore the critical role of industries, including tourism, in advancing the SDGs while addressing their own environmental and social impacts.

2.3 Tourism's Role in Promoting the SDGs

Tourism, contributing 8% of global greenhouse gas emissions, is a critical sector for advancing the SDGs while mitigating its environmental impact (Lenzen et al., 2018). The World Travel and Tourism Council (WTTC) has committed to reducing tourism-related carbon emissions by 50% by 2035 and achieving net-zero emissions by 2050 through initiatives like the "Net Zero Roadmap for Travel & Tourism" (World Travel and Tourism Council, 2021). These efforts align with the SDGs, particularly in fostering sustainable consumption patterns and promoting inclusive growth (United Nations, 2015).

Countries like Costa Rica and Slovenia have demonstrated leadership in sustainable tourism through innovative frameworks such as the Certification Sustainable Tourism program and the Green Scheme of Slovenian Tourism, respectively. These initiatives highlight the potential for destinations to balance economic growth, environmental protection and social inclusivity (Instituto Costarricense de Turismo, 2020; Green Scheme of Slovenia Tourism, n.d.).

2.4 Sustainable Tourism Frameworks

Frameworks provide structured approaches to sustainable tourism development by integrating interconnected elements of tourism ecosystems (Clarke, 1997; Leiper, 1979). For example, the System Dynamics framework identifies critical components such as attractions, infrastructure and competitive rivalry, enabling effective planning and management (Gazoni & da Silva, 2021).

Olya (2020) emphasised community involvement in sustainable tourism frameworks, asserting that resident engagement fosters ownership and enhances policy effectiveness. Methodologies like structural equation modeling and qualitative comparative analysis further support nuanced approaches to sustainable tourism planning, ensuring alignment with local contexts and stakeholder needs.

2.5 Opportunity for San Vicente

San Vicente, a municipality in Palawan, is poised to leverage sustainable tourism as a developmental strategy. As a designated Tourism Enterprise Zone (TEZ), the municipality aligns with Butler's (1980) Tourism Area Life Cycle (TALC) model, currently transitioning from the development to the consolidation stage. This phase presents a unique opportunity to integrate sustainable tourism principles into its growth trajectory, ensuring long-term resilience and socio-economic benefits (Butler, 1980).

2.6 The Role of Sustainable Tourism in Post-Pandemic Recovery

The COVID-19 pandemic underscored the vulnerabilities of tourism-dependent regions, highlighting the need for resilience and adaptability. The ASEAN Framework on Sustainable Tourism Development in the Post-COVID-19 Era provides valuable insights for regions like San Vicente, emphasising recovery strategies centered on inclusivity, digital innovation and environmental sustainability (ASEAN, 2023).

By incorporating these strategies, San Vicente can position itself as a leader in sustainable tourism, contributing to regional and global sustainability goals while enhancing its appeal as a premier destination.

3. METHODOLOGY

3.1 Methodology and Study Design

The methodological approach adopted in this study aligns with the interpretivist paradigm, which emphasises understanding the meanings, experiences and perspectives of individuals involved in the research context (Denzin et al., 2023). As a qualitative inquiry, this research aims to explore the complex socio-economic and environmental dynamics of sustainable tourism development in San Vicente. The qualitative approach is particularly suited for studying phenomena like tourism, where motivations, experiences and perceptions often require nuanced investigation (Jennings, 2010).

Tourism research benefits from qualitative methodologies, as argued by Phillimore and Goodson (2004), who highlight their ability to uncover "lived" experiences essential for understanding the intricate interactions between stakeholders. Veal (2017) further suggests that qualitative methods are invaluable for investigating areas lacking established theories, such as emerging frameworks for sustainable tourism. These methodologies allow the researcher to delve deeply into the context-specific challenges and opportunities of San Vicente, an area with limited prior academic exploration. Thus, this study employs qualitative methods to address the multifaceted social, economic and environmental dimensions of sustainable tourism (Veal, 2017).

To ensure a logical analysis, three qualitative data collection techniques were utilised: secondary data analysis, stakeholder surveys and semi-structured interviews. Secondary data analysis offered a contextual overview of San Vicente's tourism landscape, including insights into existing policies, infrastructure and tourism patterns. Stakeholder surveys provided perspectives on current tourism challenges and opportunities for sustainable development. Lastly, semi-structured interviews with local stakeholders enriched the data with insights and specialised knowledge. Together, these techniques aimed to construct a multidimensional understanding of sustainable tourism development and support the formulation of a contextually relevant framework for San Vicente.

This study did not focus on quantitative indicators primarily due to the limitations in the sample size and the researcher's geographic constraints. The researcher, based in Germany, engaged with local stakeholders in San Vicente through digital tools such as Google Forms surveys, online interviews and Google Meet video sessions. The absence of on-the-ground fieldwork in San Vicente limited the feasibility of gathering quantitative data, leading to a deliberate choice to focus on qualitative methodologies. The modest sample size, remote data collection methods, and qualitative focus mean that the findings should be interpreted as preliminary insights rather than definitive conclusions.

3.2 Data Collection Process

3.2.1 Secondary Data Collection

The first stage of data collection focused on secondary sources to establish a foundational understanding of San Vicente's tourism sector. Secondary data were obtained from a range of online resources, including government reports, legislative documents, news articles and tourism authority publications. This process shed light on the evolution of San Vicente's tourism infrastructure, particularly the San Vicente Flagship Tourism Enterprise Zone, and the legislative frameworks guiding its development.

In addition to local insights, the study examined global best practices in sustainable tourism frameworks. By reviewing models from various regions, the study identified key principles, strategies and measures that have successfully fostered sustainability. This comparative analysis aimed to discern adaptable elements for San Vicente, allowing for the customisation of a sustainable tourism framework tailored to its unique challenges and opportunities.

3.2.2 Stakeholder Surveys

Engaging local stakeholders was pivotal to understanding the ground realities of tourism in San Vicente. An online meeting via Google Meet on April 13, 2023, introduced the research objectives to key stakeholders, including municipal officials, tourism representatives and business owners. This engagement sought to build trust and ensure stakeholder participation in the subsequent survey.

The survey, disseminated via Google Forms, consisted of 20 items designed to capture both quantitative and qualitative data. Structured questions employed a 5-point Likert scale to gauge stakeholder attitudes, perceptions and opinions, while open-ended questions provided an avenue for detailed, context-rich responses. Despite efforts to maximise participation, the survey yielded 12 responses, representing government employees and officials, business operators and residents. The inclusion of a Filipino translation ensured accessibility and comprehensibility for local respondents, addressing linguistic barriers encountered during the initial phase.

3.2.3 Online Interviews with Tourism Stakeholders

To complement survey findings, semi-structured interviews were conducted with key tourism stakeholders. These interviews provided deeper insights into themes emerging from the survey data and allowed participants to articulate their experiences and perspectives in greater detail. The iterative-inductive nature of qualitative research guided the interview process, enabling the identification of emergent patterns and themes (Flick, 2018).

Four interviews were conducted between June and July 2023. Participants included a representative from Globe Telecom (a local internet and telecommunications provider), the San Vicente Flagship TEZ, TIEZA, the Municipal Tourism Office and a foreign national who is a resort owner. These interviews explored aspects of sustainable tourism, from digital infrastructure and stakeholder collaboration to the operational challenges faced by local businesses. Thematic insights from these interviews enriched the study's understanding of San Vicente's tourism ecosystem and informed the development of targeted strategies for sustainability.

3.3 Data Analysis and Methods

To analyse the collected data, this study employed Thematic Analysis and SWOT Analysis. Thematic Analysis was utilised to identify patterns and themes within the qualitative data, following Braun and Clarke's (2006) six-step process. This included data familiarisation, coding, theme identification and iterative refinement to ensure a reasonable interpretation of stakeholder experiences and perceptions. The flexibility of Thematic Analysis allowed for an exploratory approach, uncovering insights specific to San Vicente's tourism context.

In parallel, SWOT Analysis provided a structured framework for assessing internal strengths and weaknesses, as well as external opportunities and threats. By evaluating these factors, the study aimed to identify actionable strategies for enhancing sustainable tourism development. This dual-method approach ensured a systematic analysis of the data, integrating stakeholder perspectives with contextual insights to inform the proposed framework for sustainable tourism in San Vicente.

The data for the Thematic and SWOT Analyses were sourced through the survey results from the respondents as well as transcripts from the Google Meet sessions and online interviews with local leaders and stakeholders. The researcher reviewed these qualitative data sources, manually extracting key patterns, themes and insights. By coding responses and identifying recurring themes, the researcher developed the Thematic Analysis, while concurrently evaluating strengths, weaknesses, opportunities and threats to construct the SWOT analysis.

4. RESULTS

A key finding from Survey Item no. 1.A ("Sustainability is a new concept for us") revealed that stakeholders displayed varying levels of familiarity with sustainable tourism concepts. While some respondents exhibited a solid understanding, others demonstrated limited awareness, indicating the novelty of sustainable tourism to many stakeholders. However, responses to Item no. 1.B ("We would like to learn more about Sustainable Tourism") were overwhelmingly positive, highlighting stakeholders' eagerness to learn more about sustainable tourism practices.

A critical insight emerged from Item no. 2, where stakeholders ranked local tourism entities based on their perceived responsibility for sustainable tourism development. The Local Government Unit (LGU) of San Vicente was identified as bearing the most responsibility, followed by the Office of the Municipal Tourism. The San Vicente Flagship Tourism Enterprise Zone (FTEZ) and the Tourism Infrastructure and Enterprise Zone Authority (TIEZA) were ranked lower, reflecting stakeholder priorities in assigning accountability.

The survey also revealed the respondents' perceived barriers to sustainable tourism. Three major challenges emerged: (1) Lack of Government Funds; (2) Inadequate Infrastructure; and (3) Shortage of Skilled Tourism Professionals. Interestingly, when asked about political leadership (Survey Item no. 3.B), most stakeholders disagreed with the statement that there was a lack of political will to support sustainable tourism. This reflects confidence in the municipality's leadership (led by the incumbent Mayor, Amy Roa Alvarez), which could serve as a foundation for strengthening tourism development efforts. Thematic Analysis of open-ended survey responses and interview data identified recurring themes (see Figure 1), including the importance of stakeholder collaboration, the need for education on sustainable tourism practices and the critical role of leadership and governance.

Figure 1. A thematic diagram illustrating the interconnected themes impacting Sustainable Tourism Development in San Vicente. The central node denotes the primary research focus, while the surrounding nodes represent related themes. The lines depict the relationships and interactions among these themes.

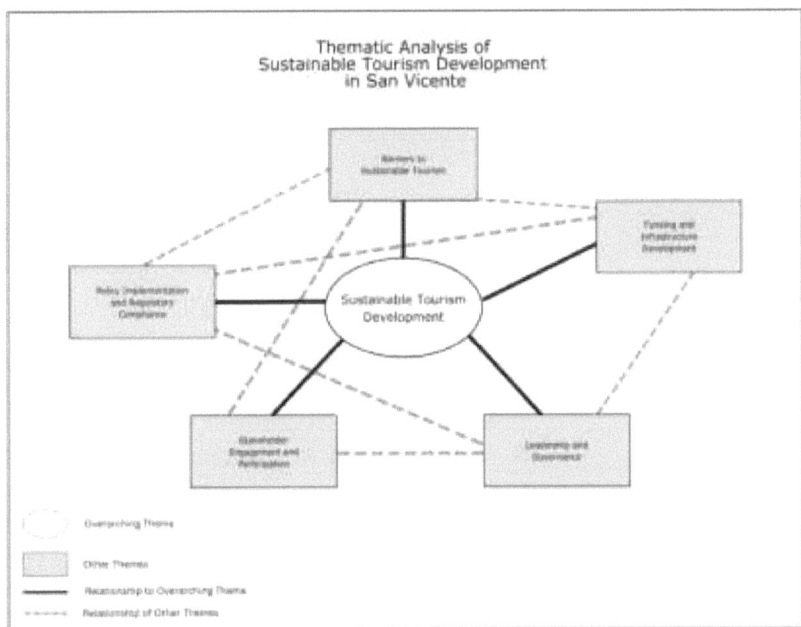

Table 1. SWOT Analysis of sustainable tourism development in San Vicente, Palawan. It identifies strengths, weaknesses, opportunities and threats of the area, providing an understanding of the current state and potential challenges and advantages for future tourism initiatives.

SWOT Analysis of Sustainable Tourism Development in San Vicente

Strengths

- San Vicente boasts an abundance of natural beauty, including pristine beaches and unique biodiversity, making it a prime spot for eco-tourism.

- The current municipal leadership, under Mayor Amy Roa Alvarez, enjoys the trust and confidence of locals and business operators, fostering a robust political will towards sustainable tourism.

- TIEZA, the LGU, and a number of private stakeholders are dedicated to sustainable practices and have shown their commitment and interest.

- The existence of a proactive master plan for tourism, even if yet to be fully actualized, sets a structured roadmap for development.

- The growth of tourism in the post-pandemic era adds to San Vicente's strength.

Weaknesses

- Infrastructure inadequacies, particularly in waste management, electricity, and internet connectivity, along with budgetary limitations, impede sustainable development.

- There is a knowledge gap and a need for more awareness about sustainable tourism among stakeholders.

- The current land classification presents an obstacle to commercial tourism development. (i.e. Port Barton, declared as Forest Land, needs to be reclassified by the Philippine Congress to become a sustainable tourism hub despite having a high number of tourism businesses in the municipality).

- A more defined Destination Management Organization (DMO) structure within the tourism sector could streamline business-related permits and clearance processes, enhancing inter-organizational cooperation among TIEZA, San Vicente Flagship TEZ, and the Local Government Unit (LGU) of San Vicente.

Opportunities

- Opportunities abound in leveraging stakeholder cooperation and embarking on community-based projects.

- Implementation of sustainability practices as prescribed in the masterplan can significantly enhance San Vicente's allure as a green tourist destination.

- Several private businesses are eager to invest in San Vicente, exemplified by Megaworld Corp's plan to invest P40 billion in developing a 462-hectare beachfront property over the next 10-15 years.

- Partnering with successful tourist destinations having similar geographical features could facilitate an effective transfer of sustainable tourism practices and knowledge.

- Reclassification of lands could pave the way for increased tourism-related businesses.

Threats

- Potential threats include a preference for short-term gains over a long-term vision.

- The lack of rigorous implementation of local laws and regulations for sustainable tourism practices poses further challenges.

- The degradation of natural resources due to activities like illegal logging and the pollution of municipal land, coastal water, and groundwater due to the absence of an efficient waste management system is another significant threat.

- The looming threats of climate change, which include rising sea levels and increased severity of weather disturbances such as typhoons, could significantly disrupt tourism activities and pose risks to infrastructure and natural attractions.

- The potential risk of over-tourism straining local resources and infrastructure.

5. DISCUSSION

The Thematic and SWOT Analyses, combined with insights gathered from stakeholder surveys and interviews, were instrumental in shaping the San Vicente Sustainable Tourism Pyramid (SVSTP). This proposed framework integrates key themes identified during the research, addressing challenges and opportunities in sustainable tourism development.

Figure 2. The San Vicente Sustainable Tourism Pyramid (SVSTP) is a tailored framework that integrates local stakeholders and tourism entities — with the San Vicente Flagship Tourism Enterprise Zone as the central DMO, showcasing an interconnected system where sustainable tourism development and infrastructure capacity are cyclically reinforced.

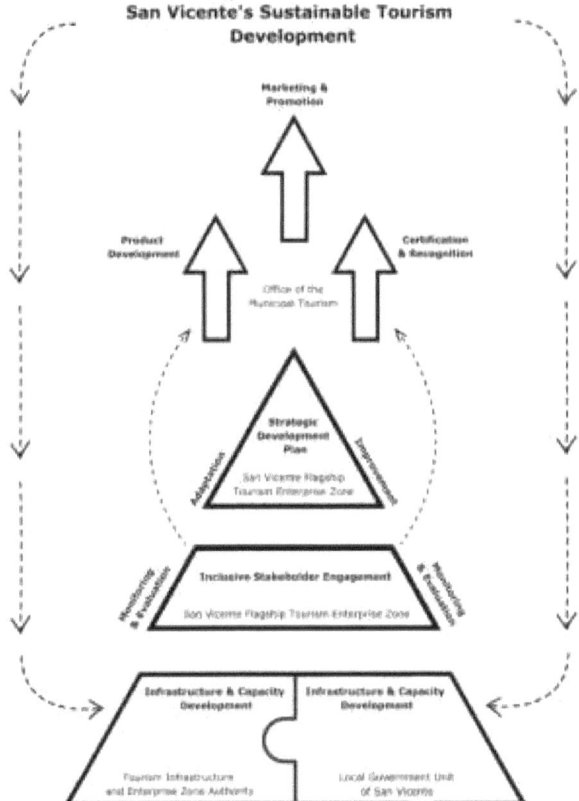

The foundation of the pyramid, **Infrastructure and Capacity Development**, prioritises basic infrastructure and human resource capacity, responding directly to gaps identified in stakeholder feedback. Above this, **Inclusive Stakeholder Engagement** ensures diverse perspectives are incorporated, fostering collaboration among government entities, private businesses and local communities. This is reinforced by legislative mandates for inclusivity in the San Vicente Flagship Tourism Enterprise Zone framework.

Monitoring and Evaluation provides a systematic approach to track progress, ensuring accountability and alignment with sustainability goals through measurable indicators. **The Strategic Development Plan**, building on the current Tourism Master Plan, emphasises adaptability to address evolving tourism trends and stakeholder needs.

At the pyramid's apex, **Product Development**, **Marketing and Promotion**, and **Certification and Recognition** work synergistically to enhance San Vicente's global competitiveness. These elements aim to differentiate the municipality while ensuring sustainable practices are incentivised and maintained.

The practical implications of the SVSTP framework extend to strategies for real-world application. For instance, the framework's emphasis on Infrastructure and Capacity Development can guide local government units in prioritising road and utility improvements, thereby supporting both tourism growth and community well-being.

Additionally, the Inclusive Stakeholder Engagement component offers a practical model for fostering public-private partnerships, enabling tourism businesses to collaborate with local communities on eco-friendly initiatives, such as mangrove reforestation and waste management programs.

Furthermore, the Certification and Recognition element could inspire San Vicente to establish a local 'Green Tourism' badge or award, promoting sustainable practices among businesses and enhancing their market competitiveness.

6. CONCLUSION

This study highlights the potential of San Vicente to become a model for sustainable tourism by integrating stakeholder collaboration, global standards and the insights gained through the proposed San Vicente Sustainable Tourism Pyramid (SVSTP). The research underscores that sustainable tourism is not merely about implementing a master plan but fostering cooperation and shared responsibility among all stakeholders, from government entities to local communities.

Strong political will, exemplified by Mayor Amy Roa Alvarez, and institutional commitment from entities like the Local Government Unit, Office of the Municipal Tourism, San Vicente Flagship TEZ and TIEZA are pivotal for driving progress. Moreover, sound fiscal management and private sector partnerships could address funding challenges, especially in the wake of pandemic-related disruptions. Rather than emulating mass-market destinations, San Vicente has the unique opportunity to carve its identity as a sustainable tourism destination, appealing to travellers who value balance between experience and environmental responsibility.

While this study offers valuable insights, it is important to acknowledge its scale and sample size limitations. As a micro-pilot study, the findings provide preliminary insights and lay a foundation for future research. Nevertheless, the study's qualitative approach offers a deeper contextual understanding of San Vicente's unique challenges and opportunities, showcasing how a tailored, destination-specific framework can effectively guide sustainable tourism development.

This approach reinforces the idea that there is no universal template for sustainable tourism frameworks, as each destination possesses distinct characteristics, challenges and opportunities. Instead, the development of bespoke frameworks that align with local contexts must be encouraged to ensure sustainability strategies are not only practical and effective but also resonant with the specific needs of different tourism destinations around the world.

REFERENCES

Association of Southeast Asian Nations (ASEAN) (2023) ASEAN launches framework on sustainable tourism development post-COVID-19. Available at: https://asean.org/asean-launches-framework-on-sustainable-tourism-development-post-covid-19/ [Accessed: 12 Mar. 2023].

Belias, D., Rossidis, I. and Valeri, M. (2022) 'Tourism in crisis: The impact of climate change on the tourism industry', in Valeri, M. (ed.) Tourism risk. Bingley: Emerald Publishing Limited, pp. 163-179. Available at: https://doi.org/10.1108/978-1-80117-708-520221012 [Accessed: 4 Jan. 2023].

Braun, V. and Clarke, V. (2012) Thematic analysis. Washington, DC: American Psychological Association.

Butler, R. (1980) 'The concept of a tourist area cycle of evolution: Implications for management of resources', The Canadian Geographer / Le Géographe canadien, 24, pp. 5-12. Available at: https://doi.org/10.1111/j.1541-0064.1980.tb00970.x [Accessed: 10 Mar. 2023].

Caradonna, J. L. (2014) Sustainability: A history. Oxford: Oxford University Press.

Clarke, J. (1997) 'A framework of approaches to sustainable tourism', Journal of Sustainable Tourism, 5(3), pp. 224-233. Available at: https://doi.org/10.1080/09669589708667287 [Accessed: 12 Jan. 2023].

Denzin, N.K., Lincoln, Y.S., Giardina, M.D. and Cannella, G.S. (2023) The Sage handbook of qualitative research. Thousand Oaks, CA: Sage Publications. Available at: https://us.sagepub.com/en-us/nam/the-sage-handbook-of-qualitative-research/book275161 [Accessed: 15 Mar. 2023].

Elkington, J. (1994) 'Towards the sustainable corporation: Win-win-win business strategies for sustainable development', California

Management Review, 36(2), pp. 90-100. Available at: https://doi.org/10.2307/41165746 [Accessed: 2 Feb. 2023].

Environmental Performance Index (2022) Yale Center for Environmental Law & Policy. Available at: https://epi.yale.edu/epi-results/2022/component/epi [Accessed: 6 Jan. 2023].

Euromonitor International (2021) Top countries for sustainable tourism. Euromonitor International. Available at: https://forumnatura.org/wp-content/uploads/2021/07/SustainableTravelIndex-v0.3.pdf [Accessed: 6 Jan. 2023].

Flick, U. (2018) An introduction to qualitative research. 6th edn. London: Sage.

Gazoni, J.L. and da Silva, E.A.M. (2021) 'System dynamics framework for tourism development management', Current Issues in Tourism, 24(20), pp. 2457-2478. Available at: https://doi.org/10.1080/13683500.2021.1970117 [Accessed: 5 March 2023].

Green Scheme of Slovenian Tourism (n.d.) Green Scheme of Slovenian Tourism. Available at: https://www.slovenia.info/en/business/green-scheme-of-slovenian-tourism [Accessed: 15 Feb. 2023].

Instituto Costarricense de Turismo (2020) CST Tourism Sustainability. Available at: https://www.ict.go.cr/en/sustainability/cst.html [Accessed: 11 Feb. 2023].

Jennings, G. (2010) Tourism research. Milton, QLD: John Wiley & Sons.

Lenzen, M., Sun, Y.-Y., Faturay, F., Ting, Y.-P., Geschke, A. and Malik, A. (2018) 'The carbon footprint of global tourism', Nature Climate Change, 8(6), pp. 522-528. Available at: https://doi.org/10.1038/s41558-018-0141-x [Accessed: 22 Jan. 2023].

Leiper, N. (1979) 'The framework of tourism: Towards a definition of tourism, tourist, and the tourist industry', Annals of Tourism Research, 6(4), pp. 390-407. Available at: https://doi.org/10.1016/0160-7383(79)90003-3 [Accessed: 5 Mar. 2023].

Meadows, D.H., Meadows, D.L., Randers, J. and Behrens, W.W. III (1972) The limits to growth. New York: Universe Books.

Meyer, W. (2020) 'Evaluation of Sustainable Development Goals between ambition and reality: How the Agenda 2030 challenges the evaluation practice', Zeitschrift für Evaluation, 19(2), pp. 221-238.

Morse, S. (2015) 'Developing sustainability indicators and indices', Sustainable Development, 23. Available at: https://doi.org/10.1002/sd.1575 [Accessed 2 Mar. 2023].

Olya, H.G.T. (2020) 'Towards advancing theory and methods on tourism development from residents' perspectives: Developing a framework on the pathway to impact', Journal of Sustainable Tourism, 29(2-3), pp. 329-349. Available at: https://doi.org/10.1080/09669582.2020.1843046 [Accessed: 17 Mar. 2023].

Palafox Associates. (n.d.). Master plan of San Vicente, Palawan as a flagship tourism enterprise zone. Available at: https://tieza.gov.ph/wp-content/uploads/2020/06/1.-San-Vicente-Master-Plan-by-Palafox.pdf [Accessed: 12 January 2023].

Phillimore, J. and Goodson, L. (2004) Qualitative research in tourism: Ontologies, epistemologies and methodologies. London: Routledge.

Republic of the Philippines (2009) Republic Act No. 9593 - An Act declaring a national policy for tourism as an engine of investment, employment, growth, and national development, and strengthening the Department of Tourism and its attached agencies to effectively and efficiently implement that policy, and appropriating funds therefor. Official Gazette of the Republic of the Philippines. Available at: https://www.officialgazette.gov.ph/2009/05/12/republic-act-no-9593/ [Accessed: 12 Jan. 2023].

Sachs, J.D. (2012) 'From millennium development goals to sustainable development goals', The Lancet, 379(9832), pp. 2206-2211. Available at: https://doi.org/10.1016/S0140-6736(12)60685-0 [Accessed: 7 Feb. 2023].

United Nations (2015) Transforming our world: The 2030 Agenda for Sustainable Development. Available at: https://sdgs.un.org/2030agenda [Accessed: 2 Mar. 2023].

United Nations (2020) The Sustainable Development Goals Report 2020. Available at: https://unstats.un.org/sdgs/report/2020/ [Accessed: 12 Jan. 2023].

Veal, A.J. (2017) Research methods for leisure and tourism: A practical guide. Harlow: Pearson Education.

Wall, G. and Badke, C. (1994). Tourism and Climate Change: An International Perspective. Journal of Sustainable Tourism, 2(3), pp. 193–203.

World Commission on Environment and Development (1987) Our common future. Oxford: Oxford University Press.

World Travel & Tourism Council (2021) A net zero roadmap for travel & tourism: Proposing a new target framework for the travel & tourism sector. London. Available at: https://wttc.org/Portals/0/Documents/Reports/2021/WTTC_Net_Zero_Roadmap.pdf [Accessed: 28 Jan 2023].

Xu, C., Kohler, T. A., Lenton, T. M., Svenning, J.-C., and Scheffer, M. (2020). Future of the Human Climate Niche. Proceedings of the National Academy of Sciences, 117(21), pp. 11350–11355. Available at: https://doi.org/10.1073/pnas.1910114117 [Accessed 4 Jan. 2023].

Cultural Determinants for the User's Acceptance of Digital Technologies for Biometric Recognition Applied by Border Control Authorities at Airports

Meriliis Sild, Sara Lestyan, Kristina Varšová,
Salzburg University of Applied Sciences,

msild.imte-m2023@fh-salzburg.ac.at, slestyan.imte-m2023@fh-salzburg.ac.at, kvarsova.imte-m2023@fh-salzburg.ac.at

Abstract

This research investigates cultural determinants that influence user acceptance of digital technologies utilized for biometric recognition by public border authorities at airports. Biometric recognition technologies (e.g. facial recognition, fingerprint scanning, and iris scanning) are increasingly being integrated into border control and travel services to enhance security and improve operational efficiency. Despite the existing gap in research regarding the cultural factors that impact the acceptance of biometric technologies, Hofstede's cultural dimensions were chosen as a valid framework for this analysis. An online survey was administered, with participant recruitment conducted at Salzburg and Munich airport. The findings reveal a substantial level of familiarity with biometric technologies, with efficiency and convenience identified as primary drivers of acceptance. Nevertheless, concerns regarding privacy, data security, and technical malfunctions emerged as considerable barriers to acceptance. Although a majority of respondents were from Western countries, variations in acceptance levels and concerns were noted across different cultural groups. The study emphasizes the importance of transparency, security measures, and opt-out options in fostering trust across diverse cultures. However, due to the limited sample size and geographical focus, further research is needed to explore cultural differences in greater depth and across broader demographics.

Keywords: biometric technologies, cultural determinants, technology acceptance

1. INTRODUCTION

The introduction of biometric technologies has revolutionized authentication technologies, offering a more secure and convenient alternative to traditional techniques like keys, passwords or PIN-codes. Unlike these standard methods, which are vulnerable to being stolen, easily forged or forgotten, biometrics rely on unique individual features, making them much more difficult to replicate or bypass. (Koichi and Takafumi, 2018) While biometrics are not entirely new – having been used in law enforcement and forensics for over a century – their technological evolution has improved accuracy, scalability, effectiveness, robustness, and user acceptance. (Jain and Kumar, 2012) Although there is a significant amount of research on biometric technology and technology acceptance among users, there appears to be a gap in studies specifically addressing the influence of cultural factors. Despite advancements in biometric systems, user adoption likely varies, for example within different countries, cultures or even contexts. Therefore, this study focuses primarily on finding out if cultural determinants, such as country of origin, influence user's acceptance of biometric technologies used at airports, which are key adopters of these authentication approach due to rising passenger numbers, stricter security measures, and the need for terrorism prevention. (Bonavita, 2016)

2. LITERATURE REVIEW

2.1 Biometric Technology in Travel and Tourism

Biometric technologies represent automated methods employing electronic devices to verify or identify individuals based on their physical and behavioral characteristics. (Wayman, et al., 2005) Physical biometrics include fingerprints, facial recognition, hand geometry, iris and retinal scans, vascular patterns, etc. Behavioral biometrics involve voice recognition, handwriting or signature analysis, and keystroke pattern analysis (voice, signature, typing). (El-Bakry and Mastorakis, 2009)

Moreover, biometrics have significantly influenced border control since the 1990s, driven by heightened security concerns after 9/11 in 2001. It has become a global billion-dollar industry with widespread adoption. (Fog Olwig, et al., 2020) Further, biometrics serve a dual purpose in tourism, not only enhancing security to protect countries from threats, but also for making border crossings faster for both people and goods. (Stodder and Warrick, 2022) The applications of this technology provide a more efficient, fluent, and secure tool for all kinds of processes (e.g. check-in/out, payments, border crossing) and even enhancing customer experience by enabling tailored services. (Neo et al., 2014)

2.2 Cultural Determinants

The meaning of culture or cultural determinants can shift in different perspectives. For example, researches have categorized cultures based on communication styles, distinguishing between high-context cultures (where communication relies heavily on implicit understanding and nonverbal cues) and low-context cultures (where communication is more explicit and direct). On the other hand, culture as a system of beliefs and behaviors that influence various aspects of life, including perceptions of nature, social structures, and daily practices such as travel and cuisine. (Hofstede, 2011) But the most well-known explanation of culture comes from Hofstede, in which he describes culture as the way people were raised, like a collective programming of the mind that separates individuals from another. Culture can be divided into six different dimensions: individualism (relative importance of each individual in the society), power distance (acceptance of unequal power distribution), masculinity (the perspective of differences between male and female roles), uncertainty avoidance (the acceptance of unknown and uncertainty in the society), long-term orientation (focus of the culture time -perceived orientation), and indulgence (individuals controlling their desire and impulses). In each of his dimensions, he analyzes different countries and their cultural tendencies, visually representing them on maps that highlight variations in those factors. (Hofstede, 2025) Although the data, as he mentions in his work, is not complete, it provides a meaningful representation. As an illustration, Western countries such as the United States, much of Europe, and Australia tend to be more individualistic, emphasizing personal choice and independence. In contrast, many Asian, African, and Eastern European countries, including Russia, often exhibit higher power distance, meaning that hierarchical structures and authority figures are more widely accepted in decision-making processes. (refer to Hofstede, 2025) While cultural determinants play a crucial role in shaping societal norms and behaviors, they also impact the acceptance of technology. The way individuals perceive and adopt new technologies is influenced by a variety of factors, including personal experiences, beliefs, and values, all of which are rooted in cultural dimensions. (Masimba, et al., 2019) Not to mention, Hofstede's model finds that higher power distance hinders technology adoption, while individualism fosters acceptance. Uncertainty avoidance has a negative impact, and masculinity shows mixed but generally positive correlations. However, Hofstede's approach is seen as reductionist, lacking cultural complexity. (Riley, et al., 2009) Furthermore, given that biometric systems in border control are implemented by government authorities, travelers possess limited influence over their adoption. Nevertheless, the acceptance of these technologies by customers is vital for improving travel experiences, making it essential to understand cultural factors in shaping perceptions of biometric technologies.

2.3 Acceptance of the Biometrics and Case Studies

The implementation of biometric technologies at airports has been extensively examined across various countries, demonstrating differing levels of acceptance that are influenced by demographic, cultural, and privacy-related factors.

Research conducted in Spain found that participants aged 45–54 report the highest satisfaction with smart airport technologies (Zamorano, et al., 2020), while in Brazil, younger passengers under 18 show the highest adoption rates. (Negria, et al., 2019) Furthermore, in Malaysia, privacy protection increased satisfaction and acceptance (refer to Neo, et. al., 2014), while in the U.S., privacy concerns hindered adoption despite positive attitudes. (Kasim, et. al., 2021) South Korean women show higher trust in biometrics, with perceived utility driving adoption. (Kim, et al., 2023) In contrast, in Greece, younger and female respondents are more accepting but worry about cloning risks and privacy. (Kitsiou, et al., 2022) Slovakian research highlights generational differences: younger users prioritized convenience, while older users had security concerns. (Taborecka, et al., 2021) Finally, in Kuwait, youth under 25 show high awareness and acceptance of fingerprint biometrics but remain skeptical about behavioral biometrics and data security. (Almayyan, 2019)

Whereas research indicates notable variations in biometric acceptance among different countries, the precise influence of culture has yet to be clearly delineated. Consequently, it becomes increasingly important to investigate the cultural determinants that shape the perceptions and responses of travelers from diverse backgrounds toward biometric technologies utilized in airports.

3. METHODOLOGY

A quantitative research design was chosen, which relies on statistical and numerical data to analyze a representative sample and draw conclusions about the populations. (Lowhorn, 2007) The method is well-suited for this study as it enables the measurement of social variables across a broad sample, allowing for statistical analysis of how cultural and demographic factors influence the acceptance of biometric technologies at airports.

For this research, an online questionnaire was conducted in English to ensure that all participants, including non-German speakers, could participate, as English serves as the no. 1 global lingua franca. The survey included 22 questions covering demographics, and biometric technologies. Moreover, as Hofstede's practices were a base for the cultural part, it was important to address the participant's country of origin and ask whether they believed their culture could influence biometric system acceptance. The choice of country of origin was made to explore potential cultural differences in the acceptance of biometric technologies, as individuals from different cultural backgrounds may have varying attitudes toward privacy, security, and technological adoption. Age was also included as a cultural determinant, recognizing that younger and older generations may have different levels of comfort and familiarity with biometric technologies, further contributing to the understanding of demographic factors in technology acceptance. This is particularly substantial when answering the hypothesis (H1) "that cultural and demographic factors influence biometric technology acceptance", while null hypothesis (H0) suggests no significant impact. In particular, the questionnaire was divided into two sections, individuals who have used biometrics before and those who have not.

Although the survey was online, participant acquisition took place at the airports, to ensure the reliability of the answers. Originally, Vienna and Munich airport were chosen due to Vienna being the largest airport in Austria and Munich being the second largest in Germany, both of which already apply biometric technologies in daily operations. (Future Travel Experience, 2022) Unfortunately, Vienna airport was not willing to cooperate, and as an alternative, Salzburg airport, which started the introduction of biometric systems in their operations in 2024 (noting, that while the survey was done on site, they did not have biometrics systems installed), was chosen instead. (ORF Salzburg, 2024)

The sample size of the responses was kept around 100 participants, as Salzburg airport is relatively small, and the passenger traffic is not as large compared to Munich airport. Considering the limitations pertaining to cultural diversity within the sample size, the emphasis transitioned towards demographic factors including age, which serves as a proxy for cultural dimensions. This methodology remains consistent with the objectives of the study, which seeks to investigate the influence of cultural factors on the acceptance of biometric technologies in airport settings. Hofstede's global map illustrates the varying cultural dimensions across countries, which may influence technology acceptance, and age-related differences could reflect generational shifts in these cultural values.

4. RESULTS

The results were obtained through the analysis of responses to the questionnaire utilizing the SPSS software. Notably, the survey was categorized into two groups: participants who have used biometric technology (as Yes-participants, n=96) and those who have not (No-participants, n=16). This categorization was based on a combination of closed and open-ended questions. The questions explored various aspects, including cultural background (as illustrated in Figure 1), familiarity with the technology, acceptance of the technology, and cultural influences on technology acceptance, which collectively form the foundation of this study. A total of 112 individuals participated in the research. The findings indicate a great dominance of younger generation, though all age groups were represented (Figure 1), as well as slight predominance of female respondents (55 % female, 44 % male and 1 % other). Due to the disproportionate number of participants from Western countries, the sample was divided into Western (68 %) and Non-Western (32 %) participants to provide a more meaningful analysis, as the low number of participants from Non-Western countries hindered drawing reliable conclusions across different cultural groups.

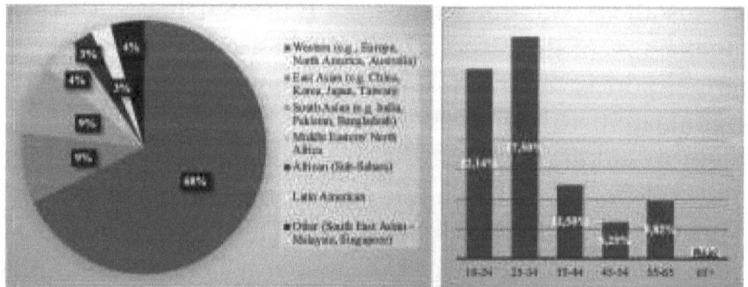

Fig. 1 Cultural Background and Age

4.1 Participants who have used Biometric Technology before

The results show a high adoption of biometric technology in travel, with over 80 % of participants (Yes-participants) reporting usage. However, when analyzing familiarity, Non-Western participants displayed a slightly higher adoption rate than Western ones, illustrated in the Figure 2. In addition, amongst the participants who had used biometrics at the airport before, the majority reported using it more than five times. In the context of inferential statistics, the chi-square test, which assesses the significance of the relationship between two variables, revealed no significant differences between Western and Non-Western participants (p=0,283). This finding suggests that the sample size may be insufficient to draw robust statistical conclusions.

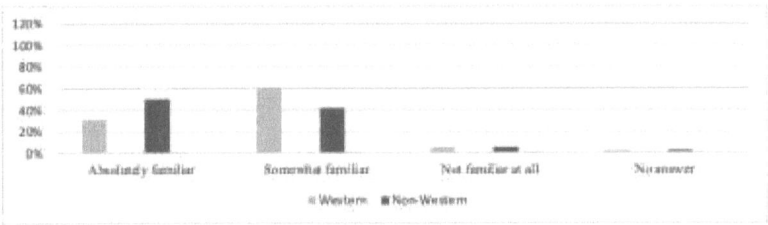

Fig. 2 Familiarity

It was also important to analyze how different cultures rated their overall experience with biometric systems among participants who had used them before. The overall feedback was positive, with Non-Western participants showing higher satisfaction, while Western participants tended to be more neutral. In addition, Non-Western (ca. 80 %) participants showed a higher overall comfort level than Western (ca. 60 %), although the inferential statistics, revealed no significance between those variables (p=0,398).

Regarding the influence of cultural background on the assessment of biometric technologies, Western participants leaned towards "yes, somewhat", whereas Non-Western participants were more likely to respond with "no". Additionally, non-Western respondents exhibited a nearly twofold inclination to indicate "unsure" (Figure 3). This could imply that non-Western participants may have been either more unsure about the impact of culture or less inclined to view it as a key factor influencing their acceptance of biometrics.

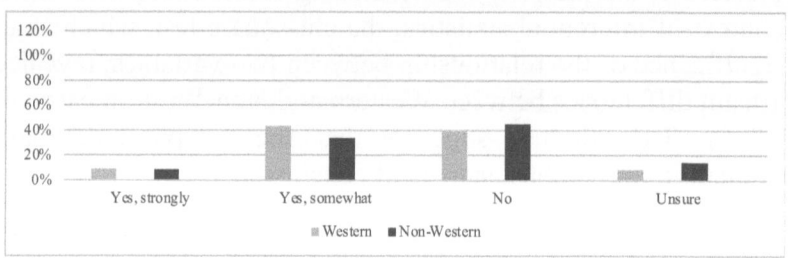

Fig. 3 Cultural Background Influences Assessment

Furthermore, both groups reported growing acceptance of biometric technologies, with Non-Western respondents showing slightly higher acceptance and less uncertainty (Figure 4). Not to mention, facial recognition was the most used biometric systems, followed by fingerprint scanning and iris scanning.

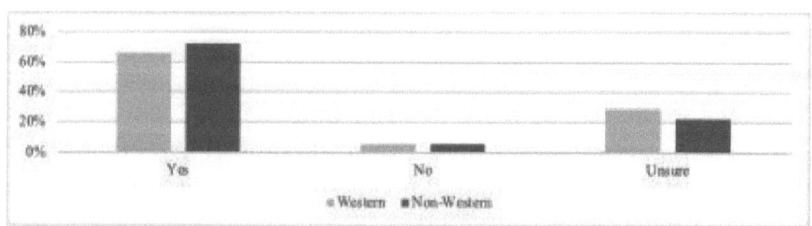

Fig. 4 Acceptance of Biometric Technologies

Additional outputs show that the main advantages of biometric technology are faster processing and greater convenience, including contactless interactions, improved security, and better travel experience. Biometric technology was mainly used for passport verification and ePassport gates, showing widespread adoption for security, less so for boarding. The most common issue reported were technical malfunctions, followed by slow processing times and privacy concerns. Usability challenges were less frequently mentioned.

4.2 Participants who have not used Biometric Technology before

Among the 16 No-participants (81 % Western, 19 % non-Western) the predominant barriers identified were concerns regarding privacy and the potential for data misuse. These issues were followed by apprehensions related to accuracy and cultural or ethical considerations. The primary reasons for the non-adoption of biometrics included its unavailability at travel destinations and a limited array of options. Additionally, concerns pertaining to distrust, privacy, and cultural factors were noted. Key elements of the adoption of biometric technology encompass assurances regarding privacy, an enhanced understanding of the technology, and improved data security measures. Insignificant factors were recommendations, positive feedback, and increased accessibility. The results demonstrate the need for transparency and clear communication, in order to foster trust and facilitate the adoption of biometric technology.

4.3 Open-ended questions

In response to the open-ended question on cultural values and biometric technology use, 63 participants identified seven key factors: privacy concerns, trust in technology and authority, cultural differences, generational gaps, security, technophobia, and normalization, as in technology being part of everyday life. Privacy concerns were most common with Asian respondents noting greater familiarity with biometrics. Older individuals were less willing to adopt biometrics than younger ones.

Furthermore, when asked about factors influencing biometric technology acceptance, 67 participants emphasized both positive (security, convenience, technological progress) and negative (privacy concerns, distrust in government) characteristics. Cultural values like privacy, trust, and familiarity shaped acceptance, with normalization increasing comfort.

In conclusion, to boost acceptance, 63 participants suggested focusing on data security, transparency, educating users, offering opt-out options, and improving system performance.

5. LIMITATIONS

Throughout this study, several limitations became evident. Firstly, the sample size of 112 participants, with a majority under 34 years old and more Western than Non-Western respondents, may not fully represent global travelers or older demographics, introducing potential biases. The small sample size limits the inferential statistical power, making it difficult to draw definitive conclusions regarding cultural differences in biometric technology acceptance.

Secondly, focusing on Salzburg and Munich airport limits applicability to other regions with different demographics and infrastructures. The findings may not fully reflect the experiences of travelers at smaller or less busy airports where biometric technology adoption might be at a different stage. The broad cultural categorization of respondents as Western or Non-Western oversimplifies the differences, and future studies may benefit from more nuanced cultural distinctions, such as those offered by Hofstede's dimensions. Such an approach would facilitate a more profound understanding of the cultural influences that affect the acceptance of biometric technology. Lastly, language barriers and potential misinterpretation of the survey questions being in English may have also impacted the clarity of responses, introducing bias and limiting the reliability of some responses.

Despite these limitations, the study offers valuable insights into the cultural determinants of biometric technology acceptance and provides a foundation for further research to address these gaps.

6. CONCLUSION

Overall, it can be stated that biometric technologies are becoming more essential to modern day society and offer numerous possibilities, especially in tourism industry.

While Hofstede's model is widely used, its reductionist approach presented some limitations regarding cultural determinants. These had to be modified due to the small sample size of the participants, by defining cultural determinants as demographics and including age. Based on the survey results, non-Western participants showed higher adoption rates and more positive experiences compared to Western participants, who leaned toward cautious neutrality. Non-Western respondents also reported greater acceptance of biometrics and perceived increases in their use. However, inferential statistical analysis showed no significant difference between the cultural groups, possibly due to the small sample size.

What is more, facial recognition was the most commonly used biometric technology, mainly for security and passport control. Key adoption drivers were efficiency and convenience, while technical issues and delays need improvement. Privacy concerns and data misuse emerged as major barriers, highlighting the importance of security, transparency, and clear communication. Open-ended responses showed that older generations are less likely to adopt biometrics, but education and cultural familiarity can reduce skepticism. Flexibility, like opt-out options, is crucial for smoother adoption.

In conclusion, the results suggest that cultural and demographic factors may influence the acceptance of biometric technologies. While descriptive data indicated differences between Western and Non-Western participants, the statistical analysis found no significant evidence to support or reject Hypothesis 1. This suggests that a larger sample size is needed for definitive conclusions. Consequently, the null hypothesis is accepted, indicating that cultural determinants do not significantly impact biometric technology acceptance.

Understanding cultural determinants is essential for governments, corporations, and stakeholders engaged in the introduction of new technologies. Although Hofstede's cultural dimensions provide a valuable framework for identifying implementation strategies, their limitations should be considered. Future research should focus on examining cultural backgrounds, levels of trust, demographic factors, and methods to enhance transparency. As culture evolves, its impact on technology acceptance remains significant despite challenges in measurement.

REFERENCES

Almayyan, W. (2019). *Social Acceptance Of Biometrics Technologies In Kuwait: A Survey. International Journal of Computer Science and Information Security (IJCSIS), 17(12).*

Bonavita, R. (2016). *Biometric Identification Systems in Airports A study regarding the impact of biometric technologies on air passengers' satisfaction.*

El-Bakry, H. M., & Mastorakis, N. E. (2009). *Personal identification through biometric technology.* Retrieved from https://www.researchgate.net/profile/Hazem-El Bakry/publication/262158503_Personal_identification_through_bio metric_technology/links/55e46c8d08aecb1a7ccb7949/Personal-identification-through-biometric-technology.pdf

Fog Olwig, K., Grünenberg, K., Mohl, P., & Simonsen, A. (2020). *The Biometric Border World: Technologies, Bodies and Identities on the Move.* Retrieved from https://www.researchgate.net/publication/336745664_The_Biometri c_Border_World_Technologies_Bodies_and_Identities_on_the_Mo ve . pp. 2-9

Future Travel Experience. (2022, August). *Munich Airport implements biometric screening for secure ID control - Future Travel Experience.* . Retrieved from https://www.futuretravelexperience.com/press-release/munich-airport-implements-biometric-screening-for-secure-id-control/

Hofstede, G. (2011). *Dimensionalizing Cultures: The Hofstede Model in Context.* Retrieved from https://scholarworks.gvsu.edu/cgi/viewcontent.cgi?article=1014&context=orpc . pp. 4-22

Hofstede, G. (2025). Retrieved from https://geerthofstede.com/culture-geert-hofstede-gert-jan-hofstede/6d-model-of-national-culture/

Jain, A. K., & Kumar, A. (2012). *Biometric recognition: An Overview. chapter from Second Generation Biometrics: The Ethical, Legal and Social Context.*

Kasim, K. O., Winter, S. R., Liu, D., Keebler, J. R., & Spence, T. B. (2021). *Passengers' perceptions on the use of biometrics at airports: A statistical model of the extended theory of planned behavior.*

Kim, J. H., Song, W.-K., & Lee, H. C. (2023). *Exploring the Determinants of Travelers' Intention to Use the Airport Biometric System: A Korean Case Study.*

Kitsiou, A., Despotidi , C., Kalloniatis, C., & Gritzalis, S. (2022). *The Role of Users' Demographic and Social Attributes for Accepting Biometric Systems: A Greek Case Study.*

Koichi, I., & Takafumi, A. (2018). *Recent Advances in Biometric Recognition.*

Lowhorn, G. L. (2007). *Qualitative and Quantitative Research: How to Choose the Best Design.* Retrieved from https://papers.ssrn.com/sol3/papers.cfm?abstract_id=2235986

Masimba, F., Appiah, M., & Zuva, T. (2019). *A Review of Cultural Influence on Technology Acceptance.* Retrieved from https://ieeexplore.ieee.org/abstract/document/9015877

Negria, N. A., Borillea, G. M., & Falcão, V. A. (2019). *Acceptance of biometric technology in airport check-in.*

ORF Salzburg. (2024, August 30). *Salzburg Airport installs biometric scanners.* Retrieved from https://salzburg.orf.at/stories/3271051/

Riley, C., Buckner, K., Johnson, G., & Benyon, D. (2009). *Culture & biometrics: regional differences in the perception of biometric authentication technologies.*

Stodder, S., & Warrick, S. T. (2022). *Biometrics at the Border: Balancing Security, Convenience, and Civil Liberties* . Retrieved from https://www.atlanticcouncil.org/wp-content/uploads/2022/01/Biometrics-at-the-Border_FDHS-Project.pdf

Taborecka, J., Martinkovicova, M., & Sipulova, M. (2021). *Ethical aspects and consumer perspectives on biometric technologies: A generational comparison. Matej Bel University, Faculty of Economics.* .

Wayman, J., Jain, A., Maltoni, D., & Maio, D. (2005). *An introduction to Biometrics Authentification Systems.* Springer.

Zamorano, M. M., Fernández-Laso, M. C., & Curiel, J. d. (2020). *Smart airports: acceptance of technology by passengers.*

The future's generation in the present moment: How does social media affect Generation Z's tourism experiences?

Zsuzsanna Csoh,

IMC University of Applied Sciences Krems

csoh.zsuzsanna@gmail.com

Abstract

Generation Z is often characterized as "chronically online" due to lifelong exposure to digitalization. While connectivity offers access to information, social interaction, and entertainment, it can foster dependency and digital fatigue. This study explores whether mindful, digital-free tourism can offer a counterbalance, examining the factors that make such experiences appealing.

Through semi-structured interviews with 10 Hungarian digital natives, the study investigates how travel environments naturally reduce social media consumption, the conditions enabling digital-free tourism acceptance, and the role of locus of control in shaping detox experiences. While participants exhibited lower social media engagement during travel, behavioural changes were due to environmental stimulation. Full digital detox proved challenging, raising safety concerns, navigation reliance, and deeply embedded digital habits.

The study contributes to slow tourism theory by demonstrating how disconnecting and Joy of Missing Out manifests in travel contexts. It also highlights how an individual's internal locus of control mediates their openness to digital detox. From a practical standpoint, tourism providers may benefit from offering tiered detox experiences ranging from tech-light zones to full-disconnection retreats rather than enforcing binary digital/analogue choices. Future research should expand on these insights using experimental methods to measure actual detox behaviours across diverse cultural contexts.

Keywords: social media, generation Z, travel behaviour, digital detox tourism, mindful tourism

1. INTRODUCTION

Social media use can be driven by numerous motivations, from keeping in touch and gathering information to staying entertained (Whiting, Williams, 2013). Generation Z is a major contributor to social media, both in the form of consuming content and sharing. Algorithms provide users with instant gratification, validation, and a sense of social connection. The age group is particularly likely to share their travel experiences, showcasing an aesthetic highlight reel of their lives (Oliveira et al. 2020).

However, since the generation experienced technology from early, formative years (Pasztor and Bak 2020), it has become an integral part of their days, creating unique challenges like addiction or FoMO (Hassan et al. 2022). One potential solution could be a digital detox, meaning a conscious reduction of screen time to improve well-being (Mirbabaie et al. 2022). While previous studies have explored digital-free tourism in Generation Y, Generation Z faces distinct challenges, raising the need for further research.

This paper explores the role of social media in Generation Z's tourism experiences and the relevance and feasibility of digital-free tourism. To gain an in-depth understanding, qualitative research was conducted in the form of interviews with 10 Hungarian participants aged 21 to 25. The study intended to measure their daily social media use, both sharing and consuming content and compare it during travel. with a focus on their attitude towards digital-free tourism: how present they are during their experiences, how much they are able to distance themselves from the digital world, and what factors could encourage them to embrace digital detoxes.

The interviews concluded that participants naturally engaged less with social media during travelling, although digital-free tourism proved to be unrealistic as a result of the high levels of digitalisation surrounding them. Respondents exhibited mixed reactions from curiosity, to concern for safety and convenience.

However, certain conditions could help ease their apprehension: adequate information, the destination's infrastructure, locals' attitude, travel companions and sources of entertainment could create a relaxing environment to disconnect.

Exploring Generation Z's views on social media and digital-free tourism can provide insight into the daily challenges they face and their needs while travelling. This understanding allows tourism providers to develop services and opportunities to encourage disconnection and engage visitors mindfully, thus making members of Generation Z part of their new target audience.

2. LITERATURE REVIEW

The following chapter entails the academic sources used for this research, related to social media, Generation Z, their travel experiences, and digital detox.

Social media and Generation Z

Social media provides its users with a platform to stay connected, generate new discussions, and fill lonely, idle moments with stimuli. Consuming online content can redirect attention, allowing for relaxation and escapism from daily stress, as it doesn't particularly require thinking (Whiting, Williams, 2013).

Generation Z's life is simultaneously private and public, as they live and express themselves virtually (Gabriel, 2014). However, most of the content on social media is still created by a minority of users, while the majority primarily consume content. Many prefer to keep their private lives hidden, often due to a lack of confidence that prevents them from posting. Conversely, content creators may also experience anxiety, which they try to alleviate through posting as a means of seeking validation and maintaining social connections (Oliveira, Araujo, & Tam, 2020). Social media algorithms give instant gratification through notifications and reactions to posts, therefore providing users with a sense of connection and belonging. Positive feedback encourages users to post more frequently, helping them maintain their ideal online self-image (Ribeiro, 2021). The majority of consumers also feel manipulated by algorithms prompting them for extensive use (Chan et al. 2022). Previous studies have shown the power of platforms like TikTok, turning entertainment into addictive, mindless scrolling (Schellewald, 2021). According to the Digital 2022 Global Overview Report created by Datareportal.com, the global average daily screen time is 6 hours 58 minutes, which can reach 9 hours in the case of Generation Z.

Social media addiction can lead to nomophobia, an irrational fear of being without a mobile phone, or FoMO, short for fear of missing out, (Hassan et al. 2022). As users try to alleviate their negative feelings with further content consumption, FoMO can turn into a habitual, vicious cycle of anxiety (Chan et al. 2022). However, distancing oneself from the online world can lead to increased mood, receptivity, attention, and mindful presence during experiences. This phenomenon is called JoMO, which, in contrast to FoMO, means Joy of Missing Out, a more conscious, reduced social media use and fuller immersion of experiences (Irimiás, 2023). A technical glitch in 2021 illustrated the two phenomena perfectly when Facebook, Whatsapp, and Instagram were unavailable for hours. Some users were outraged and frustrated, but others found being offline relieving (Barry et al. 2023).

The integrated role of mobile phones makes it increasingly difficult to abstain from using them. Ideally, consumers can recognize their need to disconnect and regulate their online presence. Research by Aranda and Baig (2018) suggests that short-term, voluntary restrictions on screen time have the most positive effects.

Travel and content creation

The hashtag #travel consistently ranks among the ten most used search terms on Instagram. The willingness to share travel information online is higher than in any other area of life. Generation Z confidently forms and expresses opinions publicly and is receptive to recommendations, forums, blogs, images, and videos, which provide richer information and serve as a medium for sharing experiences. Those who share travel-related content on social media do so because it boosts their self-confidence, allows them to offer advice to others (altruism), and, in some cases, because they see content sharing as an integral part of their personality. (Oliveira, Araujo, & Tam, 2020).

With the emergence of the experience economy (Pine & Gilmore, 1998), people increasingly seek to purchase and showcase experiences rather than objects. This shift transformed how Generation Z engages with tourism and social media, with marketing professionals and travel agents utilizing FoMO while promoting travel campaigns (Hodkinson, 2016). Social media has become a powerful tool in this context, as Generation Z perceives user-generated content as more authentic and trustworthy since businesses cannot alter or retouch such posts. (Bulchand-Gidumal, 2023). This prompts them to rely primarily on information from fellow travellers (Sotiriadis, 2017) suggesting, that UGC creators take on roles similar to travel agents promoting destinations and igniting FoMO.

Digital Detox

As technology becomes a key part of most aspects of our lives, users can note emerging challenges. Newfound problems require new defence mechanisms, creating a need for solutions like *digital detox*. Digital detox is focused on the conscious withdrawal from technology over a period of time to restore and maintain mental health and well-being. It can range from reducing time spent on social media to going completely digital-free, not using any devices. These practices can assist in coping with already present problems like addiction, and they also have a preventative role (Mirbabaie, Stieglitz, Marx, 2022). Excessive time spent with technology can dampen the mood in professional settings and daily lives, but also when travelling. This has given way to *digital-tree tourism (DFT)*, the need to travel without digital devices or the internet. Today, in many destinations such as the Maldives, the UK and the US, tourism businesses are trying to create the right conditions to encourage tourists to go offline and forgo using their mobile phones. This can range from creating offline areas, limiting

Wi-Fi access or collecting travellers' devices upon arrival. It has many benefits, like increasing creativity, and curiosity, encouraging interpersonal relationships, removing expectations, and helping visitors to truly immerse themselves in the experience. Floros et al. (2019) investigated Generation Y's attitudes toward DFT. In their sample, they included 17 participants who are regular social media users in their daily lives. The subjects had positive attitudes towards digital detox, but often experienced difficulties when arriving at destinations, such as when booking transfers and tickets online, or even at the bus or train station, due to the high level of digitalisation in tourism. In big cities, the fear of getting lost made them less able to immerse themselves in the experience, but in smaller, quieter villages, the simplicity of the environment provided scope for offline recreation. Beyond the individual's positive attitude an appropriate infrastructure within the destination is needed to allow offline recreation to flourish.

Hassan, Salem and Saleh (2022) conducted a study of Generation Y members who have incorporated digital detox into their travel habits. The research was based on the concept of locus of control. The results suggest those who had a greater belief in internal control - that is, they personally felt in control of the situations they encountered - enjoyed the offline time, paid attention to detail, and socialized more easily. Those who put the outside world in control experienced difficulties such as stress due to a lack of information, language barriers, and orientation problems. Although the participants in the study had different experiences, a periodic detachment from the digital world may increase belief in internal control long term, reduce extreme reactions, and improve quality of life.

The concept of digital detox, and digital-free tourism are relatively new, therefore extensive research results are not yet available, raising further questions regarding the complex nature of different personality traits and social media use. For extroverted individuals distancing from their online social presence can prove to be more challenging, while ones with more introverted tendencies could find spending time away from the community presumably less difficult, leading to more conscious online habits (Barry et al. 2023).

At the date of publication limited research has been conducted about digital-free tourism specifically in the case of Generation Z. Since this group is the first to grow up surrounded by digitalization from a young age, they face unique challenges related to their online presence and consumption, raising further questions. This paper explores the generation's attitudes toward social media, travelling, and the rise of digital-free tourism.

3. RESEARCH METHODS

This study employed a qualitative research approach to explore Generation Z's relationship with social media during travel and assess the feasibility of digital-free tourism. The methodology was designed to gather in-depth data that could provide insights into participants' behaviours and perceptions.

Ten Hungarian participants aged 21 to 25 were selected for semi-structured individual interviews. The choice of Hungarian participants was motivated by access to and familiarity with the Hungarian higher education system, facilitating recruitment and cultural understanding. A combination of convenience and snowball sampling methods was used, initially recruiting through university networks, with subsequent referrals from the participants. This approach allowed to reach a diverse range of Generation Z individuals with varying ages, genders and levels of social media engagement, from professional influencers to minimal users, thus creating a heterogeneous group.

The following table summarizes the participants' characteristics:

Table 1. Characteristics of sample, Source: own research

Code	Gender	Age	Average daily screen time	Attitude towards digital detox holidays
R1	Female	22	9 hours	couldn't do
R2	Female	22	4 hours	couldn't do
R3	Female	22	4 hours	would try
R4	Female	23	3,5 hours	couldn't do
R5	Female	22	8 hours	would try
R6	Female	24	9 hours	couldn't do
R7	Female	25	9 hours	would try
R8	Male	22	3,5 hours	would try
R9	Male	21	8 hours	couldn't do
R10	Male	21	3,5 hours	couldn't do

Participants were informed of their right to withdraw from the study at any time. All gave consent before the interviews and were assigned a code to keep anonymity. The interviews lasted between 30 to 45 minutes and were conducted in person or online in October and November 2023. The interview guide included 25 open-ended questions and projective techniques such as word association and photo elicitation to capture both broad and specific views on digital-free tourism. Responses were transcribed using Alrite.com and translated with DeepL Translator.

Limitations

The following limitations should be considered when interpreting the results of this study.

Due to the small sample size (n=10) and qualitative nature of the study, results are not generalizable to the broader Generation Z population. The focus on Hungarian participants may limit cross-cultural comparisons and sampling may have introduced biases during selection. Additionally, participants assessed digital-free tourism hypothetically, as they had no direct experience, therefore future research should employ observational methods, such as diary studies to evaluate actual behaviours.

While this sample cannot represent global trends, it provides valuable insights into how young adults in an emerging European economy engage with digital technologies during travel. Future research could combat these limitations by using larger, more diverse samples, with cross-cultural comparisons, and including experimental designs where participants actually experience digital-free tourism.

4. FINDINGS

This chapter details key findings regarding how social media affects individuals' travel experiences. The results expand on three main themes social media consumption during travelling, experiences and content creation, and attitudes towards digital detox.

Social media use during travel

When asked about their daily lives, no participants considered themselves to be taking part in below-average social media consumption. They cited involuntary urges and addiction as the primary reasons, which were both perceived as universal problems among the generation. The average daily screen time in the sample ranged from 3,5 to 9 hours. Even when not actively using their devices, participants sought out passive stimulation, such as listening to videos, and podcasts during other activities.

Social media's entertainment value lures subjects into the habit of mindless scrolling, which they justify with both being over- and understimulated. When daily responsibilities prove to be intellectually demanding they associate scrolling with unwinding, while after mundane tasks, during procrastinating, or feeling lonely or tired they turn to social media to fill them with impulses. Although respondents could provide reasons for scrolling, the action rarely resulted in satisfaction. Instead, excessive screen time often left them battling shame, aware of the time that had been wasted.

In contrast, participants generally reported a lower online presence during travelling, which they attributed to feeling filled with rich stimuli. A change in scenery at a new destination provides them with new pastimes and enough excitement, making social media's entertainment function unnecessary. The exceptions were certain "dead times", such as waiting in a long queue alone, when they instinctively reverted to scrolling.

Participants' reduced social media use during travel was rarely a conscious choice. While some made deliberate efforts to avoid certain platforms or limit scrolling, others prioritized freedom and spontaneity over limiting themselves with rules. For most, the decrease in social media engagement occurred naturally as a result of the travel experience itself. Group travel, in particular, seemed to diminish the need for online interactions, as the social aspects typically fulfilled by social media were satisfied through in-person connections. This shift contributed to the organic reduction in social media use, as travellers focused more on immediate, real-world experiences rather than digital engagement.

FoMO and JoMO

Although the need for daily scrolling temporarily subsided, time spent away from both social media and their familiar environments triggered varying degrees of FoMO. Those travelling with loved ones or keeping in touch online with their social circle reported feeling less affected. These individuals often viewed their travel experiences as unique opportunities, prioritizing them over potential missed events at home, which they felt they could easily make up for. Only one participant recalled a real sense of FoMO when having had to choose between attending a festival and travel, in which case the sacrificed experience felt more tangible.

Even a participant who completely embraced the opportunity to disconnect during their vacation admitted to compensating for missed screen time upon returning home. This suggests that while the need for stimuli can be adequately satisfied during a trip, the need for connectivity remains. For others, this showed up in the form of concern about falling behind on work or study commitments, highlighting the pressures of having to be constantly accessible digitally.

Missing out wasn't necessarily perceived as negative in every case, with the JoMO phenomenon also being present during travels: *"I absolutely feel like I'm missing out, but in a positive way, because I see this as a bit of time off." (R1)*. For these individuals not being occupied with others' online activities provided a sense of relief and a heightened focus on their experiences, resulting in a deeper appreciation.

In conclusion, while travel naturally reduces social media use among Generation Z, the psychological impact of this reduction varies. For some, it offers a refreshing break from digital engagement, while for others, it creates a tension between enjoying present experiences and staying connected to their broader social and professional networks. In order to truly immerse themselves during travelling, it is important to let go of distracting and anxiety-inducing factors that generally consume their minds. Since their online presence becomes limited, the sense of obligation to be constantly available briefly subsides, and they can shift their focus on their loved ones surrounding them during their trips, reevaluating their new experiences. Spending their time actively and meaningfully can help absorb new stimuli and reduce the need for pointless screen time.

Experiences and content creation

Participants exhibited diverse content-creation habits in their daily lives. While some never or rarely posted, others shared more frequently, monthly, or weekly. The sample also included a professional influencer to assess a wide range of behaviours and attitudes.

On their personal social media pages, participants tended to share content they considered valuable, memorable, or aesthetically pleasing. These posts served the purpose of reflecting their personalities in the form of snapshots of daily life, candid moments, unique experiences, and group photos showcasing their social circles.

During travel, participants created significantly more content than in their regular lives. Two opposing tendencies could be noted about sharing: some posted about their adventures as they were experiencing them, while others deliberately delayed sharing until later in their day or after the trip. For some participants, extensive and planned content creation during their trips turned into a negative experience, as it shifted focus away from enjoying the moment. Instead, the goal became capturing the perfect content for others' consumption. These individuals benefitted from delayed posting, as it allowed them to be truly present, and absorb experiences before publishing to social media.

However, the pressure of social media expectations did not diminish for delayed posters. Participants used the additional time to carefully curate their content, selecting the best ones to share while keeping the ones they deemed to be lower quality or less interesting to themselves.

Another emerging phenomenon was anticipating and evaluating moments and destinations for their potential as social media content. Many respondents admitted to mentally framing scenes in terms of their 'Instagrammability', with some even choosing travel destinations solely for their well-known photo opportunities. In these cases, it quickly diminished the enjoyment of the trip when popular photo spots became crowded with tourists all waiting for their turn to capture the perfect shot. Conversely, their anticipation of photography wasn't inherently negative, but rather a tool to evoke joy and preserve memories for many. Some participants naturally found artistic self-expression in the form of taking pictures and sharing: *Photography is a field I love, so when I see something, I already have a composition in mind—my thinking naturally starts from an image." (R6)*.

In conclusion, participants' documentation increased during travelling, however their social media sharing differed. While some individuals posted in real-time, others exhibited a need for mindfulness, opting for delayed sharing to avoid shifting focus from the experience. Social media influences their travel behaviour from choosing a destination to visiting attractions, capturing and sharing their experiences. Although documenting their adventures didn't inherently affect them negatively it does pose the risk of prioritizing content creation over true immersion.

Digital detox attempts

Nearly all participants had attempted to limit their online consumption at one point in their lives or felt the need to do so in the future. Their strategies included relying on their willpower, specific screen time restrictions on their smartphones, or deleting certain apps, in order to boost productivity, facilitate meaningful pastimes, and combat overstimulation. While many felt victorious by regaining self-control, others struggled to maintain a digital detox, leading to feelings of defeat as they broke the restrictions. Over time participants developed FoMO, not wanting to miss others' posts, messages, or potential emerging opportunities. Disconnecting from digital devices during daily life proved to be challenging for all.

Perceptions of digital-free tourism

Participants assessed the prospect of digital-free tourism hypothetically, as they had no similar experience before. Individuals voiced contrasting views regarding the potential benefits and disadvantages. They associated a smartphone-free trip with calmness and a heightened sense of presence, believing it could be eye-opening. Without the distraction of notifications, they envisioned spending their time more meaningfully, replacing social media engagement with lasting memories. They also felt they would be more attentive to their surroundings and details, which could lead to a greater appreciation of their environment. Additionally, the absence of digital devices could encourage resourcefulness, turning everyday challenges into opportunities for problem-solving and a sense of achievement.

On the contrary, respondents deemed smartphones essential for daily communication, gaining important updates, or alleviating the potential risks of finding themselves in an emergency without the ability to call for help. Among young, female participants, both outside dangers or getting lost could feel like a disastrous risk without their devices at hand. The most repeated concern among all participants was the lack of navigation, which they saw as crucial for safe travel experiences. These difficulties could arise during domestic travel as well, as there are many areas still unknown to them, but international travel induces a higher uneasiness, due to the additional language barriers. Since the generation hasn't had to rely on traditional navigation tools such as compasses or maps, they anticipated facing difficulties using them.

Digitalization has been a major focus in recent tourism, as businesses adapt to online registration, booking and payment systems. When it comes to creating a seamless customer experience, smartphones are a necessity, providing safety, convenience and efficiency. One participant highlighted their smartphone as encompassing all necessities into one device, eliminating the need for maps, tickets, and wallets.

Participants associated the following words with offline destinations: *panic, anxiety, despair, uncertainty, unusual, unimaginable, positive, exciting, and freeing.* While participants recognised the potential benefits of disconnecting, many felt that the disadvantages outweighed the benefits, both due to habit and reliance on smartphones. The loss of control associated with being without smart devices was notable among both male and female participants, leaving them feeling isolated and vulnerable.

However, the concept of digital-free tourism didn't inherently sound frustrating for all participants: *"...it would make me feel lost, and then it might actually make me feel in control, that I can be lost. It's a good thing that I can just go with the flow." (R1).* This highlights, that those with an internal locus of control could view this as a positive challenge to tackle, suggesting that personality traits affect receptiveness to digital detox experiences.

Challenges of adopting digital-free tourism

When considering a digital-free holiday, lack of communication would be the most taxing on participants, if they were unable to make calls or send texts. Respondents emphasized the need to keep up a two-way communication; both to stay informed and be able to inform. Not all participants owned a camera, therefore also making their phones an essential part of travelling and capturing memories. Participants also highlighted special tendencies that would be challenging to forgo, with one participant expressing their desire to be able to choose what music they listen to.

Although participants presumed being able to give up scrolling, they would miss accessing information easily, as it is an integral part of their lives: *"if I can't remember something, I can find it in a second, I do it quite often..." (R7)."* This shows, that beyond the necessities their devices can provide, individuals perceive the provided convenience as a need. Even having their smartphones with them can feel essential, with some citing nomophobia.

It can be concluded that numerous factors would make it difficult for them to completely abandon their devices during travelling: from enhancing their sense of security to navigation, payments, and photography. Nevertheless, many were open to reducing social media use and content consumption, as long as it didn't require them to forgo essential functions like keeping in touch with loved ones. As a result, digital detox during travel seems more feasible as a partial or time-limited practice rather than a complete withdrawal from the digital world.

Key to digital-free tourism

Overall, the feasibility of digital-free tourism remained a divisive topic. Finally, participants identified several key factors and services that would allow them to successfully embrace offline travelling. The following section contains their needs and potential solutions.

Participants would require an engaging destination with attractions, pre-arranged programs in an itinerary, and activities that provide meaningful ways to fill their days. Some respondents believed travelling without using their devices could be more possible at an all-inclusive resort where everything is at their disposal, while others preferred trying nature-based tourism like camping or a meditation retreat.

They expressed a need for access to educational materials and brochures about the city's landmarks, nearby shops, and restaurants. Navigation leading to these destinations, along with transport schedules near the accommodation, maps, and advertised guided tours eliminate the need for smart devices. To accommodate diverse needs information should be available in multiple ways and languages, including pictograms, informational boards at transportation hubs, a reception desk at the accommodation, or a nearby information desk where visitors can ask questions in person. Providing sufficient information before arrival can also help eliminate potential uncertainties.

Choosing the right travel companions, especially if they also take part in a digital detox, could hold participants accountable, or keep them occupied and engaged enough. Beyond their travel partners, the destination's residents also hold a key role: *"It's really helpful if the people at the destination are kind and willing to help because, in that case, you can solve everything." (R9).*

For capturing memories in tangible ways cameras, stationed photographers, or photo booths could provide a solution. In terms of entertainment, music according to their taste and tabloids could serve as alternatives to social media.

Finally, providing the appropriate infrastructure is needed to ensure their safety. Reliable power and network coverage that allows phone calls in emergencies without internet or social media access can affirm travellers.

In conclusion, several conditions account for a successful digital-free holiday. The destination is crucial from the accommodations, residents, and activities aspect. Sufficient information before and during travels, alternative forms of entertainment, and the right companions could provide them with safety and stimulation. Finally, they need to have the option and infrastructure to use their devices in case of an emergency.

Relevance of findings

These findings provide valuable insights into Generation Z's complex relationship with social media and digital technology during travel experiences. While often characterised as a social media-addicted age group, their responses reveal a more nuanced picture, highlighting the importance of investigating the broad effects of social media beyond generalizations.

The impact of online impulses on Generation Z's lives and experiences varies significantly on a personal level, as online consumption and sharing habits result from complex internal processes. This diversity was evident even within this small sample, where vastly different attitudes and perceptions towards digital-free tourism emerged. Some respondents expressed a desire and openness to restrict their screen time during travel, indicating that digital-free destinations can be relevant for a segment of this age group.

However, it's crucial to recognize that there isn't a universal solution for Generation Z when it comes to digital-free tourism. Many participants viewed complete digital detox as an extreme measure, suggesting that a more nuanced approach might be more effective.

This study highlights possible conditions and ways to accommodate different needs and reach a target market within the generation. For tourism providers seeking to attract Generation Z travellers, implementing tiered solutions could be a valuable strategy. This approach would offer a spectrum of digital detox options, from tech-light zones to full disconnection retreats. Rather than aiming for strict and total disconnection, the goal of tourism businesses should be to create opportunities and support mindful tourism within guests' comfort zones. Such flexibility would allow young travellers to experiment with digital-free experiences gradually, potentially increasing their comfort with more extensive disconnection over time.

Further exploratory research is needed to gain a more comprehensive understanding of Generation Z's attitudes towards digital-free tourism. Future studies could employ experiments, diary studies, or large-scale representative surveys to provide a general assessment of the generation's perspectives and preferences regarding digital detox during travel.

5. CONCLUSION

This study explored Generation Z's relationship with social media during travel experiences and the feasibility of digital-free tourism through 10 individual interviews. The sample included a diverse group of different ages, genders, and contrasting social media use. Examining their consumption and content creation habits, as well as their attitudes toward digital detox, provided broad insights into their technology use during travel.

Previous academic research demonstrated typical tendencies and behaviours like scrolling, addiction, FoMO, and the effects of digital detox, which can vary based on personality traits. Participants confirmed the ingrained role of social media in their daily lives, many citing a generational problem involving involuntary urges and habitual use. They spend significant time on their devices, often consuming content both actively and passively throughout the day. Social media offers entertainment, escapism, and a sense of belonging, but also results in cycles of usage that are difficult to break. However, when travelling, participants reported a reduction in their online presence. The stimulating new experiences, combined with the immersive nature of travel, often diminished their urge to scroll, allowing them to focus more on their surroundings and companions. This suggests that travel itself can act as a motivator for digital detox, even if unintended.

Their content production increased during a unique experience, highlighting the role of social media as both a documentation tool and a source of pressure. To what extent and when these documents were published varied from individual to individual. While some participants enjoyed capturing and sharing moments, the act of content curation can diminish others' experiences. The desire to both be present in the moment and create aesthetically pleasing content shows the effects social media has on Generation Z.

Regarding digital-free tourism, the study revealed mixed attitudes. While participants reacted with curiosity and recognized the relevance and potential benefits of disconnecting, they also expressed concerns about convenience and the safety of navigating an unfamiliar environment without devices. The reliance on smartphones for communication, navigation, payments, and entertainment made the prospect of a completely digital-free holiday hard to imagine. Their sense of control depended on several conditions to have a successful digital detox holiday. Destinations with engaging activities, reliable resources, and clear travel information can help ease their anxiety. The right travel companions, local community, and access to emergency communication, traditional navigation tools, and alternative forms of entertainment can enhance the feasibility of digital-free experiences.

Digital-free tourism is not a universal solution in the case of Generation Z. While some travelers seek disconnection, others may benefit more from less extreme detox experiences allowing them to reduce their screen time without feeling completely isolated.

This research contributes to the recent discourse on the effects of digital detox, by providing a nuanced perspective on Generation Z's travel habits. While the study was limited to small sample size and qualitative methods, it offers insights into the attitude toward digital-free travel among young travellers. These findings only allow for a theoretical assessment of their reactions to a digital-free holiday, therefore future research is warranted in the forms of conducting large-scale surveys, and experimental or diary studies.

In conclusion, exploring the challenges surrounding social media is necessary and relevant, as it has become part of everyday life, but its impact varies. As tourism continues to evolve, understanding the generations' demands can help design travel experiences that fulfill their needs, providing a mindful immersion into experiences.

REFERENCES

Aranda, J. H., & Baig, S. (2018). Toward „JOMO": The joy of missing out and the freedom of disconnecting. Proceedings of the 20th International Conference on Human-Computer Interaction with Mobile Devices and Services, 1–8. https://doi.org/10.1145/3229434.3229468

Barry, C., Smith, E., Murphy, M., Halter, B., & Briggs, J. (2023). JOMO: Joy of Missing Out and its Association with Social Media Use, Self-Perception, and Mental Health. Telematics and Informatics Reports, 10, 100054. https://doi.org/10.1016/j.teler.2023.100054

Bulchand-Gidumal, J. (2023). The case of BeReal and spontaneous online social networks and their impact on tourism: Research agenda. Current Issues in Tourism, 0(0), 1–5. https://doi.org/10.1080/13683500.2023.2191174

Chan, S. S., Van Solt, M., Cruz, R. E., Philp, M., Bahl, S., Serin, N., Amaral, N. B., Schindler, R., Bartosiak, A., Kumar, S., & Canbulut, M. (2022). Social media and mindfulness: From the fear of missing out (FOMO) to the joy of missing out (JOMO). Journal of Consumer Affairs, 56(3), 1312–1331. https://doi.org/10.1111/joca.12476

Christina Floros, Wenjie Cai, Brad McKenna & Dimah Ajeeb (2019): Imagine being off-the-grid: millennials' perceptions of digital-free travel, Journal of Sustainable Tourism, DOI: 10.1080/09669582.2019.1675676

Datareportal.com (2022): https://datareportal.com/reports/digital-2022-global-overview-report Accessed: 2023.11.20.

Gabriel, F. (2014). Sexting, Selfies and Self-Harm: Young People, Social Media and the Performance of Self-Development. Media International

Australia, 151(1), 104–112.
https://doi.org/10.1177/1329878X1415100114

Hassan, T. H., Salem, A. E., & Saleh, M. I. (2022). Digital-Free Tourism Holiday as a New Approach for Tourism Well-Being: Tourists' Attributional Approach. International Journal of Environmental Research and Public Health, 19(10), Article 10. https://doi.org/10.3390/ijerph19105974

Hodkinson, C., (2016). 'Fear of Missing Out' (FOMO) marketing appeals: A conceptual model. Journal of Marketing Communications

Irimiás, A. (2023). The Youth Tourist: Motives, Experiences and Travel Behaviour. Emerald Publishing Limited. http://ebookcentral.proquest.com/lib/corvinus/detail.action?docID=72 13767

Mirbabaie, M., Stieglitz, S., & Marx, J. (2022). Digital Detox. Business & Information Systems Engineering, 64(2), 239–246. https://doi.org/10.1007/s12599-022-00747-x

Oliveira, T., Araujo, B., & Tam, C. (2020). Why do people share their travel experiences on social media? Tourism Management, 78, 104041. https://doi.org/10.1016/j.tourman.2019.104041

Pásztor, J., Bak, G., (2020): Digital Divide: A Technological Generation Gap. MEB2020 — Proceedings of 18th International Conference on Management, Enterprise, Benchmarking. Óbuda University.

Pine, B.J. and Gilmore, J.H., 1998. Welcome to the experience economy. Harvard Business Review, 76(4), pp.97-105.

Ribeiro, J. F. (2021). The Relationship Between Instant Gratification and Actual Social Media Use.

Schellewald, A. (2021). ON GETTING CARRIED AWAY BY THE TIKTOK ALGORITHM. AoIR Selected Papers of Internet Research.

Sotiriadis, M. D. (2017). Sharing tourism experiences in social media: A literature review and a set of suggested business strategies. International Journal of Contemporary Hospitality Management, 29(1), 179–225. https://doi.org/10.1108/IJCHM-05-2016-0300

Whiting, A., & Williams, D. (2013). Why people use social media: A uses and gratifications approach. Qualitative Market Research, 16. https://doi.org/10.1108/QMR-06-2013-0041

HafenCity: Balancing tourism and livability

Jaqueline Reusch
Harz University of Applied Sciences
jreusch@hs-harz.de

Abstract

This study analyses the integration of living space and tourism in Hamburg's HafenCity, Germany, and develops recommendations for the development of future city districts. HafenCity serves as a research area to analyse the effects of tourism on the quality of life of the residents and to identify factors of success for the interaction of urban development and tourism. A particular focus is placed on social sustainability and the management of overtourism. The resulting recommendations for action demonstrate that the interlinking of habitat and tourism planning as well as the active participation of the local community are essential for the success of such urban development projects.

Keywords: Urban tourism, HafenCity, Hamburg, quality of life, social sustainability

1. INTRODUCTION

HafenCity, Hamburg's largest inner-city urban development project, is a prime example of sustainable urbanisation along the waterfront. Central to this vision is a comprehensive approach to sustainability that integrates social, ecological, and economic dimensions. The dual function of HafenCity as both a residential and commercial hub (Landis, 2022, p. 407), in conjunction with its status as a prominent tourist destination, underscores the imperative to address the diverse needs of its stakeholders, including residents and visitors (HafenCity Hamburg GmbH, 2021). The coexistence of tourism and residential life in HafenCity emphasises the necessity for a harmonious interaction between these spheres. As tourists engage with the public spaces of residents, shifts in perceived quality of life and community acceptance of tourism become critical areas of focus (Reif, 2019, p. 262). This dynamic becomes particularly relevant with the planned introduction of major attractions, such as the Westfield Hamburg Überseequartier, which aims to draw both local and international visitors and raises concerns about the potential for overtourism and its effects on the social fabric of the district (Univail-Rodamco ÜSQ Süd Quartiersmanagement GmbH, 2021). Notwithstanding its modern infrastructure and central location, recent public discourse has called into question the alignment of urban planning objectives with the lived experiences of HafenCity's residents (Diem et al., 2024). These discrepancies highlight the critical need for a more profound comprehension of the strategies necessary to effectively integrate tourism with residential life in comparable urban projects.

Prior research has explored waterfront revitalization and urban tourism. Kostopoulou (2013) highlights the potential for revitalized waterfronts to act as creative milieus, attracting 'creative tourists'. Meanwhile, Keyvanfar et al. (2018) emphasize sustainable waterfront revitalization (SWR) and offer a decision support tool, though focused on historic waterfronts. However, a significant gap remains in the understanding of the specific dynamics of balancing tourism and livability in modern, mixed-use developments such as HafenCity. In contrast to existing studies, this research shifts the focus from quantitative sustainability assessments toward a qualitative understanding of resident experiences. Recognizing the absence of a dedicated case study on HafenCity, this comprehensive research aims to investigate strategies for integrating tourism with residential life, ultimately providing actionable recommendations for local stakeholders and decision-makers. The study employs an in-depth exploration of resident and expert perspectives to address the nuanced social and economic dynamics within HafenCity and to contribute valuable insights for analogous urban projects. To this end, the study pursues three core research objectives:

RO1: What factors affect the quality of life of stakeholders, particularly HafenCity residents?

RO2: How does tourism impact the equilibrium between living space and quality of life in HafenCity?

RO3: What lessons can be extracted for the development of analogous urban projects?

By addressing these objectives, the study aims to contribute to the broader discourse on sustainable urban development, highlighting HafenCity as both a case study and a blueprint for balancing residential and tourism interests.

2. THEORETICAL BACKGROUND

This section provides the foundational context for understanding the interplay between tourism and urban living spaces in Hamburg's HafenCity. Additionally, key concepts such as destination development, urban tourism, and social sustainability are introduced. It explores HafenCity's historical and urban planning framework while addressing the challenges of integrating residential life with tourism. It highlights areas where existing theoretical frameworks fall short and underscores the need for a nuanced case study. By examining these elements, this section establishes the theoretical underpinnings necessary for analysing the district's dynamics and drawing actionable insights for future urban projects.

2.1 Hamburg's HafenCity

Hamburg's HafenCity represents one of the most ambitious inner-city development projects in Europe and has held the status of an independent city district since 2008. Its planning began in the 1990s with the aim of redesigning the inner-city harbour of Hamburg, Germany. A key milestone was the adoption of the master plan in 2000, which serves as a flexible framework to address the evolving requirements of urban development and the economy. The construction process extends from west to east and north to south, with notable milestones such as the development of the first neighbourhood on Sandtorkai in 2003, the district's reserved status in 2006, and a master plan revision in 2010 (HafenCity Hamburg GmbH, 2006). HafenCity Hamburg GmbH plays a pivotal role in this development, overseeing the entire project as the authoritative body. The implementation of a multi-stage development process ensures close collaboration between property developers and city administrators. This collaborative approach not only supports coherent urban planning but also guarantees adherence to high-quality standards, contributing to risk minimization and cost reduction (HafenCity Hamburg GmbH, 2006, p. 18).

A central aspect of the master plan is positioning HafenCity as a model for sustainable and integrative urban development in the 21st century. The vision emphasizes diverse mixed-use development comprising residential, work, leisure, and cultural areas. This approach seeks to foster a dynamic urban environment capable of housing approximately 12,000 residents and creating jobs for up to 20,000 individuals (HafenCity Hamburg GmbH, 2006, p. 23). Innovative solutions, such as the terp model for flood protection and the creation of accessible neighbourhood structures, reflect the district's commitment to sustainability (HafenCity Hamburg GmbH, 2006, p. 21). Furthermore, participatory processes in housing allocation aim to promote balanced social interaction and inclusivity (HafenCity Hamburg GmbH, 2006, p.55).

The current demographic structure of HafenCity reflects a diverse age profile, with young adults and families particularly prominent (Statistisches Amt für Hamburg und Schleswig-Holstein, 2024). However, infrastructural shortcomings, such as the lack of a secondary school, detract from the district's quality of life. Residents also report unmet expectations regarding local amenities and a vibrant neighbourhood atmosphere. The high volume of car traffic and environmental issues, such as heat generation from construction materials, further exacerbate these challenges (Diem et al., 2024). These factors highlight the gap between the ambitious goals of HafenCity's planners and the lived experiences of its residents. This disparity underscores the necessity of subsequent research aimed at identifying the factors that genuinely influence residents' quality of life (RO1).

2.2 Defining Destination Development in the Context of HafenCity

A destination, as defined by UN Tourism, is a place that forms the core reason for travel decisions (UN Tourism, 2024). Volgger, Erschbamer and Pechlaner (2021) expand this definition, describing a tourist destination as a location outside a person's everyday environment where they stay for at least one night. In contrast, Scherhag (2018) highlights the infrastructural perspective, identifying a destination as a geographical area equipped with the necessary accommodations, attractions, and facilities to support tourism. Eisenstein (2014) further distinguishes between tourism communities, tourism regions, and destinations, noting that while the former are supply-oriented, destinations are demand-oriented. Moretti (2017) complements these views with a synthetic perspective, combining supply and demand aspects to provide a holistic understanding of a destination as a complex system integrating tourism, residential, and administrative spaces.

Letzner's (2014) classification of destination types, which include natural landscapes, cultural landscapes, urban landscapes, and artificial leisure spaces, positions HafenCity predominantly within the urban landscape category, albeit with elements of cultural and artificial spaces. Additionally, Beritelli and Bieger's (2014) concepts of Destination Governance and Leadership highlight the importance of participatory decision-making and integrated management strategies. This approach is crucial for HafenCity, given its complexity and the potential conflicts between tourism-driven activities and the everyday lives of its residents. The integration of diverse perspectives and proactive management are essential for mitigating potential negative impacts of tourism on residents' quality of life, a key focus of RO2.

By adopting a comprehensive and inclusive understanding of destination development, HafenCity can serve as a model for urban spaces that successfully integrate tourism and residential life. This perspective supports the overarching goals of this research to identify strategies that harmonize living spaces with tourism while promoting sustainability and stakeholder collaboration.

2.3 Urban tourism and living space in the context of HafenCity

City tourism encompasses all forms of visits by non-residents to urban areas, whether for business or leisure purposes, with or without an overnight stay (Freytag and Popp, 2009, p. 7). Urban spaces serve as destinations driven by diverse motives such as leisure, business, education, and culture (Eisenstein, Kampen and Reif, 2020, p. 106). However, the characteristics of city tourism often depend on the type of city in question (Anton-Quack and Quack, 2007, p.194). Cities can be categorized by attributes such as location, demographics, or cultural significance. In Germany, classifications include population size and central functions, distinguishing cities from rural areas (Heineberg, 2018, pp. 2528).

The concept of "living space" adds another dimension to urban tourism. Defined sociologically, living space is the socially constructed environment claimed or inhabited by a group or society (Bendel, 2022). Rapid increases in a city's attractiveness can strain its tourism carrying capacity, a phenomenon known as overtourism (Peeters et al., 2018, p. 21). This occurs when excessive tourist numbers lead to negative perceptions among both visitors and locals, undermining cultural authenticity and altering the city's role as a living space. If tourism-driven changes deviate too far from a city's original culture, the destination risks losing its unique identity and competitive advantage (Dreyer and Antz, 2020, p. 42).

Hamburg has implemented measures to mitigate such risks, particularly by addressing housing availability. The Hamburgische Wohnraumschutzgesetz (HmbWoSchG) has played a pivotal role in protecting residential spaces and reducing the misuse of housing for illegal short-term rentals, such as those offered on platforms like Airbnb. In 2021, this law enabled the return of 1,259 previously misused apartments to the rental market (Bürgerschaft der Freien und Hansestadt Hamburg, 2023, p. 3). By safeguarding housing and limiting its misuse, the law helps counteract rising rents and property prices, mitigating gentrification—a process characterized by the displacement of original residents and changes to the social fabric of neighbourhoods (Kronauer, 2018).

Overtourism poses additional challenges to social sustainability, a key dimension of the sustainability triad alongside ecological and economic sustainability (Von Hauff and Kleine, 2005, pp. 5). Social sustainability emphasizes creating stable and inclusive societies while securing basic needs across generations. However, overtourism can undermine this by exceeding the physical, social, and ecological carrying capacities of a destination (Peeters et al., 2018, p. 21). Indicators of overtourism include tourism density, Airbnb prevalence, proximity to cruise terminals, and infrastructure strain. Encounters between locals and visitors within cultural offerings can counteract overtourism, fostering authenticity when both groups engage with these activities (Mandel, 2020, p. 60). These experiences often occur outside the so-called "tourist bubbles," which are concentrated areas tailored to visitor demand, such as historical city centers or cultural hotspots. However, when tourists venture into residential neighbourhoods seeking authenticity, it can be perceived by locals as spatial appropriation. Although this has not been observed in Hamburg's day tourism, overnight tourists have triggered such sentiments (Reif, 2019, p. 273). Surveys from 2017 indicated early signs of anti-tourist attitudes in HafenCity and St. Pauli (Reif, 2019, p. 267). The impacts of overtourism extend beyond social dimensions. Economically, it can lead to inflation and gentrification by increasing demand for goods, services, and housing, often displacing lower-income residents (Kronauer, 2018). Ecologically, the overuse of resources like water and energy exacerbates pollution and stresses infrastructure (Peeters et al., 2018, p. 39) To address these challenges, cities must employ tailored strategies, such as visitor management, redistribution of tourism, and promotion of less-frequented attractions. Regulatory measures like limiting Airbnb listings and implementing tourist taxes are also essential (Kagermeier, 2021, p. 143).

Hamburg's Metropolitan Region exemplifies urban-rural cooperation to manage tourism sustainably. By integrating areas from neighbouring states, the region fosters joint economic and living space initiatives while enhancing mobility, energy, and cultural offerings (Metropolregion Hamburg, 2024). HafenCity, as a hybrid space blending tourism and residential life, offers valuable insights into how urban tourism can balance authenticity with sustainable development, ensuring a harmonious coexistence between visitors and locals.

3. RESEARCH METHODOLOGY

Preliminary examinations in HafenCity and private observations in everyday life were conducted in order to identify relevant themes and questions. These findings then guided the unsystematic literature review using the snowball method to identify further relevant works and aspects. Based on these findings, this section details the methodological approach and research design of the master's thesis that formed the foundation of this paper.

3.1 Research design

Given that the topic and the formulated research questions had not previously been scientifically investigated within the planned framework, an explorative research design was selected (Pohlmann, 2022, p. 78). This approach, common in qualitative research, emphasizes openness, flexibility, and comprehensiveness to understand and interpret complex scientific contexts (Pohlmann, 2022, p. 50). To collect the necessary data, interviews were conducted with professionals and (former) residents of HafenCity. The selected sample, typical for qualitative research, comprised a small group to enable an in-depth exploration of the research topic (Voss, 2022, p. 42). The sample size for this study was determined using the principle of "information power" as described by Malterud, Siersma and Guassora (2016). According to this approach, the required sample size in qualitative research is not fixed but depends on several factors that collectively determine the adequacy of the sample to provide robust and meaningful insights. These factors include the study aim, sample specificity, use of established theory, quality of dialogue, and analysis strategy. This choice diverges from the more common saturation approach, which seeks to continue collecting data until no new insights emerge. The decision to use 'information power' was based on the specific objectives of the study and the need to balance depth with time and resource constraints. However, this approach may introduce bias by potentially underestimating the diversity of experiences within HafenCity. In addition, it must be recognised that reliance on a small sample size may limit the generalisability of the findings. Future studies could benefit from larger samples or mixed methods approaches to increase generalisability.

The interviews were problem-centred and semi-structured, allowing for both guidance and flexibility during the conversations. The objectives derived from preliminary literature analysis and observations informed the design of the interview guidelines for professionals and residents (Mayring, 2023, pp. 60).

3.2 Data collection

The identification of interview partners involved researching experts relevant to HafenCity, including stakeholders, tourism representatives, and professionals who reconcile economic interests with public welfare. Contacts were facilitated by professors from the West Coast University of Applied Sciences (FH Westküste), and additional inquiries were made via email and telephone. Despite the unanswered inquiries, including those directed at HafenCity Hamburg GmbH and Westfield Hamburg Überseequartier, to enhance the information power as outlined by (Malterud, Siersma and Guassora, 2016), a suitable group of six experts agreed to participate. The final group of experts included representatives from neighbourhood management, tour guides, the Elbphilharmonie as a major attraction, and Hamburg Tourismus GmbH as a destination management organisation. The decision to proceed with this number of participants was influenced by the time constraints of the research project, which restricted the possibility of securing additional interviews.

A multi-faceted approach was employed to recruit residents. Leaflets were distributed in local food service establishments and mailboxes across HafenCity to reach a broad audience. Additionally, the network of Hamburg's regional group of Foundation of German Business (SDW) was utilised to access a wider pool of potential participants. This network facilitated further recruitment through referrals from existing contacts, allowing for the inclusion of additional neighbours. The participants were selected to ensure a diversity of personal backgrounds, including their location of residence within HafenCity, age, profession, relationship status and gender, as these factors may influence perceptions of tourism and livability. Nonetheless, it is important to acknowledge the possibility that the selection process may have introduced biases, such as self-selection by participants who are more engaged or have stronger opinions on the topic. Consequently, efforts were made to balance these characteristics and obtain a comprehensive overview of the situation. Six residents living in different parts of HafenCity, representing diverse sociodemographic characteristics, participated in the study. During the interview process, it became apparent that responses from residents began to converge, with recurring themes and insights. This suggested that further interviews were unlikely to yield significantly new findings. The decision to limit the number of residents interviewed was also taken to ensure a balanced representation of opinions from both residents and experts, thus creating an equitable basis for the analysis of the interplay between residential and professional perspectives.

Participants were invited via email and provided with a consent form, which they signed prior to the interviews. They also received the interview guidelines in advance to prepare their responses. Depending on their preferences and availabilty, interviews were conducted via video conference (Microsoft Teams), telephone, or in-person. For example, an interview with representatives of the Elbphilharmonie included three professionals who complemented each other's responses. Similarly, the exchange with a HafenCity Infocenter Kesselhaus representative included a guided tour, during which notes were taken, followed by a 30-minute interview to address remaining questions. Other interviews lasted 45 minutes (residents) or 60 minutes (professionals). The interviews were recorded and transcribed for data processing using MS Teams (interview via video conference) or NoScript (interviews via phone call or in person) software, adhering to data protection regulations and the content-semantic transcription system (Dresing and Pehl, 2018, pp. 21). Transcriptions were then manually revised to ensure that they are standardized and dialects translated into standard language.

3.3 Methods of analysis

The chosen approach applied a content-based structuring and combined deductive and inductive categorization (Mayring, 2015). Text passages relevant to predefined, theory-based categories were paraphrased according to interpretation rules. Categories were derived from the research questions and existing theoretical frameworks, ensuring alignment with the study's objectives. Coding rules defined for each category facilitated the accurate assignment of text passages. Subsequently, paraphrases were generalized under defined abstraction levels, with redundant paraphrases removed in a two-step reduction process. Separate category systems were developed for expert interviews and resident interviews to accurately capture differing perspectives. Following the deductive categorization phase, an inductive category development process was conducted to address data elements not adequately captured by the initial categories. Through iterative analysis, new categories were generated directly from the data, ensuring emergent themes were recognized and integrated into the analytical framework. This step allowed the study to capture unexpected or context-specific insights, thereby enriching the analysis. The combination of these approaches facilitated the development of a final, cohesive set of codes. These codes provided a structured yet flexible representation of the data, capturing both theoretical expectations and novel findings. This methodological rigor ensured that the results section delivers a comprehensive and representative summary of the relevant findings, enabling actionable recommendations for urban development and tourism planning in HafenCity.

3.4 Method evaluation

To ensure quality, the study adhered to the principles of openness, communication, process orientation, and reflection as outlined in qualitative social research (Pohlmann, 2022, pp. 50). Six general quality criteria for qualitative research were considered (Mayring, 2023, pp. 122): procedural documentation, argumentative validation of interpretations, rule orientation, subject proximity, communicative validation, and triangulation. Procedural documentation was ensured through detailed transcription and analysis. Interpretations were justified with reference to the theoretical background. Rule orientation was maintained via the structured application of Mayring's process model (2015, p. 104). Subject proximity was achieved by including stakeholders and residents of HafenCity in the study, ensuring their perspectives were heard. Communicative validation occurred during interviews, as interviewees confirmed or clarified their responses when summarized by the interviewer. Triangulation was achieved by comparing data from stakeholders and residents with existing literature and observational data (Mayring, 2015, p. 125).

The exploratory research design and qualitative methodology offered valuable insights into HafenCity's development. However, the study was subject to certain limitations, including technical challenges such as internet issues and background noise, as well as the inherent limitations of qualitative studies due to their small sample size. These limitations can affect the generalisability of the findings. To enhance the generalisability of future research, larger samples and mixed-method approaches might be considered. Additionally, the original quotes from the study's participants were in German, which could have introduced a language barrier. The process of translating these quotes into English introduces a potential risk of distortion, as nuances and meanings may be misinterpreted during the translation process. This poses a challenge for accurately conveying the participants' perspectives and could influence the interpretation of findings. The chosen explorative research design and qualitative methodologies effectively addressed the study's research objectives, allowing for comprehensive insights into HafenCity's development. Despite the limitations of the methods applied, the study offered actionable recommendations and meaningful conclusions, underscoring the alignment between the research objectives and the methodological choices.

4. RESULTS AND DISCUSSION

Mayring (2015) qualitative content analysis produced coding codes for the professional interviews and a further coding list for the resident interviews (see Table 1). These were used to systematically analyse the transcripts of the interviews and to identify key quotations that underpin the findings. It should be noted that the original quotes are in German and were translated into English for this paper. Data will be provided upon request in the interests of scientific transparency.

Table 1. Codes

Residents	Experts
Quality of living	Urban planning
Social infrastructure	Habitat design
Social integration	Social & economical sustainability
Tourism challenges	Tourism compatibility measuers

4.1 Resident perspectives

The perspectives of the residents highlight the balance between the modern amenities of HafenCity and the practical and social challenges it presents. Their experiences offer insights into key aspects such as quality of life, infrastructure, social integration and the impact of tourism, and provide a basis for evaluating life in this unique urban environment. The sub-sections below are an in-depth examination of these themes, based on observations and first-hand accounts from residents.

The following findings concur with the theoretical underpinnings of urban tourism and living space, wherein the concept of "living space" is delineated sociologically as the socially constructed environment claimed or inhabited by a group or society (Bendel, 2022). The perceived quality of life in HafenCity is influenced by both physical and social factors, thereby underscoring the significance of addressing these dimensions in urban planning. This corroborates RO1 by emphasising factors pertinent to residents' quality of life.

4.1.1 Quality of living

The residents provided a number of observations on the merits and drawbacks of residing in HafenCity. The architectural quality of the residential buildings was frequently lauded, with features such as underfloor heating and triple-glazed windows that effectively reduced external noise being singled out for particular praise (Reusch, 2024, Appendix P). However, concerns regarding privacy due to glass facades were also commonly expressed, with the perception that they limited the personal scope for design expressed: *"If a building has a glass facade, you can't cover that up. It's probably not meant to be used as a hiding space"* (Reusch, 2024, Appendix N). Ongoing construction was frequently mentioned as a detriment to daily life, with noise, dust, and access issues reported. Despite these challenges, proximity to promenades and waterfronts contributed positively to quality of life, offering opportunities for recreation and relaxation (Reusch, 2024, Appendix O). Green spaces were appreciated for their aesthetic value, but questions were raised about their functionality and ecological balance. Residents noted a need for more usable green areas to mitigate heat and improve recreational opportunities (Reusch, 2024, Appendices Q, L). This is consistent with Kostopoulou's (2013) theory that green spaces enhance an area's appeal, creating an environment conducive to creativity that benefits residents and visitors.

The district's low traffic levels were found to have a positive impact on parents' sense of safety for their children (Reusch, 2024, Appendix L). It was noted that children would meet in the courtyard and be able to live relatively independently, due to the low level of car traffic in the area. However, concerns were raised about parking availability and costs, with visitors and residents struggling with high fees and limited spaces (Reusch, 2024, Appendix P). Public transport was widely praised for its reliability and convenience. The addition of two subway stations in proximity has significantly enhanced connectivity, ensuring efficient and accessible commuting (Reusch, 2024, Appendix O). While cycling infrastructure in newer districts was acknowledged to be satisfactory, older districts were found to have an absence of dedicated cycle lanes, resulting in cyclists having to share the thoroughfares with motor vehicles. This situation was reported to be a source of frustration for residents (Reusch, 2024, Appendix O).

4.1.2 Social infrastructure & social integration

Social infrastructure was identified as a pivotal domain for enhancement. Concerns were voiced by residents regarding the affordability and diversity of local options, as well as their opening hours. The accessibility of childcare facilities and educational institutions was scrutinised, with parents highlighting overcrowded childcare centres and a paucity of secondary education options. The healthcare infrastructure was deemed inadequate, particularly in specialised fields like paediatricians: *"A bit of infrastructure for living is also lacking. So paediatricians, all kinds of other doctors are missing"* (Reusch, 2024, Appendix L). The presence of an intact social infrastructure, encompassing a healthcare system with adequate medical provision, is of paramount importance for the tourism industry. This is due to the fact that visitors can rely on such an infrastructure when necessary, thereby impacting the quality of their experience. Additionally, it can lead to overcrowding and strain on resources. Public transport and shared bicycle services, such as StadtRad, utilised by both groups, are another notable example, impacting its efficiency and accessibility (Reusch, 2024, Appendix N). In addition to these social infrastructure challenges, fostering community integration is essential for enhancing the quality of life in HafenCity. Existing meeting places, such as courtyards, and temporary events like markets and festivals have fostered social interactions (Reusch, 2024, Appendix

O). However, residents have articulated a need for more non-commercial spaces to enhance community cohesion (Reusch, 2024, Appendix N). The district's social and age-related diversity has been recognised, yet the lack of a distinct neighbourhood identity persists due to its planned origins (Reusch, 2024, Appendix M, N). Communication initiatives, including newsletters and local meetings, have been implemented to enhance participation, yet uptake remains limited (Reusch, 2024, Appendix N, Q). The current social integration in HafenCity is characterised by a combination of positive developments and unmet needs, as perceived by residents.

The establishment of non-commercial spaces is crucial for enhancing social integration and community identity, supporting RO2 by highlighting the impact of tourism on the equilibrium between living space and quality of life. Integrating tourism with residential life is essential to foster social cohesion and mitigate negative tourism impacts. A comprehensive urban planning approach is necessary to address these challenges. This approach involves incorporating traffic management strategies into sustainable development frameworks, ensuring mobility solutions support both residents and tourists while minimizing environmental impacts. The concept of a SWR index provides a structured framework for evaluating and enhancing the sustainability of projects like HafenCity, addressing environmental, social, and economic dimensions. By applying such a framework, policymakers can identify areas needing social infrastructure improvements, supporting a more sustainable and inclusive urban environment. This aligns with the broader goal of balancing tourism development with residential needs, emphasizing participatory planning and social sustainability in urban projects.

4.1.3 Tourism challenges

Beyond the issues of noise and overcrowding, HafenCity faces challenges related to waste management and the prestige associated with iconic attractions. Residents perceive existing disposal facilities as insufficient and primarily designed for tourists rather than locals (Reusch, 2024, Appendices P, Q), highlighting a need for improved waste management services to alleviate strain on shared resources and ensure adequate recycling options. This underscores the importance of integrating environmental sustainability into urban planning, addressing the ecological dimension of the sustainability triad (Von Hauff and Kleine, 2005).

Iconic attractions such as the Elbphilharmonie serve as a source of pride for residents, who regard it as a "prestige object" (Reusch, 2024, Appendix O) that enhances the district's cultural reputation (Dreyer, 2020, p. 50). However, the area's growing popularity has led to increased tourism-related pressures, which has in turn highlighted the need for more thoughtful urban planning that can balance the needs of residents and visitors (Kronauer, 2018). This aligns with theoretical discussions on the role of cultural attractions in urban tourism, where such landmarks can both attract tourists and enhance local identity (Dreyer, 2020). However, the prestige associated with these attractions can also contribute to gentrification, as rising property values and rental costs displace local businesses (Reusch, 2024, Appendix O) and residents, undermining social sustainability (Kronauer, 2018). Therefore, the implementation of strategies that mitigate these effects is crucial. Such strategies may include participatory planning and the creation of affordable housing options, ensuring that the benefits of tourism are equitably distributed among stakeholders. By addressing these challenges, HafenCity can serve as a model for sustainable urban development, providing lessons for analogous urban projects. This aligns with RO3 by highlighting the importance of balancing tourism development with residential needs and social sustainability.

4.2 Professional perspective

The professional perspective section explores how experts approach urban planning and sustainability in HafenCity. It examines how professional insights balance residential needs with tourism, focusing on safety, space utility and quality of life. This approach aligns with the broader vision of HafenCity as a model for sustainable urban development, integrating social, ecological, and economic dimensions (HafenCity Hamburg GmbH, 2006).

4.2.1 Urban Planning & Habitat Design

HafenCity's urban planning incorporates innovative principles to balance livability, authenticity, and community with the challenges posed by tourism and urban density. This approach aligns with theoretical discussions on the role of urban design in fostering community safety and livability (Kostopoulou, 2013; Landis, 2022). Activating ground floors is a key strategy for improving community safety. As one expert explained, *"Where there are no ground floor uses, you feel much less safe, especially in the evening when it's dark. It's different when there are shops that are lit up and provide some brightness"* (Reusch, 2024, Appendix K).

Open spaces are emphasised for their role in increasing the district's attractiveness and fostering creativity by providing much needed space for the creative scene (Reusch, 2024, Appendices I, J). As one expert noted: *"We should pay a little more attention to having a centre where people 'have to' or 'want to' meet. That's why I'm recommending a market square, which I think is completely ignored in today's urban planning"* (Reusch, 2024, Appendix K). The district's authenticity stems from a mix of uses, including living, working, and cultural activities. Experts highlighted the importance of organically developed neighbourhoods, emphasising that such neighbourhoods, integrating life, production, and cultural activities, are particularly attractive (Reusch 2024, Appendix I). In order to maximise the use of space, HafenCity's planners have adopted a multifaceted approach, as articulated by one expert who stated that "*maximising the use of space was at least a sub-goal*" (Reusch, 2024, Appendix H). This commitment to optimising the use of space is evident in the meticulous orientation of residential buildings, which is intended to minimise noise disturbance. This is exemplified by the design of courtyards, which are intended to provide a barrier against external noise (Reusch, 2024, Appendix J). Furthermore, the strategic positioning of entrances serves to mitigate the impact of emissions and noise on residents. While certain experts propose the tolerance of elevated noise levels during nocturnal hours in specific areas, this strategy emphasises the district's capacity for balancing urban density with resident needs (Reusch, 2024,

H, I). Given the limited availability of land, HafenCity has adopted creative solutions such as integrating playgrounds and kindergartens on rooftops, demonstrating adaptability while meeting residents' needs (Reusch, 2024, Appendix K). These strategies are indicative of HafenCity's proficiency in achieving a balance between urban density and innovative, resident-centred planning, thus establishing itself as a model for sustainable urban development. Consequently, this contributes to RO3 by offering valuable insights and lessons for analogous urban projects.

The integration of these design elements serves to enhance HafenCity's appeal as a vibrant and inclusive urban environment, aligning with theoretical frameworks that accentuate the significance of mixed-use development and community engagement in urban planning. The emphasis on the creation of authentic neighbourhoods through the provision of affordable housing and non-commercial spaces aligns with broader goals of social sustainability and community cohesion, underscoring the district's potential as a creative milieu that attracts both residents and visitors (Kostopoulou, 2013).

4.2.2 Social & economical sustainability

HafenCity's approach is characterised by its commitment to integrating social and economic sustainability, with a focus on fostering inclusivity and resilience. The importance of effective communication and citizen participation in this context has been articulated by several experts, with one individual emphasising the significance of citizen participation, stating: *"We live in times where citizen participation is crucial. It's about communication, respect for people, and addressing concerns and needs through honesty and transparency"* (Reusch, 2024, Appendix I). Tools like a citizen participation portal, developed with HafenCity University, support these efforts, though experts caution that participation must be balanced with decisive leadership: *„Citizen participation is a double-edged sword. It brings great ideas, but development also needs leaders to guide the process"* (Reusch, 2024, Appendix I).

Achieving economic sustainability necessitates a balanced approach, navigating the tension between tourism-driven growth and meeting local needs. Rising rental costs and the displacement of essential services pose significant risks, compounded by the seasonal dependency of businesses from March to October. One expert cautioned that rent escalation is a concern, as it can lead to the displacement of everyday amenities and essential services, potentially reaching a critical tipping point (Reusch, 2024, Appendix H). Experts have emphasised the need for balanced retail development, with the Westfield Center Überseequartier anticipated to reshape the retail landscape in Hamburg (Reusch, 2024, Appendix J). Experts also advocate for equitable revenue distribution from events and the avoidance of excessive concentration of hotels and hotspots: *"While the necessity for hotels is acknowledged, it is paramount to ensure their judicious distribution across the city to circumvent the creation of concentrated hubs"* (Reusch, 2024, Appendix H). This is in accordance with theoretical discussions on the importance of destination governance and leadership in managing tourism impacts (Beritelli and Bieger, 2014).

4.2.3 Tourism compatibility measures

In the context of HafenCity's development, a core aspect of the planning process is the balancing of tourism and residential needs. As one expert has noted, *"A destination that is attractive for its residents is also automatically attractive for travelers"* (Reusch, 2024, Appendix I), thereby prioritising the creation of liveable spaces that attract visitors. This perspective emphasises the quality of life for residents over purely tourist-driven development. Inclusive planning is vital for fostering compatibility, with experts advocating for the involvement of cultural stakeholders and tourism professionals through workshops to ensure diverse and functional designs (Reusch, 2024, Appendix H) that result in more comprehensive outcomes. Neighbourhood management acts as a core link between residents, businesses, and decision-makers, fostering cohesive development. Visitor management strategies adopt advanced technologies and thoughtful urban design, such as pre-booking fees, ticket limitations, and artificial intelligence to manage flows and prevent overtourism. Features like cruise terminals with integrated bus facilities streamline movement: terminals designed to allow direct disembarkation for passengers help reduce congestion (Reusch, 2024, Appendix K). Wider pedestrian pathways and open spaces further enhance public areas and mitigate crowding (Reusch, 2024, Appendix J). The enhancement of infrastructure in HafenCity, including cultural offerings and improved public transportation services, is a significant benefit of tourism, supporting both residents and visitors (Reusch, 2024, Appendix H). Furthermore, hotels and restaurants are encouraged to provide cultural programmes that foster community connections. The effective communication of the value of tourism is crucial for maintaining public acceptance of tourism, as experts emphasise the need to showcase the positive contributions of tourism to the community (Reusch, 2024, Appendix I). These findings highlight the importance of social sustainability in managing tourism impacts, ensuring that tourism benefits are equitably distributed and negative impacts are mitigated (Von Hauff and Kleine, 2005).

5. LIMITATIONS AND SCOPE FOR FUTURE RESEARCH

While the explorative research design and qualitative methodology provided in-depth insights into the quality of life and touristic development of HafenCity, limitations included technical challenges (e.g., internet issues, background noise) and the small sample size typical of qualitative studies. These limitations affect generalizability. Future research could benefit from larger samples and mixed-method approaches to enhance generalizability and incorporate additional perspectives. An additional limitation lies in the fact that the original quotes from the study's participants were in German. Translating these quotes into English introduces a potential risk of distortion, as nuances and meanings might be misinterpreted during the translation process. This poses a challenge for accurately conveying the participants' perspectives and could influence the interpretation of findings. Participant selection bias, such as self-selection, may have influenced the study's outcomes, highlighting the importance of acknowledging these biases to enhance credibility. The chosen explorative research design and qualitative methodologies effectively addressed the study's research objects, allowing for comprehensive insights into HafenCity's development. Despite limitations, the methods provided actionable recommendations and meaningful conclusions, underscoring the alignment between research objectives and methodological choices.

It is recommended that future studies explore targeted research questions or recommend mixed-method approaches to guide subsequent investigations. For instance, integrating quantitative methods could provide a more comprehensive understanding of the impacts of tourism on HafenCity's residents. Additionally, examining the effectiveness of participatory planning processes and the role of stakeholder engagement in managing overtourism could offer valuable insights for sustainable urban development. The study's primary focus on social sustainability and the management of overtourism underscores the necessity for ongoing research into strategies that balance tourism growth with residential needs, ensuring that urban projects like HafenCity serve as models for sustainable and inclusive development.

6. CONCLUSION AND IMPLICATIONS

This study set out to investigate the complex interplay between residential life and tourism in Hamburg's HafenCity, a district striving to balance urban living with a burgeoning tourist presence. The study drew from the theoretical framework and qualitative insights from stakeholders and residents, and the findings offer critical implications for decision makers in HafenCity's development and similar urban projects. The conclusions are structured around the three research objectives (ROs).

RO1: The quality of life in HafenCity is shaped by a multifaceted set of factors. Architectural design, green spaces, and proximity to promenades and public transport have been identified as positive influences. However, challenges such as ongoing construction, noise pollution, limited parking, and inadequate healthcare and educational infrastructure have been identified as constraints on resident satisfaction. The lack of non-commercial spaces for social interaction and a distinctive neighbourhood identity have been found to further exacerbate these issues. Social integration, while progressing through shared spaces and events, remains hindered by the district's planned origins and limited community participation. The improvement of social infrastructure, the establishment of inclusivity, and the addressing of spatial inequities are therefore imperative in order to increase the overall livability of the area.

RO2: The impact of tourism on HafenCity has been a subject of considerable interest, with the district experiencing both positive and negative consequences as a result. Cultural landmarks, such as the Elbphilharmonie, serve to establish the district as a tourist destination, yet the concomitant increase in visitors has been shown to intensify infrastructural strain and accentuate socio-economic challenges. The phenomenon of overtourism has been demonstrated to disrupt local routines through a number of channels, including overcrowding, inflated housing costs and increased demand for public resources. However, it should be noted that tourism has also been shown to stimulate improvements in public transport and cultural offerings, benefiting both visitors and locals alike. The management of these dynamics necessitates the implementation of innovative visitor management strategies, including pre-booking systems, the redistribution of tourist flows, and participatory planning processes. The study emphasises the importance of aligning tourism development with resident-centric urban planning to facilitate a sustainable coexistence.

RO3: HafenCity's experience highlights essential strategies for integrating tourism and residential life in future urban projects. Firstly, participatory planning that incorporates stakeholder feedback ensures that development aligns with community needs. Measures such as the creation of non-commercial meeting spaces and the fostering of affordable housing are vital for promoting social cohesion. Secondly, proactive management of tourism impacts through zoning, infrastructure planning, and the equitable distribution of amenities can mitigate the risks of overtourism. Thirdly, the integration of sustainability principles in urban planning across the social, economic, and environmental dimensions is essential for ensuring long-term resilience and inclusivity. HafenCity serves as a model for leveraging tourism as a driver of urban renewal while maintaining the integrity of living spaces.

The following table summarises the theoretical and practical implications for sustainable urban development in HafenCity and similar projects, building on these findings:

Table 2. Theoretical and practical implications

Aspect	Theoretical implication	Practical implication
Participatory planning	Aligns with destination governance and leadership theories, emphasising stakeholder engagement (Beritelli and Bieger, 2014).	Essential for balancing tourism and residential needs through inclusive decision-making processes like community workshops and citizen participation portals.
Urban tourism and living space	Contributes to the discourse on urban tourism by demonstrating the benefits of mixed-use development (Kostopoulou, 2013).	Integration of cultural attractions and public spaces catering both residents and visitors, enhancing livability for residents while fostering a vibrant tourist environment
Non-commercial spaces	Supports theoretical discussions on community engagement and social cohesion (Kostopoulou, 2013).	Creation of public squares or marketplaces that serve as hubs for social interaction fostering community identity and mitigating overtourism effects.
Visitor management	Aligns with theoretical perspectives on managing tourism impacts, emphasising the need to alleviate overtourism	Use of pre-booking system and ticket limitations to mitigate infrastructure strain

	effects (Peeters et al., 2018).	and enhance residents' quality of life.
Affordable housing	Reflects theoretical concerns about gentrification and social inclusivity (Kronauer, 2018).	Implementation of rent control policies and promotion of affordable housing options to prevent gentrification and maintain social inclusivity.

In conclusion, the HafenCity project illustrates the intricate balance required to harmonise urban living with tourism. By addressing the outlined challenges and leveraging the identified opportunities, HafenCity can achieve its vision as a sustainable and integrative urban district. The findings of this study provide actionable recommendations for policymakers, urban planners, and tourism stakeholders, ensuring that future urban developments resonate with the needs of all stakeholders while fostering sustainable growth.

REFERENCES

Anton-Quack, C. and Quack, H.-D., 2007. Städtetourismus - eine Einführung. In: Geographie der Freizeit und des Tourismus: Bilanz und Ausblick. München: Oldenbourg Verlag. pp.193–203. https://doi.org/10.1524/9783486700015.193.

Bendel, O., 2022. Lebensraum. [online] Available at: <https://wirtschaftslexikon.gabler.de/definition/lebensraum-124738/version-386982> [Accessed 19 August 2024].

Beritelli, P. and Bieger, T., 2014. From destination governance to destination leadership – defining and exploring the significance with the help of a systemic perspective. Tourism Review, 69(1), pp.25–46. https://doi.org/10.1108/TR-07-2013-0043.

Bürgerschaft der Freien und Hansestadt Hamburg, 2023. Wohnraumschutzbericht 2021. [online] Hamburg. Available at: <https://www.buergerschaft-hh.de/parldok/dokument/84677/wohnraumschutzbericht_2021.pdf> [Accessed 14 August 2024].

Diem, V., Hamm, M., Heinemann, C., Läsker, C., Ramsel, Y., Rossbauer, M., Tschaikowski, B., Twickel, C., Woltjen, G. and Zinnecker, F., 2024. Wie lebt es sich in der HafenCity? Die Zeit № 41. Hamburg, 26 Sep., pp.2–5.

Dresing, T. and Pehl, T., 2018. Praxisbuch_Transkription. 8. Auflage ed. [online] Marburg. Available at: <https://www.audiotranskription.de/wp-content/uploads/2020/11/Praxisbuch_08_01_web.pdf> [Accessed 5 August 2024].

Dreyer, A., 2020. 2. Kulturtourismus – eine Einführung. In: Kulturtourismus. De Gruyter. pp.29–52. https://doi.org/10.1515/9783486711028-002.

Dreyer, A. and Antz, C., 2020. Kulturtourismus. [online] De Gruyter. https://doi.org/10.1515/9783486711028.

Eisenstein, B., 2014. Grundlagen des Destinationsmanagements. OLDENBOURG WISSENSCHAFTSVERLAG. https://doi.org/10.1524/9783486779950.

Eisenstein, B., Kampen, J. and Reif, J., 2020. 7. Städtereisen. In: A. Dreyer and C. Antz, eds. Kulturtourismus. [online] Berlin, Boston: De Gruyter Oldenbourg. pp.105–114. https://doi.org/doi:10.1515/9783486711028-007.

Freytag, T. and Popp, M., 2009. Der Erfolg des europäischen Städtetourismus. Grundlagen, Entwicklungen, Wirkungen. Geographische Rundschau, 61(2), pp.4–11.

HafenCity Hamburg GmbH, 2006. HafenCityHamburg. The Masterplan. [online] Hamburg. Available at: <https://www.hafencity.com/_Resources/Persistent/c/7/1/d/c71db692487a55836aa17c935cb54d973e403384/z_de_broschueren_24_Masterplan_end.pdf> [Accessed 5 September 2024].

HafenCity Hamburg GmbH, 2021. Facts & figures. Important information about HafenCity. [online] Available at: <https://www.hafencity.com/_Resources/Persistent/5/0/1/b/501bc0d8dcc763292c0fb4397dfb8a0edf0394c6/HafenCity_Daten%20und%20Fakten%20EN.pdf> [Accessed 7 January 2025].

Von Hauff, M. and Kleine, A., 2005. Methodischer Ansatz zur Systematisierung von Handlungsfeldern und Indikatoren einer Nachhaltigkeitsstrategie-Das Integrierende Nachhaltigkeits-Dreieck. [online] Available at: <https://kluedo.ub.rptu.de/frontdoor/deliver/index/docId/1597/file/Das_Integrierende_Nachhaltigkeits-Dreieck.pdf> [Accessed 30 August 2024].

Heineberg, H., 2018. Stadttypen. [online] Hannover: ARL - Akademie für Raumforschung und Landesplanung. Available at: <https://www.arl-net.de/system/files/media-shop/pdf/HWB%202018/Stadttypen.pdf> [Accessed 15 July 2024].

Kagermeier, A., 2021. Managementansätze zum Umgang mit Overtourism. In: Overtourism. Stuttgart: utb GmbH. pp.137–182.

Keyvanfar, A., Shafaghat, A., Mohamad, S., Abdullahi, M.M., Ahmad, H., Derus, N.H.M. and Khorami, M., 2018. A sustainable historicwaterfront revitalization decision support tool for attracting tourists. Sustainability (Switzerland), 10(2). https://doi.org/10.3390/su10020215.

Kostopoulou, S., 2013. On the revitalized waterfront: Creative milieu for creative tourism. Sustainability (Switzerland), 5(11), pp.4578–4593. https://doi.org/10.3390/su5114578.

Kronauer, M., 2018. Gentrifizierung: Ursachen, Formen und Folgen. [online] Available at: <https://www.bpb.de/themen/stadt-land/stadt-und-gesellschaft/216871/gentrifizierung-ursachen-formen-und-folgen/> [Accessed 14 August 2024].

Landis, J.D., 2022. Urban regeneration meets sustainability - HafenCity, Hamburg. In: Megaprojects for Megacities. Edward Elgar Publishing. pp.407–428. https://doi.org/10.4337/9781803920634.00019.

Letzner, Volker., 2014. Tourismusökonomie : Volkswirtschaftliche Aspekte rund ums Reisen. De Gruyter. https://doi.org/10.1524/9783110369922.

Malterud, K., Siersma, V.D. and Guassora, A.D., 2016. Sample Size in Qualitative Interview Studies. Qualitative Health Research, 26(13), pp.1753–1760. https://doi.org/10.1177/1049732315617444.

Mandel, B., 2020. 3. Kulturvermittlung im Tourismus. In: Kulturtourismus. De Gruyter. pp.53–62. https://doi.org/10.1515/9783486711028-003.

Mayring, P., 2015. Qualitative Inhaltsanalyse. Grundlagen und Techniken. 12th ed. Weinheim: Beltz Verlagsgruppe.

Mayring, P., 2023. Einführung in die qualitative Sozialforschung. 7th ed. Weinheim Basel: Beltz Pädagogik.

Metropolregion Hamburg, 2024. Metropolregion Hamburg. [online] Available at: <https://metropolregion.hamburg.de/ueber-uns> [Accessed 28 July 2024].

Moretti, A., 2017. The Network Organization. A Governance Perspective on Structure, Dynamics and Performance. [online] Cham: Springer International Publishing. https://doi.org/10.1007/978-3-319-52093-3.

Peeters, P., Gössling, S., Klijs, J., Milano, C., Novelli, M., Dijkmans, C., Eijgelaar, E., Hartman, S., Heslinga, J., Isaac, R., Mitas, O., Moretti, S., Nawijn, J., Papp, B. and Postma, A., 2018. Research for TRAN Committee - Overtourism: impact and possible policy responses.

Pohlmann, M., 2022. Einführung in die Qualitative Sozialforschung. [online] Stuttgart, Deutschland: utb GmbH. https://doi.org/10.36198/9783838555300.

Reif, J., 2019. Touristische Aktionsräume und die Wahrnehmung von Crowding. Zeitschrift für Tourismuswissenschaft, [online] 11(2), pp.257–287. https://doi.org/10.1515/tw-2019-0015.

Reusch, J., 2024. Hamburg's HafenCity als touristische Destination und Lebensraum: Situationsanalyse und Handlungsempfehlungen für Oberbillwerder. FH Westküste.

Scherhag, K., 2018. Destination. [online] Gabler Wirtschaftslexikon. Available at: <https://wirtschaftslexikon.gabler.de/definition/destination-29114/version-252731> [Accessed 17 June 2024].

Statistisches Amt für Hamburg und Schleswig-Holstein, 2024. Regionaldaten für HafenCity. [online] Available at: <https://region.statistik-nord.de/detail/1010011111010100110/2/1715/227679/> [Accessed 6 September 2024].

UN Tourism, 2024. Glossary of tourism terms. [online] Available at: <https://www.unwto.org/glossary-tourism-terms#:~:text=Destination%20(main%20destination%20of%20a,decision%20to%20take%20the%20trip.> [Accessed 17 June 2024].

Univail-Rodamco ÜSQ Süd Quartiersmanagement GmbH, 2021. Unforgettable Events and Entertainment. [online] Available at: <https://b2b.ueberseequartier.de/en/entertainment-leisure/> [Accessed 29 January 2025].

Volgger, M., Erschbamer, G. and Pechlaner, H., 2021. Destination design: New perspectives for tourism destination development. Journal of Destination Marketing and Management, 19. https://doi.org/10.1016/j.jdmm.2021.100561.

Voss, R., 2022. Wissenschaftliches Arbeiten. [online] Stuttgart, Deutschland: utb GmbH. https://doi.org/10.36198/9783838588124.

The Role of Innovation Policy in Shaping the Future of Sustainable Tourism Development: Insights from Austria

Master Thesis submitted to Salzburg University of Applied Sciences
in partial fulfilment of the requirements for obtaining the academic degree of
"Master of Arts in Business"

Author: Dennis Kamau Muniu
Email adress: kamaudennis96@gmail.com

Abstract

This paper explores how innovation policy shapes sustainable tourism development in Austria using a qualitative research approach. It explores the perspectives of key stakeholders, including government policymakers, tourism businesses, destination management organizations (DMOs), and local communities. Semi-structured expert interviews with government policymakers, tourism businesses, DMO representatives, and community leaders provide insights into the implementation and effectiveness of Austria's innovation policies in promoting sustainable tourism practices. A content analysis of policy documents, including the Research, Technology, and Innovation (RTI) Strategy 2030; RTI Pact 2024-2026; Austrian Research and Technology Report 2023; and Plan T - Master Plan for Tourism, reveals the policy landscape and the status quo. Austria's innovation policies emphasize sustainability, digitalization, and stakeholder engagement. Environmental outcomes include the integration of renewable energy and energy-efficient technologies in tourism infrastructure. Economic outcomes are mixed, as R&D investments contribute to sustainable tourism growth, yet the sector faces challenges such as economic leakage through international booking platforms and difficulties in SMEs accessing funding. Social outcomes indicate community participation, educational programs, and cultural preservation efforts. Nevertheless, there is a lack of specific focus on tourism within these policy frameworks. Additionally, fully achieving the intended policy outcomes faces hurdles such as greenwashing, bureaucratic hurdles, and stakeholder engagement. Successful initiatives such as the Alpine Pearls Network, a collaboration of Alpine destinations focused on sustainable mobility, demonstrate the potential for integrating sustainable practices into tourism offerings. The network promotes car-free holidays and provides efficient public transport solutions. These initiatives have successfully reduced reliance on private vehicles and decreased environmental impact, offering a practical model for achieving policy goals related to sustainable tourism. Based on these findings, this paper offers policy recommendations, including developing dedicated funding for tourism innovation, enhancing stakeholder collaboration platforms, fostering a data-driven decision-making approach, supporting SMEs, and implementing robust monitoring and certification schemes. This study underscores the importance of a holistic, long-term approach to innovation policies for sustainable tourism development. Aligning these policies with the specific needs of the tourism sector and engaging diverse stakeholders can strengthen Austria's position as a leader in sustainable tourism. The findings bridge the gap between academia and industry, offering practical insights for policymakers and industry stakeholders that if implemented, can drive sustainable growth in Austria.

Keywords: Tourism, innovation, sustainable development, innovation policy, stakeholder engagement, policy implementation

1. INTRODUCTION

The global tourism industry, currently valued at an estimated 9.5 trillion USD and representing 7.7% of the global GDP, is experiencing a notable recovery post-pandemic, signalling resilience and potential for further growth (Statista, 2024). Sustainable recovery however necessitates addressing the relationship between tourism and the environment through strategies that account for the long-term economic, social, and environmental impacts (Ilić & Kostić, 2021). This aligns with global and regional sustainable tourism policies, such as the UN Sustainable Development Goals and the European Green Deal, which emphasize the need for innovative and sustainable approaches to tourism development (European Commission, n.d; UNWTO, 2020).

This paper explores how innovation policies promote sustainable tourism development in Austria, focusing on the design, implementation, and stakeholder perceptions of these policies. It emphasizes the need for innovative approaches to sustainability that integrate environmental stewardship, economic viability, and social well-being (UNWTO, 2020). These innovative approaches include technology-driven solutions, such as digital platforms, artificial intelligence, and data analytics, alongside social innovations that foster community involvement and responsible tourism practices. The study offers insights into how Austria can more effectively align its innovation policies with sustainability goals. This research aims to provide practical recommendations for enhancing policy frameworks, improving collaboration between stakeholders, and supporting sustainable tourism development within Austria and potentially informing similar efforts in other regions.

The main research question is "How does innovation policy shape sustainable tourism development in Austria?" This thesis aims to enhance the scholarly understanding of how innovation policy shapes the future trajectory of sustainable tourism. It assesses the policy's current status quo, explores stakeholder perspectives, and identifies areas for strategic improvement. This research provides actionable insights for industry stakeholders and policymakers, aligning academic studies with practical applications. The objectives of this study are as follows:

To examine the current status quo and characteristics of Austria's innovation policy relevant to the tourism sector, focusing specifically on Research Technology and Innovation Strategy and Plan T: Master Plan for Tourism.

To evaluate the extent to which innovation policies in Austria have achieved their intended environmental, economic, and social outcomes.

To explore the views of stakeholders, particularly those involved in sustainability initiatives such as Alpine Pearls, on the implementation of innovation policies in sustainable tourism development.

To formulate policy recommendations aimed at enhancing Austria's innovation strategy for the sustainable development of tourism based on a comprehensive analysis of current practices and stakeholder feedback.

1.1 Problem Statement

According to Hjalager (2012), literature has extensively examined the nature, scope, and implications of innovation within the tourism industry. However, policies that influence transformative changes within destinations and the tourism sector have not been conceptualized equally from a theoretical standpoint or analyzed through empirical research. The policy statement on tourism policies for sustainable and inclusive growth by the OECD (2017) acknowledges the significance of innovation and sustainability separately. Nonetheless, there remains a lack of understanding and clarity regarding the connection between innovation policies and sustainable tourism development, particularly in Austria.

The 'COVID-19' pandemic profoundly impacted tourism, causing significant declines in tourist arrivals and industry disruptions. However, this presents an opportunity to revise tourism policies and practices to enhance long-term sustainability (Lama & Rai, 2021). The pandemic heightened awareness of sustainability issues and exposed significant weaknesses in existing tourism policies. Effective innovation policies must incorporate environmental management strategies such as eco-friendly practices, energy management, and waste reduction to protect natural resources. Additionally, economic instruments, such as sustainable tourism taxes and revenue management, can support financial stability while encouraging sustainable practices.

Policymakers need to focus on integrating sustainability into all aspects of tourism development, ensuring that post-pandemic recovery efforts do not compromise long-term sustainability goals (Schönherr et al., 2023). Moreover, the literature identifies a 'science-policy gap' in implementing 'sustainable tourism practices' due to lack of adequate knowledge of effective procedures, approaches, and instruments for evidence-based sustainable tourism policies. These factors make it challenging to translate scientific knowledge into policy (Scuttari et al., 2023). Furthermore, understanding the specific role of innovation policy in driving sustainable tourism development is crucial, as current research primarily focuses on the general impact of innovation and tourism on sustainability (Ahmad et al., 2022).

Despite advancements in innovation policies in the tourism sector, evaluations of their effectiveness are limited. This gap complicates the assessment of the true impact of these policies and hinders informed decision making (Fayos-Solà & Cooper, 2019; OECD, 2024). Baidal et al. (2014) identify significant challenges and limitations in achieving desired outcomes, necessitating systematic research. Consequently, understanding and enhancing the contribution of innovation policies are essential for advancing the tourism industry.

The OECD report "Tourism Trends and Policies 2024" underscores the importance of coordinated, forward-looking policies to address challenges and harness tourism's potential for a more resilient, sustainable, and inclusive future (OECD, 2024). It emphasizes strategic planning focused on workforce improvement, sustainable practices, and international cooperation. However, many countries struggle to effectively implement sustainable tourism policies and practices. Research has identified various barriers, including lack of long-term vision, insufficient government integration, excessive bureaucracy, and unclear policies (Fayos-Solà & Cooper, 2019). This gap between policy recommendations and on-the-ground implementation has led to inefficiencies and missed opportunities for sustainable development in the tourism sector. Therefore, these findings reinforce the necessity for detailed evaluations to effectively refine and advance tourism innovation policies. This forms the central focus of this paper: "How does innovation policy shape sustainable tourism development in Austria?"

2. LITERATURE REVIEW

According to Stenberg (2017), innovation involves looking into the future and thinking beyond the present. Innovation in tourism can manifest in various forms, including processes, products, marketing, and organizational innovation (Boldureanu, 2015). The literature suggests that tourism innovations are predominantly incremental, with radical innovations being scarce. This incremental nature of innovation may be due to the service-oriented characteristics of tourism, where changes often involve enhancements to existing offerings rather than complete overhauls. While radical innovations are rare, incremental innovations remain essential as they enable gradual improvements that shape industry transformation at the ground level (Egresi, 2016). These innovations are a driving force in the tourism industry, offering destinations a means to adapt to global changes and improve their competitive edge (Kuchumov et al., 2020; Şahin, 2024). Innovations in tourism also comprise new business models, marketing strategies, and service enhancements that collectively improve the tourist experience and operational efficiency (Clausen & Madsen, 2014).

Innovation policies can be defined as strategies that guide and foster innovation by setting up frameworks for research and development (R&D), regulatory improvements, and creating environments conducive for innovation (ITIF, 2020; World Bank, 2010). Innovation policies are increasingly recognized as essential drivers of sustainability. As the global tourism industry faces mounting environmental and socio-economic challenges, it becomes clear that achieving long-term sustainability requires the integration of innovative solutions at all levels of policy and industry practice (OECD, 2020). Further research reveals that eco-innovation, eco-tourism policies, and the expansion of sustainable tourism are positively correlated (Firman et al., 2022). This relationship manifests in the development of new tourism products that are environmentally friendly and culturally sensitive, thereby supporting the long-term sustainability of tourism destinations. Long-term sustainability in tourism requires innovation policies that transform industry practices. Policies that encourage co-creation address deficiencies in sustainable tourism management (Eraqi, 2013). Co-creation is a collaborative process, where multiple stakeholders, including governments, academia, investors, SMES, suppliers, and other actors, come together to develop new solutions (UNWTO, n.d.).

Figure 1 illustrates innovative co-creation among multiple stakeholders including suppliers, SMEs, investors, governments, and universities.

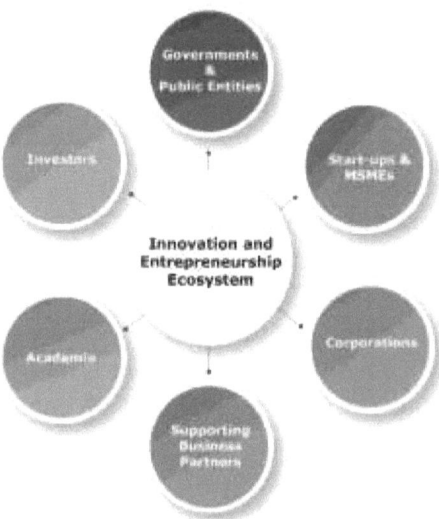

Figure 1: The ecosystem of innovation
Source: UNWTO (n.d).

2.1 Drivers and barriers of innovation in tourism

Several studies have identified key drivers of innovation in the tourism sector. For instance, Divisekera and Nguyen (2018) reveal that collaboration can lead to innovation by enabling the exchange of ideas and resources among firms, institutions, or individuals. Additionally, partnerships with other firms or institutions are significant determinants of service and marketing innovation. Furthermore, human capital plays a critical role in generating product and organizational innovation and in shaping the propensity of people to accept these innovations. Creative human resources and the implementation of new ideas in the tourism sector are strongly associated with skilled and knowledgeable employees. Another significant driver is information and communication technology (ICT). ICT promotes innovation in operational processes, enables organizational changes, and develops new forms of interaction between tourists and providers (Divisekera & Nguyen, 2018; Jiménez-Zarco et al.,2011).

However, there are barriers to innovation in the tourism industry, specifically affecting small and medium-sized tourist enterprises (MSMTEs). Most of these barriers are internal management-inherent issues, such as low financial resources, staff shortages of skilled personnel, and resistance to change. Other factors inhibiting MSMTEs include knowledge management, technology transfer, and network analysis. The lack of resources, access to technology, and weak networking among MSMTEs are the major contributors to these challenges. Moreover, the external environment can pose significant obstacles. For example, strict regulations, lack of cooperation among local stakeholders, and poor infrastructure negatively affect the intensity of innovation efforts (Najda-Janoszka & Kopera, 2014). Furthermore, the innovation process can be challenging because of the multiple interactions required by stakeholders.

The geographic and spatial aspects also hinder innovation. The geographical position of the market, its size, and its location determine the extent and nature of the innovations that can be undertaken. Enterprises located in geographically less favoured positions or small markets often face relatively low levels of access to resources, such as information and knowledge, making innovation difficult for them (Olah & Alpek, 2021). In addition, innovative initiatives face cultural and social hindrances, including reluctance from local communities and traditional business practices that are not conducive to innovation. Cultural resistance to change and low levels of social capital can limit the adoption of novel ideas (Trunfio & Campana, 2019).

2.2 Innovation policies and sustainable tourism development

Innovation policies in tourism have evolved. Initially, these policies focused on removing barriers but have progressively evolved to embrace more complex systems that facilitate collaboration and knowledge transfer (Hjalager, 2012). Booyens and Brouder (2022) highlight that, despite the presence of policies, practical implementation remains a challenge. Translating policy objectives into measurable outcomes is difficult, particularly due to the limited engagement of diverse stakeholders. Traditionally, tourism policies have prioritized growth. However, sustainability is receiving greater attention (Hall & Williams, 2019). Policies can shape innovation, either supporting or hindering sustainability efforts. Tourism-specific innovation policies remain rare. Yet, they are increasingly recognized as essential for fostering sustainable development. At the same time, Austria has broader innovation policies that apply across sectors. Some of these indirectly influence tourism innovation. Recognizing this overlap is crucial for understanding how tourism innovation evolves within the wider policy landscape.

Furthermore, limited awareness and understanding of sustainability among tourists and industry stakeholders may hinder the implementation of sustainable practices (Madar & Neaşu, 2020). Similarly, Xu and Sofield (2013) critique the effectiveness of current tourism policies in promoting sustainability. They argue that, while sustainability is often highlighted as a goal, specific guidance on implementing sustainable practices is lacking. To make innovation policies more effective for sustainable tourism, a clear and practical approach is required. There is a disconnect between policy goals and implementation that often leads to poor outcomes. Engaging stakeholders in discussions can help align policies with on-the-ground needs (Bramwell & Lane, 2011; Dredge & Jenkins, 2007). In this regard, adequate funding is essential. Governments must allocate sufficient money for research, training, and infrastructure to ensure that these policies work (Dredge & Jenkins, 2007).

Therefore, strong monitoring and evaluation systems are required. These systems should use detailed assessment methods to understand the actual influence of policies (Ruhanen, 2013). Therefore, knowledge sharing is vital. Platforms such as industry forums and research networks help to spread best practices and encourage collective learning (Hjalager, 2002). Fostering a culture of innovation and experimentation is equally important. Governments can support this by offering incentives, removing barriers, and celebrating success. This helps to create an environment in which sustainable tourism can thrive (Hall & Williams, 2008).

2.3 Policymaking

The policymaking process consists of several stages: agenda-setting, policy formation, decision-making, implementation, and evaluation or termination (Young & Roederer-Rynning, 2020). It is important to note that these phases do not necessarily follow a strict sequence because policies may be modified and refined at any stage (Hill & Hupe, 2015). Agenda setting involves identifying issues that require government action, such as promoting eco-friendly tourism practices (European Geosciences Union [EGU], 2024). Following this, policy formulation establishes policy goals, implications, costs, and stakeholder reactions, such as deciding between subsidies for sustainable tourism businesses or incentives for tourists to choose eco-friendly options (EGU, 2024). Adoption is the next phase in which policies are approved through necessary legislative processes. Subsequently, implementation is performed, during which appropriate resources and partners are mobilized, and the policy is executed. In the evaluation stage, the policy's effectiveness is assessed, and any unforeseen effects are detected. The final stage involves determining whether a policy should be continued, modified, or terminated. Figure 2 illustrates the policy cycle, displaying these stages and their interactions.

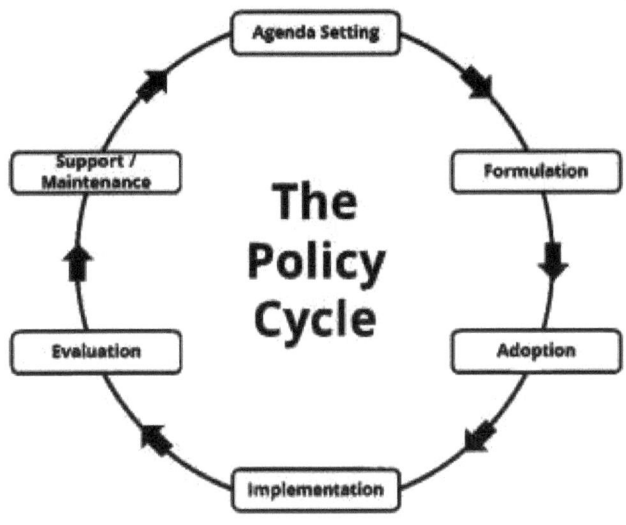

Figure 2: The policy cycle
Source: European Geoscience Union (2024).

Turning broad innovation policy into specific initiatives is a complex process that involves breaking down overarching goals into practical actions, such as economic growth, clean energy, and sustainable cities (Kergroach, 2018; United Nations, 2015). This structured approach to innovation policy aligns with the United Nations Sustainable Development Goals for promoting sustainable tourism development (United Nations, 2015). It is also important that those policies target the enablers and barriers to innovation as discussed (see section drivers and barriers of innovation).

Figure 3 illustrates the progression from broad policy goals to specific elements of an innovation policy initiative. It shows the essential linkages that guide this transition, mapping out how broad objectives are systematically converted into specific actionable measures.

Figure 3: From overarching policy goals to the characteristics of an innovation policy initiative
Source: Kergroach, S. (2018)

The framework also details the characteristics of innovation policy measures, including policy rationale, instruments, target populations, implementation stages, timeframes, governance mechanisms, and budget allocations. This strategic approach is useful for determining whether innovation policies support sustainable tourism. This foundational understanding is essential for examining Austria's innovation strategies, including the Master Plan for Tourism, RTI Strategy 2030, the RTI Pact 2024-2026, and the RTI Report 2023. These policy documents are useful for understanding how Austria's policies align with the broader goal of sustainable tourism development.

The 'Plan T – Master Plan for Tourism' provides guidelines to enhance cooperation among stakeholders and integrate sustainability into the tourism sector (BMAW, 2019). This policy promotes digitalization and supports SMEs in adopting sustainable practices. The 'RTI Strategy 2030' sets Austria's long-term vision for innovation, focusing on sustainable economic growth and addressing climate goals. This strategy encourages collaboration between public institutions, research bodies, and private enterprises. The 'RTI Pact 2024-2026' operationalizes these strategies through specific funding allocations and research priorities, particularly emphasizing climate neutrality and energy efficiency (RTI Strategy 2030, 2020; RTI Pact 2024-2026, 2022). Collectively, these policies provide a coherent framework that integrates innovation, sustainability, and stakeholder engagement to support Austria's tourism sector.

2.4 Gaps in the literature

Despite substantial literature on innovation and sustainability in tourism, significant research gaps persist. One of the most notable gaps is the lack of studies that examine the longitudinal impacts of innovation policies on the tourism sector's responsibility toward sustainability. Much of the existing research focuses on the short-term impacts of policy implementation, with few studies exploring the long-term effectiveness of innovation policies in shaping industry behaviour (Bramwell & Lane, 2011). Additionally, there is a limited focus on how these policies affect SMEs, despite their critical role in the tourism sector. Understanding how innovation policies can better support SMEs in adopting sustainable practices is an area that requires further exploration. Another gap is the lack of in-depth analysis of stakeholder perspectives on the effectiveness of innovation policies. While some research has explored policy outcomes from a theoretical perspective, there is a dearth of qualitative studies that capture the views of those directly involved in policy implementation and the adoption of sustainable practices, particularly in the Austrian context (Waligo et al., 2013).

The existing literature highlights the crucial role of innovation policies in achieving sustainable tourism outcomes, emphasizing collaborative governance and stakeholder engagement. Researchers identify incremental innovation as predominant in tourism, emphasizing the importance of gradual improvements rather than radical changes (Egresi, 2016; Boldureanu, 2015). Additionally, the literature discusses barriers such as limited financial resources and resistance to change within SMEs, alongside external challenges such as regulatory constraints (Najda-Janoszka & Kopera, 2014). Considering these insights, this study employs an integrated theoretical framework comprising the Triple Helix Model, Triple Bottom Line Model, and Stakeholder Theory. The theoretical framework enables a systematic exploration of how innovation policies facilitate stakeholder cooperation, address sustainability across economic, social, and environmental dimensions, and ultimately shape the future trajectory of sustainable tourism development in Austria.

3. THEORETICAL FRAMEWORK

The theoretical framework for this study integrates the Triple Helix Model, Triple Bottom Line (TBL) Model, and Stakeholder Theory to understand the relationship between innovation policies and sustainable tourism development effectively. These frameworks offer insights into the roles and interactions of various stakeholders; the balance of economic, social, and environmental factors; and the mechanisms by which innovation can be fostered and sustained. This study draws on the three primary theories for an exhaustive analysis.

First, the Triple Helix Model emphasizes collaboration between academia, industry, and the government in fostering innovation. This model highlights the importance of these three sectors working together to drive economic growth, thereby ensuring that innovation is not only encouraged but also effectively implemented and maintained. In addition, the Triple Bottom-line Framework assesses sustainability by considering economic, social, and environmental impacts. It provides a holistic view that ensures that all dimensions are balanced and integrated into tourism practices, thus promoting sustainable development that does not compromise any one aspect for the sake of another.

Furthermore, Stakeholder Theory underscores the importance of involving all relevant parties such as local communities, businesses, and governments in the development and implementation of sustainable tourism practices. Ensuring that all stakeholders are engaged, and their interests are considered increases the likelihood that sustainable tourism practices can be successfully adopted and maintained. Integrating these theoretical perspectives allows for an in-depth comprehension of how innovation policies can support sustainable tourism development. This approach helps to identify best practices, challenges, and opportunities, thereby contributing to both academic knowledge and practical solutions in the field of sustainable tourism.

3.1 Triple Helix Model

The Triple Helix Model proposes how collaboration between academia, business, and the government promotes innovation and economic growth (Etzkowitz & Leydesdorff, 2000). Specifically, the exchange of knowledge, technology, and best practices among these sectors is crucial for fostering sustainable tourism development (Etzkowitz & Zhou, 2017). Numerous policies and programs designed to promote innovation draw influence from the triple helix model (Rodrigues & Melo, 2012).

In this model, the government's role is to create policies and establish regulations that support sustainable tourism. In addition, they provide funding and infrastructure to promote sustainability and competitiveness. Academic institutions contribute expertise, research findings, and educational programs that inform innovation policies and practices in the tourism sector (Etzkowitz & Zhou, 2017). Businesses such as Alpine Pearls implement innovations and adopt new technologies. Furthermore, they offer practical insights and, through partnerships with academia and the government, apply the research findings to develop sustainable tourism products. They also align their business strategies with innovation policies (Ranga & Etzkowitz, 2013).

The Triple Helix model fosters an innovation ecosystem where the boundaries between academia, industry, and government are increasingly blurred, leading to the creation of hybrid organizations and networks (Etzkowitz & Leydesdorff, 2000). This blurring of boundaries facilitates a more dynamic and responsive approach to innovation, which is crucial in the rapidly evolving tourism sector. Additionally, the model can be applied to regional innovation systems, emphasizing the role of regional policies and local contexts in shaping the effectiveness of triple-helix interactions (Rodrigues & Melo, 2012). By tailoring the triple-helix model to regional specifics, stakeholders can address unique challenges and leverage local strengths more effectively.

Over time, the Triple Helix model has evolved to include the quadruple and quintuple helices. The Quadruple Helix adds the media and public as a fourth helix, embedding civil society and cultural aspects into the innovation process. While the Triple Helix focuses on knowledge production and innovation in the economy, the Quadruple Helix broadens this by emphasizing the 'knowledge society and knowledge democracy.' This model suggests that the sustainable development of a knowledge economy must co-evolve with knowledge society. The Quintuple Helix model goes further by incorporating the natural environment and stressing the importance of socio-ecological transitions in driving innovation. Quintuple Helix views natural environments as key drivers of knowledge production and innovation, defining new opportunities in the knowledge economy. This model supports the creation of synergies between the economy, society, and democracy to foster sustainable development. Socioecological transition presents a major challenge for future development (European Commission, 2009, as cited in Carayannis & Campbell, 2010). The Quintuple Helix model addresses this challenge by creating win-win scenarios for ecology, knowledge, and innovation. These extensions are particularly relevant to sustainable tourism as they emphasize the importance of public engagement and environmental considerations in innovation processes (Carayannis & Campbell, 2010).

Figure 4 illustrates the Quadruple and Quintuple Helix models, highlighting the inclusion of media, public, and natural environments as key components in driving innovation and fostering sustainable development.

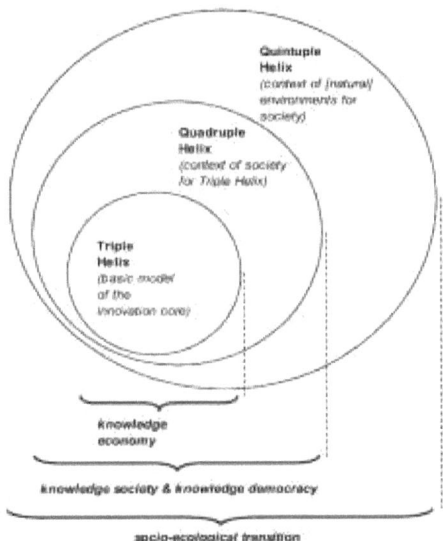

Figure 4: The Quintuple Helix Model
Source: Carayannis et al. (2010).

This study applies the Triple Helix model to examine the interactions between academia, businesses, and government on the design, implementation, and outcomes of innovation policies in shaping sustainable tourism development in Austria. Specifically, the model helps assess the effectiveness of current policies, identify gaps in collaboration, and propose strategies to strengthen partnerships that promote sustainable tourism practices. This paper draws from the Triple Helix model and its extensions to formulate policy recommendations that capitalize on the strengths of these collaborations.

Figure 5 illustrates the Triple Helix model, showing the dynamic interactions between government, academia, and industry in promoting innovation and sustainable tourism development.

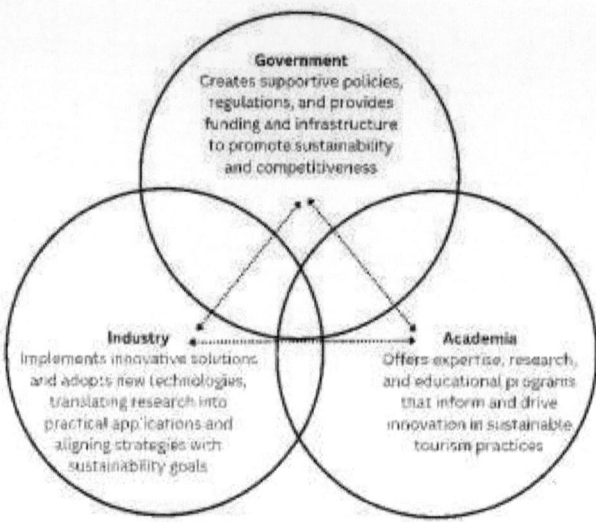

Figure 5: The Triple Helix Model
Source: Author's own illustration adapted from Yang, H. (2022).

3.2 The Triple Bottom Line (TBL) model

The Triple Bottom Line (TBL) model evaluates performance across three dimensions: 'economic, social, and environmental,' thus expanding on the traditional focus solely on financial performance (Elkington, 1998). Economic sustainability ensures that tourism initiatives are financially viable, generating profits while contributing to the local economy. Policies encourage businesses to adopt eco-friendly practices and invest in sustainable tourism projects by providing financial incentives (Dwyer, 2005). Social sustainability emphasizes the well-being of local communities and the fair distribution of tourism benefits. It advocates for improved quality of life for residents and ensures that tourism development respects local cultures and traditions. Innovation policies can enhance social sustainability by involving community stakeholders in decision-making and supporting initiatives that benefit local populations (Gibson, 2016). Environmental sustainability addresses the impact of tourism on natural resources and ecosystems. It aims to minimize negative environmental impacts and promote the conservation of natural areas.

According to Buckley (2012), innovation policies can support environmental sustainability by advocating for funding research focused on green technologies. Moreover, they can enforce regulations aimed at limiting environmental damage.

The Triple Bottom Line model provides an evaluation framework for assessing Austria's innovation policies in sustainable tourism. Economic sustainability was evaluated through grants and tax incentives for businesses that focused on green practices. Environmental sustainability was examined by analyzing funding for eco-friendly infrastructure and initiatives to protect natural sites. Social sustainability focused on the involvement of local communities in planning and ensuring that tourism revenue supports the local services and infrastructure. This approach allows for a thorough assessment of how effectively Austria's innovation policies have achieved their economic, environmental, and social objectives in promoting a sustainable tourism industry. The model used in this evaluation is illustrated in Figure 6.

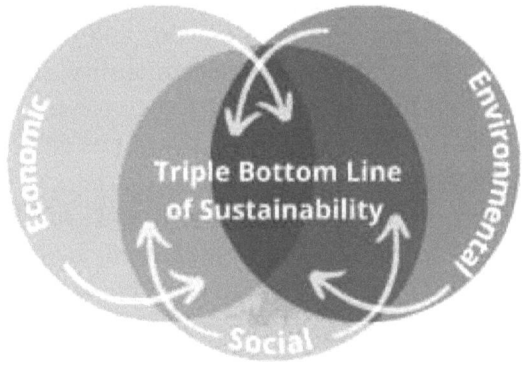

Figure 6: The Triple Bottom Line Model
Source: ImpactNV (2024).

3.3 The Stakeholder Theory

The stakeholder theory, first introduced by Freeman (1984), offers a framework for understanding the diverse perceptions and influences of stakeholders in the tourism sector. This theory underscores the need to engage a broad spectrum of stakeholders, including local communities, tourists, business owners, environmental organizations, and governmental bodies (Freeman, 1984). Engaging stakeholders is essential for developing inclusive tourism practices that are culturally respectful and environmentally responsible.

Active participation by stakeholders ensures that tourism initiatives align with the needs and expectations of all parties involved. Moreover, effective engagement necessitates resolving conflicts and ensuring equitable distribution of tourism benefits among stakeholders. Nonetheless, managing stakeholders in the tourism industry faces conflicts of interest, compounded by a lack of awareness and resistance to change. Addressing these issues requires inclusive policies and practices that foster stakeholder engagement and collaboration (Benckendorff & Lund-Durlacher, 2013; Freeman, 1984). The success of the Alpine Pearls Network exemplifies the significance of stakeholder management and collaborative processes in achieving sustainable tourism goals. By accommodating the needs and interests of all stakeholders, tourism initiatives can attain greater sustainability, inclusivity, and resilience (Benckendorff & Lund-Durlacher, 2013).

Effective stakeholder identification involves systematically mapping out all entities that influence or are influenced by tourism activities, comprehending their interests, and analyzing their power and influence (Freeman, 1984). Several key stakeholders have been identified in the context of innovation policy and sustainable tourism development. Government entities at both local and national levels provide the necessary regulatory framework and financial incentives to promote sustainable tourism practices. The Austrian government's "Plan T" for tourism underscores the pivotal role of government involvement (BMAW, 2019). Destination Management Organizations (DMOs) play a critical role in coordinating tourism-related activities and implementing policies (Waligo et al., 2013). Tourism businesses such as Alpine Pearls are crucial for the practical implementation of sustainable practices. Their involvement ensures that sustainability measures are economically viable and effectively integrated into daily operations (Hardy & Pearson, 2018). Engaging host communities in governance processes such as

Living Labs can foster more inclusive and effective tourism policies (Thees et al., 2020). The stakeholder groups identified as the most impactful, and therefore prioritized for interviews, include government policymakers, tourism businesses such as Alpine Pearls, DMOs, and local communities. Figure 7 illustrates a stakeholder map depicting the relationships between tourism and innovation policies.

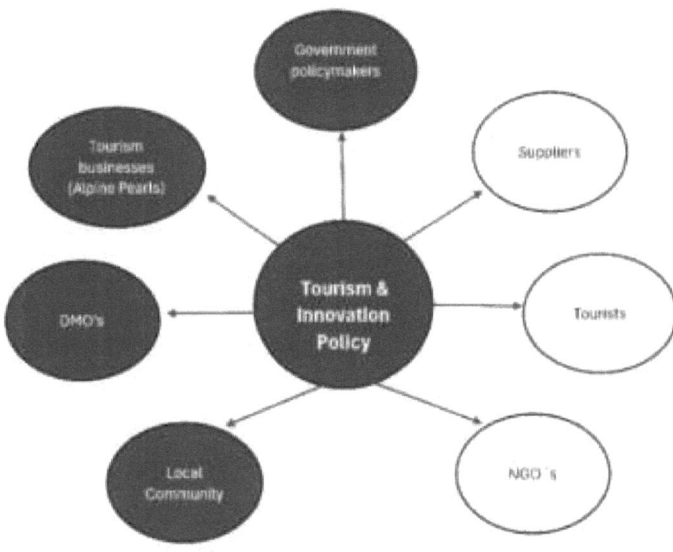

Figure 7: Stakeholder mapping
Source: Author

Although the stakeholder map above illustrates the presence of many stakeholder groups, only representatives from selected groups were interviewed due to availability constraints and the limited scope of the paper.

4. METHODOLOGY

This paper explores how innovation policy shapes sustainable tourism development in Austria using qualitative research methodology and an interpretivist approach. The study investigates the perspectives and experiences of key stakeholders, including government policymakers, tourism businesses, Destination Management Organizations (DMOs), and local communities. The central research question is: "How does innovation policy shape sustainable tourism development in Austria?" An exploratory research framework was employed to investigate these ideas thoroughly, given the limited existing research on the connection between innovation policies and sustainable tourism (Stebbins, 2001). This method is also suitable for understanding how these policies are perceived, interpreted, and acted upon by stakeholders (Bryman, 2012).

Primary data were collected through semi-structured interviews with key stakeholders actively involved in innovation policies and sustainable tourism practices (Ayres, 2008). These stakeholders included government officials responsible for developing and implementing tourism-related policies, representatives from tourism businesses, DMOs, and local community members. Nine in-depth interviews provided rich and detailed insights into the experiences, perspectives, and challenges faced by these stakeholders (Creswell & Creswell, 2017). Each interview lasted approximately 30 to 60 minutes and was conducted online with participants located in Austria. All interviews were conducted in English. Ethical considerations included obtaining informed consent, ensuring confidentiality, voluntary participation, clearly communicating the participants' right to withdraw, and ensuring anonymity throughout the reporting process.

Secondary data, including policy documents and reports, provided valuable contextual information and a broader understanding of the policy landscape. These data were gathered through an analysis of relevant materials such as Austria's Research Technology and Innovation Report 2023, RTI Strategy 2030, RTI Pact 2024-2026, and The Master Plan T for Tourism. These documents offered insights into Austria's goals and strategies for promoting sustainability and innovation within the tourism sector. Purposive sampling ensured the selection of information-rich participants and documents directly relevant to the research objectives (Bryman, 2012). Interview participants were chosen based on their significant expertise and experience in innovation policies and sustainable tourism, ensuring they could provide in-depth insights based on their practical knowledge. Key policy documents were selected based on their relevance to Austria's innovation policies and sustainable tourism strategies.

An inductive content analysis approach was used to analyze qualitative data gathered from interviews and policy documents (Elo et al., 2014). This method allowed for the identification of emergent themes, patterns, and meanings without imposing preexisting categories or theoretical frameworks. The analysis involved several systematic steps: transcription of interview recordings, familiarization with the data, inductive coding, theme development, reliability and validity checks, and synthesis of themes to inform policy recommendations. Combining insights from expert interviews and policy document analysis, the study sheds light on the interplay between innovation and sustainability in Austrian tourism. Government policymakers are shifting from technology-centric to holistic innovation policies, prioritizing societal goals and sustainability. However, challenges in implementing transformative strategies include navigating bureaucratic systems and fostering continuous collaboration.

5. FINDINGS

This research identifies key outcomes related to environmental, economic, and social dimensions of sustainable tourism in Austria. A central finding is the notable shift in Austria's innovation policies from a narrow technology focus towards broader sustainability goals. Policy documents such as the RTI Strategy 2030 and Plan T emphasize sustainability, renewable energy, and responsible tourism infrastructure. Stakeholders acknowledged that these policies effectively encourage tourism businesses and Destination Management Organizations (DMOs) to adopt sustainable initiatives. Nevertheless, implementation faces notable challenges. Participants highlighted issues such as greenwashing, where sustainability claims are exaggerated without meaningful action. Bureaucratic inefficiencies also impede achieving environmental objectives.

From an economic perspective, stakeholders noted positive impacts from innovation policies, particularly through increased research and development (R&D) investments. These investments have encouraged innovative practices among tourism enterprises. Despite this progress, participants reported concerns about economic leakage. They highlighted how reliance on international online booking platforms redirects revenue away from local businesses. Respondents suggested the importance of promoting local platforms and authentic products. This would help retain more economic benefits within local communities and strengthen local economies.

Social outcomes were positively associated with community involvement and stakeholder collaboration. Interviewees emphasized the benefits arising from community participation in tourism planning. They also cited successful educational programs and cultural preservation initiatives as evidence of strengthened social sustainability. Despite these achievements, stakeholders pointed out challenges such as inadequate funding and barriers to effective collaboration. These factors limit the full potential of community engagement initiatives. Stakeholders stressed the importance of targeted funding and more effective intersectoral collaboration. Addressing these factors, they argued, could substantially enhance the implementation of sustainable tourism objectives in Austria.

6. CONCLUSION

This study highlights the significant role innovation policies play in shaping sustainable tourism in Austria. Environmental, economic, and social dimensions were each positively influenced by strategic policies, although implementation barriers remain. Policymakers and stakeholders alike emphasized the need for improved collaboration, targeted funding, and strategies to counteract economic leakage and greenwashing. Addressing these challenges can help Austria fully realize the potential of its innovation policies, driving sustainable development effectively within the tourism sector.

6.1 Policy Implications

To support sustainable tourism in Austria, this study suggests policy measures across three main stakeholder groups: policymakers, businesses, and communities.

6.1.1 Policymakers

i. Increase Funding: Establish a dedicated funding program for tourism innovation similar to R&D tax credits, with expanded Austrian Research Promotion Agency (FFG) initiatives to streamline funding access through Austria's Wirtschaftsservice (aws).

ii. Foster Cross-sector Collaboration: Implement regular tourism innovation forums led by the Federal Ministry for Digital and Economic Affairs to strengthen cooperation across sectors such as transport and agriculture.

iii. Address Economic Leakage: Develop a national strategy promoting direct bookings through local platforms with tax incentives, aiming to reduce high commission rates from international booking sites such as Booking.com.

iv. Integrate Data-Driven Decision-Making: Establish a national tourism data platform to collect tourism-specific data and introduce a standardized sustainability reporting system aligned with Global Sustainable Tourism Council (GSTC) criteria.

6.1.2 Businesses and DMOs

i. Sustainable Mobility and Sector Partnerships: Promote eco-friendly transportation options such as the Werfenweng card and encourage collaboration with agriculture and transport to bolster sustainable tourism.

ii. Combat Greenwashing: Adopt reliable certification schemes, such as the Austrian environmental label, to educate consumers on genuine sustainable practices and distinguish authentic sustainable offerings.

iii. Digital Transformation and Seasonal Management: Leverage technology to enhance booking systems and manage tourist flows by introducing programs to attract tourists in low seasons.

6.1.3 Community Engagement

i. Support Local Involvement: Involve communities in tourism planning and decision-making to ensure benefits are fairly distributed, along with regular forums for addressing concerns.

ii.   Promote Sustainability Education: Develop initiatives that educate communities on sustainable tourism practices and encourage adoption of sustainable practices in daily life.

REFERENCES

Ahmad, N., Youjin, L., & Hdia, M. (2022). The role of innovation and tourism in sustainability: Why is environmentally friendly tourism necessary for entrepreneurship? Journal of Cleaner Production, 379, 134799. https://doi.org/10.1016/j.jclepro.2022.134799

Ayres, L. (2008). Semi-structured interview. In L. M. Given (Ed.) SAGE Encyclopedia of Qualitative Research Methods (1), 811-812. Sage.

Benckendorff, P., & Lund-Durlacher, D. (2013). International cases in sustainable travel & tourism. Retrieved from https://www.researchgate.net/publication/323446628_International_Cases_I n_Sustainable_Travel_Tourism

Boldureanu, G. (2015). Innovative activities of travel companies. Yearbook of the "gh. zane, " Institute of Economic Research, 24(1), 67–74. Retrieved from https://www.semanticscholar.org/paper/Innovative-Activities-Of-Travel-Companies-Boldureanu/0ddaf744bab60d9e224c8f5897a12f1cc1dfc7ed

Boldureanu, G. (2015). Innovative activities of travel companies. Yearbook of the "gh. zane," Institute of Economic Research, 24(1), 67–74. Retrieved from https://www.semanticscholar.org/paper/Innovative-Activities-Of-Travel-Companies-Boldureanu/0ddaf744bab60d9e224c8f5897a12f1cc1dfc7ed

Booyens, I., & Brouder, P. (2022). Social innovation for sustainable tourism development. Edward Elgar Publishing EBooks, 193–209. https://doi.org/10.4337/9781800372740.00020

Booyens, I., & Brouder, P. (2022). Social innovation for sustainable tourism development. Edward Elgar Publishing EBooks, 193–209. https://doi.org/10.4337/9781800372740.00020

Bramwell, B., & Lane, B. (2000). 1 Collaboration and partnerships in tourism planning. Multilingual Matters eBooks (pp. 1–19). https://doi.org/10.21832/9780585354224-003

Bramwell, B., & Lane, B. (2011). Critical research on the governance of tourism and sustainability. Journal of Sustainable Tourism, 19(4-5), 411–421. https://doi.org/10.1080/09669582.2011.580586

Bramwell, B., & Lane, B. (2011). Critical research on the governance of tourism and sustainability. Journal of Sustainable Tourism, 19(4-5), 411–421. https://doi.org/10.1080/09669582.2011.580586

Bryman, A. (2012). Social Research Methods (4th Ed.). Oxford: Oxford University Press.

Buckley, R. (2012). Sustainable tourism: Research and reality. Annals of Tourism Research, 39(2), 528-546. https://doi.org/10.1016/j.annals.2012.02.003

Carayannis, E. G., & Campbell, D. F. (2010). Triple helix, quadruple helix and quintuple helix And how do knowledge, innovation and the environment relate to each other? International Journal of Social Ecology and Sustainable Development, 1(1), 41–69. https://doi.org/10.4018/jsesd.2010010105

Chaminade, C., Lundvall, B., Vang, J., & Joseph, K. J. (2009). Designing Innovation Policies for Development: towards a systemic experimentation-based approach. Edward Elgar Publishing eBooks. https://doi.org/10.4337/9781849803427.00022

Creswell, J. W., & Creswell, J. D. (2017). Research design: Qualitative, quantitative, and mixed methods approaches. (4th ed.)Sage publications.

Divisekera, S., & Nguyen, V. K. (2018). Drivers of innovation in tourism: An econometric study. Tourism Economics, 24(8), 998–1014. https://doi.org/10.1177/1354816618794708

Dodds, R., & Butler, R. (2009). Barriers to Implementing Sustainable Tourism Policy in Mass Tourism Destinations - Munich Personal RePEc Archive. Uni-Muenchen.de, 5(1). https://mpra.ub.uni-muenchen.de/25162/1/MPRA_paper_25162.pdfDwyer, L. (2005). Relevance of triple bottom line reporting to achievement of sustainable tourism: A scoping study. Tourism Review International, 9(1), 79–938. https://doi.org/10.3727/154427205774791726

Dredge, D., & Jenkins, J. (2007). Tourism planning and policy. John Wiley & Sons.

EGU - European Geosciences Union. (2024). EGU The policy cycle. Retrieved from https://www.egu.eu/policy/cycle/#:~:text=The%20policy%20cycle%20is%20an,cycle%20as%20an%20optimal%20model.

Elkington, J. (1998). Partnerships from cannibals with forks: The triple bottom line of 21st-century business. Environmental Quality Management, 8(1), 37–51. https://doi.org/10.1002/tqem.3310080106

Elo, S., Kääriäinen, M., Kanste, O., Pölkki, T., Utriainen, K., & Kyngäs, H. (2014). Qualitative Content Analysis: A Focus on Trustworthiness. SAGE Open, 4(1), 2158244014522633. https://doi.org/10.1177/2158244014522633

Eraqi, M. I. (2013). Innovation co-creation for effective sustainable tourism development management in Egypt. International Journal of Sustainable Strategic Management, 4(2), 105. https://doi.org/10.1504/ijssm.2013.058590

Eraqi, M. I. (2013). Innovation co-creation for effective sustainable tourism development management in Egypt. International Journal of Sustainable Strategic Management, 4(2), 105. https://doi.org/10.1504/ijssm.2013.058590

Etzkowitz, H., & Leydesdorff, L. (2000). The dynamics of innovation: From National Systems and "Mode 2" to a Triple Helix of university–industry–government relations. Research Policy, 29(2), 109-123. https://doi.org/10.1016/S0048-7333(99)00055-4

Etzkowitz, H., & Zhou, C. (2017). The Triple Helix: University–Industry–Government Innovation and Entrepreneurship. Routledge. https://doi.org/10.4324/9781315620183

European Commission. (n.d.). A European Green Deal. Retrieved from https://commission.europa.eu/strategy-and-policy/priorities-2019-2024/european-green-deal_en

Fayos-Solà, E., & Cooper, C. (2019). The future of tourism. Springer eBooks. https://doi.org/10.1007/978-3-319-89941-1

Federal Government of the Republic of Austria. (2020). RTI Strategy 2030. Retrieved from https://era.gv.at/public/documents/4489/RTI_Strategy_2030-1-1.pdf

Federal Government of the Republic of Austria. (2022). RTI Pact 2024 –2026. Retrieved from https://era.gv.at/public/documents/4835/RTI_Pact_2024-2026.pdf

Federal Ministry for Sustainability and Tourism. (2019). Plan T: Master Plan for Tourism. Retrieved from https://www.bmaw.gv.at

Firman, A., Moslehpour, M., Qiu, R., Lin, P.-K., Ismail, T., & Rahman, F. F. (2022). The impact of eco-innovation, ecotourism policy and social media on sustainable tourism development: evidence from the tourism sector of Indonesia. Economic Research-Ekonomska Istraživanja, 36(2), 1–21. https://doi.org/10.1080/1331677x.2022.2143847

Freeman, R. E. (1984). Strategic Management: A Stakeholder Approach. Boston: Pitman.

Gibson, R. (Ed.). (2016). Sustainability Assessment: Applications and opportunities (1st ed.). Routledge. https://doi.org/10.4324/9781315754048

Gonca Güzel Şahin. (2024). The Synergy Between Tourism, Aviation, and Digital Transformation. Advances in Mechatronics and Mechanical Engineering

(AMME) Book Series, 112–132. https://doi.org/10.4018/979-8-3693-0732-8.ch007

Gretzel, U., Sigala, M., Xiang, Z., & Koo, C. (2015). Smart tourism: Foundations and developments. Electronic Markets, 25(3), 179-188. https://doi.org/10.1007/s12525-015-0196-8

Hall, C. M., & Williams, A. M. (2008). Tourism and innovation. Routledge.

Hall, C. M., & Williams, A. M. (2019). Tourism and Innovation. Routledge eBooks. https://doi.org/10.4324/9781315162836

Hardy, A., & Pearson, L. J. (2018). Examining stakeholder group specificity: An innovative sustainable tourism approach. Journal of Destination Marketing & Management, 8, 247–258. https://doi.org/10.1016/j.jdmm.2017.05.001

Hill, M., & Hupe, P. (2015). Policy failure and the policy-implementation gap: can policy support programs help? Policy Design and Practice, 1(2), 1-14. https://doi.org/10.1080/25741292.2018.1540378

Hjalager, A. (2012). Innovation policies for tourism. International Journal of Tourism Policy, 4(4), 336. https://doi.org/10.1504/ijtp.2012.052565

Hjalager, A. (2012). Innovation policies for tourism. International Journal of Tourism Policy, 4(4), 336. https://doi.org/10.1504/ijtp.2012.052565

Hjalager, A. M. (2002). Repairing innovation defectiveness in tourism. Tourism Management, 23(5), 465–474. https://doi.org/10.1016/s0261-5177(02)00013-4

Ilić, B., & Kostić, M. (2021). The impact of the COVID-19 pandemic on tourism: A new conceptual framework. Tourism Management Perspectives, 39, 100854.

ImpactNV - Nevada Sustainability Alliance. (2024). ImpactNV Our impact. Retrieved from https://impact-nv.org/our-impact/

ITIF - Information Technology and Innovation Foundation. (2020). ITIF National Innovation Policies: What Countries Do Best and How They Can Improve. Retrieved from https://itif.org/publications/2020/03/23/national-innovation-policies-what-countries-do-best-and-how-they-can-improve

Jiménez-Zarco, A. I., Martínez-Ruiz, M. P., & Izquierdo-Yusta, A. (2011). Key service innovation drivers in the tourism sector: empirical evidence and managerial implications. Service Business, 5(4), 339–360. https://doi.org/10.1007/s11628-011-0118-6

Kergroach, S. (2018). National innovation policies for technology upgrading through GVCs: A Crosscountry comparison. Technological Forecasting and Social Change. https://doi.org/10.1016/j.techfore.2018.04.033

Kuchumov, A., Testina, Y., Chaikovskaya, A., & Maslova, E. (2020). Influence of Digital Innovations on Environmentalization of Tourist Destinations. Proceedings of the 2nd International Scientific Conference on Innovations in Digital Economy: SPBPU IDE-2020. https://doi.org/10.1145/3444465.3444466

Lama, R., & Rai, A. (2021). Challenges in Developing Sustainable Tourism Post COVID-19 Pandemic. Tourism Destination Management in a Post-Pandemic Context, 233–244. https://doi.org/10.1108/978-1-80071-511-020211016

Liburd, J. J. (2018). Understanding collaboration and sustainable tourism development. Collaboration for sustainable tourism development (pp. 8-34). Goodfellow Publishers.

Liu, F. L. (2014). Green Management of Tourist Attractions Region under the Background of Circular Economy. Advanced Materials Research, 989-994, 5592–5595. https://doi.org/10.4028/www.scientific.net/amr.989-994.5592

Madar, A., & Neaşu, N.A. (2020). Tourists' vision about the implementation of sustainable development practices in the hospitality industry in Romania. Proceedings of the International Conference on Business Excellence, 14, 769 - 779.

Najda-Janoszka, M., & Kopera, S. (2014). Exploring Barriers to Innovation in Tourism Industry – The Case of Southern Region of Poland. Procedia - Social and Behavioral Sciences, 110, 190–201. https://doi.org/10.1016/j.sbspro.2013.12.862

Najda-Janoszka, M., & Kopera, S. (2014). Exploring Barriers to Innovation in Tourism Industry – The Case of Southern Region of Poland. Procedia - Social and Behavioral Sciences, 110, 190–201. https://doi.org/10.1016/j.sbspro.2013.12.862

OECD - Organisation for Economic Co-operation and Development. (2017). OECD Tourism policies for sustainable and inclusive growth. Policy Statement. Retrieved from https://www.oecd.org/cfe/tourism/OECD-Policy-Statement-Tourism-Policies-for-Sustainable-and-Inclusive-Growth.pdf

OECD - Organisation for Economic Co-operation and Development. (2020). OECD Tourism Trends and Policies. OECD Publishing, Paris. https://doi.org/10.1787/6b47b985-en

OECD - Organisation for Economic Co-operation and Development. (2024). OECD Tourism Trends and Policies. Retrieved from https://www.oecd.org/en/publications/oecd-tourism-trends-and-policies-2024_80885d8b-en.html

Olah, D., & Alpek, B. L. (2021). The theoretical model of spatial production for innovation. Journal of Innovation and Entrepreneurship, 10(1), 1-24. https://doi.org/10.1186/s13731-021-00182-4

Ranga, M., & Etzkowitz, H. (2013). Triple Helix Systems: An Analytical Framework for Innovation Policy and Practice in the Knowledge Society. Industry and Higher Education, 27(4), 237-262. https://doi.org/10.5367/ihe.2013.0165

Rodrigues, C., & Melo, A. I. (2012). The Triple Helix Model as Inspiration for Local Development Policies: An Experience-Based Perspective. International Journal of Urban and Regional Research, 37(5), 1675–1687. https://doi.org/10.1111/j.1468-2427.2012.01117.x

Ruhanen, L. (2013). Local government: facilitator or inhibitor of sustainable tourism development? Journal of Sustainable Tourism, 21(1), 80–98. https://doi.org/10.1080/09669582.2012.680463

Schoenefeld, J. J., Hildén, M., & Schulze, K. (2022). Policy innovation for sustainable development. Edward Elgar Publishing EBooks, 161–174. https://doi.org/10.4337/9781789904321.00019

Schönherr, S., Peters, M., & Kuščer, K. (2023). Sustainable tourism policies: From crisis-related awareness to agendas towards measures. Journal of Destination Marketing & Management, 27, 100762. https://doi.org/10.1016/j.jdmm.2023.100762

Scott, N., Baggio, R., & Cooper, C. (2008). Network Analysis and Tourism. Multilingual Matters eBooks. https://doi.org/10.21832/9781845410896

Scuttari, A., Windegger, F., Wallnöfer, V., & Harald Pechlaner. (2023). Bridging the science-policy gap in sustainable tourism: evidence from a multiple case study analysis of UNWTO INSTO sustainable tourism observatories. Journal of Sustainable Tourism, 1–25. https://doi.org/10.1080/09669582.2023.2279023

Statista. (2024). Travel and Tourism. Retrieved from https://www.statista.com/outlook/mmo/travel-tourism/worldwide

Statista. (2024). Travel and tourism: contribution to global GDP 2023. Retrieved from https://www.statista.com/statistics/233223/travel-and-tourism-total-economic-contribution-worldwide/

Stenberg, A. (2017). What does Innovation mean - a term without a clear definition. Retrieved from https://www.diva-portal.org/smash/get/diva2:1064843/FULLTEXT01.pdf

Thees, H., Pechlaner, H., Olbrich, N., & Schuhbert, A. (2020). The Living Lab as a Tool to Promote Residents' Participation in Destination Governance. Sustainability, 12(3), 1120. https://doi.org/10.3390/su12031120

Trunfio, M., & Campana, S. (2019). Drivers and emerging innovations in knowledge-based destinations: Towards a research agenda. Journal of Destination Marketing & Management, 14, 100370. https://doi.org/10.1016/j.jdmm.2019.100370

UN - United Nations. (2015). UN Sustainable Development Goals. Retrieved from https://sdgs.un.org/goals.

UNEP- United Nations Environment Programme, & World Tourism Organization. (2005). Making tourism more sustainable: a guide for policy makers. Division Of Technology, Industry And Economics; Madrid.

UNWTO. (2020). Sustainable tourism. World Tourism Organization. Retrieved from https://www.unwto.org/sustainable-tourism

Waligo, V. M., Clarke, J., & Hawkins, R. (2013). Implementing sustainable tourism: A multi-stakeholder involvement management framework. Tourism Management, 36(36), 342–353. https://doi.org/10.1016/j.tourman.2012.10.008

Waligo, V. M., Clarke, J., & Hawkins, R. (2013). Implementing sustainable tourism: A multi-stakeholder involvement management framework. Tourism Management, 36(36), 342–353. https://doi.org/10.1016/j.tourman.2012.10.008

Walters, G., & Clulow, V. (2013). Issues in Sustainable Tourism. The International Journal of Sustainability Policy and Practice, 8(3), 11–19. https://doi.org/10.18848/2325-1166/cgp/v08i03/55381

World Bank. (2010). Innovation Policy: A Guide for Developing Countries. Retrieved from https://hdl.handle.net/10986/2460

Xu, H., & Sofield, T. (2013). Sustainability in Chinese development tourism policies. Current Issues in Tourism, 19(13), 1337–1355. https://doi.org/10.1080/13683500.2013.849665

Yang, H. (2022). A Triple Helix Model of Doctoral Education: A Case Study of an Industrial Doctorate. Sustainability, 14(17), 10942. https://doi.org/10.3390/su141710942

Young, A. R., & Roederer-Rynning, C. (2020). 3. The EU Policy Process in Comparative Perspective. Policymaking in the European Union, 43–66. https://doi.org/10.1093/hepl/9780198807605.003.0003

Segmentation of Ski Resort Visitors According to Ski Destination Choice Attributes with a Focus on Czech Families

Karolina Krupauerova, MCI | Management Center Innsbruck,
krupauerovak@gmail.com

Abstract

This study investigates the segmentation of ski resort visitors based on destination choice attributes, with a specific focus on Czech families. Given the increasing competitiveness of ski tourism, understanding visitor preferences and decision- making processes is crucial for effective marketing strategies. Employing a quantitative approach, this research identifies key pull factors influencing Czech families' selection of ski resorts and segments them accordingly. Using principal component analysis and cluster analysis, five distinct visitor segments were established: demanding tourists, passive tourists, true skiers, value-seeking tourists, and kids-oriented tourists. The study enriches the existing literature on ski tourism segmentation and provides practical insights for ski resort managers to develop targeted strategies aimed at family travellers. This research is critical in shaping the future of ski tourism by helping destinations understand family travel behaviours more effectively, thereby ensuring sustainable tourism growth and increased visitor satisfaction. The findings also provide a foundation for further research into how ski resorts can implement tailored marketing strategies to attract specific customer segments and improve overall business performance.

Keywords: ski tourism; family segmentation; consumer behaviour; pull factors; destination choice

1. INTRODUCTION

Ski tourism is a highly profitable sector with significant economic and social impacts, particularly in Europe and North America (UNWTO, 2024; Hashemi et al., 2022). Ski resorts, mainly in rural areas, drive employment and community growth (Silberman & Rees, 2010; Bätzing, 2017). However, the industry faces climate change and global competition, particularly in the Alps (Hopkins & Maclean, 2014; Moreno-Gené et al., 2018; Vanat, 2022). Maintaining competitiveness requires an effective marketing strategy that stems from market segmentation (Konu et al., 2011; Assael & Roscoe, 1976; Kara & Kaynak, 1997).

Benefit segmentation, widely used in tourism (Sarigöllü & Huang, 2005), examines tourist decision-making (Paker & Vural, 2016) through the push-pull framework (Crompton, 1979). Push factors reflect travellers' motivations (Yang et al., 2011), while pull factors relate to destination attributes (Hall et al., 2017). Studies confirm that applying push-pull factors enhances destinations' market competitiveness (Baloglu & Uysal, 1996; Hudson et al., 2004).

While segmentation research on ski tourism is extensive (Alexandris et al., 2006; Dolnicar, 2020; Konu et al., 2011; Miragaia & Martins, 2015), family tourism remains underexplored. Existing studies focus on family holiday planning (Kang et al., 2003) but overlook different stages families go through based on children's age and abilities, which have an impact on destination decision-making (Nanda et al., 2007; Amirtha & Sivakumar, 2022). Moreover, existing studies mainly focus on push factors that motivate families to travel (Shaw & Dawson, 2001; Zabriskie & McCormick, 2001; Larsen et al., 2007), but the issue of pull motivation is not sufficiently explored in this case. Despite the profitability of the family market, particularly in Austria (Lehto et al., 2012; Österreich Werbung, 2023), segmentation research on family ski tourism is limited.

This study addresses this gap by analysing Czech families, an important source market for many European ski resorts and Austria's fourth-largest winter source market (Österreich Werbung, 2023). This leads to the study's purpose, which is *to broaden the scope of research on family ski vacation decision-making by categorising different sub-segments of Czech families based on pull factors*. This study aims to contribute to scholarly research that can assist ski resort marketing managers in segmenting their family market according to pull factors.

2. THEORETICAL BACKGROUND

2.1 Destination choice

The theoretical foundation of this study is based on consumer behaviour theories (e.g. Engel et al., 1973; Kotler et al., 2022) applied to tourism. The process of selecting tourism services and destinations is a complex decision-making procedure (Solomon et al., 2019) influenced by a combination of intrinsic and extrinsic factors, which necessitate thoughtful consideration across multiple stages from the initial desire to travel to the post-travel reflection and evaluation (Sirakaya and Woodside, 2005). The literature on tourism offers various models for destination choice (e.g. Clawson and Knetsch, 1978; Van Raaij and Francken, 1984; Woodside and Lysonski, 1989, Crompton, 1992; Karl et al., 2015, Woodside & Sherrel, 1977).

One aspect is constantly emphasised in the literature: motivation. Motivation acts as a catalyst in the decision-making process. According to Moutinho (1986) and further explored by Wang et al. (2020), motivation encompasses the internal desires and external stimuli that provoke tourists to engage in travel. These motivations are often categorized into internal *push factors*, which drive individuals to seek travel experiences, and external *pull factors,* destination's attributes, which attract them to specific destinations (Dann, 1981; Hall et al., 2017). This paper focuses specifically on the more tangible motivation in the form of pull factors.

2.2 Ski destination choice based on pull factors

Previous research on ski destinations has largely examined customer loyalty, satisfaction (Hudson & Shephard, 1998; Matzler et al., 2004, 2007), and push motivations (Alexandris et al., 2006; Dolnicar & Leisch, 2003; Holden, 1999), with limited focus on pull factors and family-specific priorities.

Klenosky et al. (1993) categorized visitor values into six clusters, including terrain diversity, snow conditions, cost, and local culture. Hudson and Shephard (1998) expanded this framework by identifying 97 attributes, highlighting the importance of slope services, accommodation, and value for money. Subsequent studies reinforced these findings. Godfrey (1999) identified snow conditions and terrain variety as key factors for British skiers, noting differences in preferences based on skill level, gender, and age. Dickson and Faulks (2007) found that off-slope activities and evening entertainment were less important, reaffirming the primacy of skiing-related factors. Matzler et al. (2007) highlighted information availability, slope characteristics, and the price-quality ratio as major determinants of tourist satisfaction, varying by visitor demographics. Won et al. (2008) employed conjoint analysis to examine preferences among college skiers, emphasizing snow conditions as a universal priority. More recently, Chaudhary et al. (2023) analysed ski tourism in the Himalayas, underscoring snow quality, safety, and supporting services as critical decision factors.

Despite these insights, family ski tourism remains underexplored, revealing a research gap in understanding the specific pull factors influencing family decision-making in destination selection.

2.3 Family destination choice

A destination choice's distinctiveness stems from the extensive, intricate, and risk-laden decision-making it necessitates, regarded as a high-involvement purchase due to its low frequency and the significant financial and temporal implications involved (Solomon et al., 2019). This complexity is pronounced in family vacation planning, where decisions are typically made jointly by spouses, a dynamic supported by several studies which emphasize the shared nature of decision-making in holiday planning (Kang et al., 2003; Nanda et al., 2007; Sharp & Mott, 1956; Davis & Rigaux, 1974).

In the context of destination's pull factors, affordability and child-friendly services rank highly among important attributes for families, alongside accommodations suited to their needs (Srnec et al., 2016). Yet, the research mostly focuses on push motivation (Shaw & Dawson, 2001; Zabriskie & McCormick, 2001; Larsen et al., 2007) and is scant regarding pull factors specific to family tourism and even more so within market segmentation, which often overlooks family-oriented perspectives, even in areas like ski tourism where families are a significant demographic (Füller & Matzler, 2008; Matzler et al., 2004).

2.4 Tourist segmentation

The segmentation of travellers is a key topic in destination marketing, essential for tailoring strategies (Konu et al., 2011; Miragaia & Martins, 2015). It can be conducted using an a priori approach, where segments are predefined, or a post-hoc approach, where segments emerge from data analysis (Dolnicar, 2002; Mazanec, 2002; Myers & Tauber, 1977). The push-pull framework is widely applied in the post-hoc approach, particularly through benefit segmentation, which assesses the benefits tourists seek to refine market targeting and product differentiation (Haley, 1968; Sarigöllü & Huang, 2005).

Pull factors such as safety, accessibility, cultural heritage, nature, shopping, and entertainment play a crucial role in segmentation (Araslı & Baradarani, 2014; Baloglu & Uysal, 1996; Correia et al., 2007). For instance, Fraiz et al. (2020) segmented active Spanish tourists into health, adventure, and culture-focused groups, while Paker and Vural (2016) identified five segments among Turkish yachters based on push and pull factors. In general, however, research focuses mainly on push factor segmentation (Beh & Bruyere, 2007; Hall et al., 2017; Park & Yoon, 2014) and there is a clear gap in research on pull factor segmentation

Despite extensive segmentation research in various tourism markets, family ski tourism remains underexplored. This leads back to the study's purpose, which is *to broaden the scope of research on family ski vacation decision-making by categorising different sub-segments of Czech families based on pull factors.*

3. METHODOLOGY

3.1 Data collection

Data were collected through a self-administered structured questionnaire. Destination choice was assessed using 24 attributes derived from a literature review, with 'ski school' added after pilot testing. A 4-point Likert-type scale, avoiding neutral responses, measured the importance of these attributes (Asún et al., 2016). Classification questions covered demographics and ski-specific factors, including children's age and ski experience, reflecting family-specific decision-making (Jacobsen et al., 2008; Konu et al., 2011; Matzler et al., 2007).

The questionnaire was distributed via online platforms and the newsletter of a Czech ski resort Lipno nad Vltavou in March and April 2024. To boost participation, respondents had the chance to win ski passes.

The sample included adults raising at least one child under 18 who had undertaken a ski family holiday (leisure travel away from home for more than one day) with at least one of their children under 18 in the past two seasons. This was defined based on the definition of family holidays by Schänzel et al. (2015, p. 106). The inclusion of children's views in the research involves a high level of difficulty in execution and high ethical demands that could not be met with the limited resources of the student thesis thus, children were not questioned. This limitation is further elaborated in the discussion. Conducted in Czech, the survey targeted Czech-speaking participants. Of 521 respondents, 408 met the criteria.

3.2 Data analysis

The post-hoc segmentation approach, also known as posteriori segmentation, was used which is a standard practice in tourism marketing research (Dolnicar, 2004; Myers & Tauber, 1977; Mazanec, 2002; Masiero & Nicolau, 2012). This method's effectiveness in tourism market segmentation is well-documented (Chang, 2006; Lee & Sparks, 2007; Paker & Vural, 2016).

The data analysis involved six steps beginning with a descriptive analysis of the sample, followed by principal component analysis (PCA) with varimax rotation to simplify and explain variability among observed variables. This led to the creation of sum variables from identified factors, and Cronbach's alphas were calculated to assess the internal consistency of these factors. Subsequent K-means cluster analysis segmented the data into homogeneous clusters. ANOVA tested for statistical differences across clusters, using F-statistics to identify significant differentiators. The analysis concluded with a cross-tabulation and chi-square test to assess demographic variations across the segments.

4. RESULTS

4.1 Participants

In a survey of 521 participants, 408 met the criteria for this study, which sought to understand the demographics of ski holidaymakers. The survey found a higher percentage of female respondents (57.1%) compared to males (42.9%). The most represented age group was 41 to 50 years, comprising 47.8% of the sample, followed by 31 to 40 years at 33.1%, and 51 to 60 years at 11%. Respondents under 31 years made up 5.1%, and those over 60 years constituted 2.9%. The educational background of participants was predominantly university level (66.5%), followed by secondary education with a diploma (24%) and college education (5.4%).

The survey indicated that ski holidays tend to attract middle to upper-social-class families, evidenced by the majority (27.2%) reporting a monthly household income of over 100,001 CZK. Other significant income brackets included 60,001-80,000 CZK (24.8%) and 80,001-100,000 CZK (21.8%).

Families typically consisted of two parents (91.9%), with most households having 6-14-year-old children (58.1%). The selected age categories of children and their age ranges were chosen to correspond with the categories used by the Czech Statistical Office in their work.

Regarding skiing proficiency, 52.9% identified as advanced skiers, 39% as moderately advanced, and 8.9% as beginners. The survey also revealed that the predominant family setup included parents with one child (37%), followed by families with three children (11.3%). Only a small fraction of respondents had four or more children.

4.2 Principal component analysis

The initial factor analysis identified a six-factor solution (eigenvalues >1), explaining 58.5% of total variance. Items with factor loadings below 0.50 (Hair, 1998) were excluded, removing five variables (*parking facilities, safety, tourist information, additional activities, and ski & snowboard rental*). A second analysis with 19 remaining items produced a five-factor solution, explaining 59.5% of variance, but factor *nightlife and entertainment* was excluded due to low factor loading. A third analysis confirmed a five-factor model, accounting for 61.5% of variance.

The Kaiser-Meyer-Olkin (KMO) measure of 0.768 and Bartlett's test of sphericity ($p < 0.001$) validated the suitability of factor analysis. Table 1 presents the final factor structure. Cronbach's alpha values exceeded 0.65, confirming reliability (Taber, 2018).

Table 1. Factor analysis of ski resort choice criteria

Measure items	Factor 1	Factor 2	Factor 3	Factor 4	Factor 5	Cronbach's α
F1_Amenities						0.757
SR7_Variety of accommodation	0.771					
SR6_Variety of restaurants	0.744					
SR8_Wellness offers	0.711					
SR9_Supermarket and shops	0.631					
F2_Cost						0.818
C2_Lift ticket prices		0.875				
C3_Price of accommodation		0.808				
C1_Ski (discounted) packages		0.761				
C4_Price of food		0.722				
F3_Downhill skiing services						0.691
SR2_Number of slopes			0.818			
SR3_Variety of runs			0.748			
SR4_Crowding			0.640			
SR1_Snow quality			0.607			
F4_Convenience with kids						0.675
SR10_Offers for children in the slopes region (kids slopes, kids parks)				0.766		
SR11_Offers for children (other than skiing)				0.633		
A1_Travel time				0.616		
SR18_Ski school				0.559		
F5_Atmosphere						0.771
SR14_Atmosphere/ambience					0.882	
SR13_Friendly employees					0.837	
Initial eigenvalue	4.203	2.838	1.821	1.374	1.031	
Percentage of variance explained	23.3	14.7	10.1	7.6	5.7	
Cumulative percentage of variance explained	23.3	38	48.1	55.8	61.5	

Note: KMO measure of sampling adequacy = 0.768; chi-square = 2355.329; Bartlett's test of sphericity, p < 0.001.

Factor 1, Amenities, includes a *variety of restaurants, accommodation variety, wellness offers,* and *supermarkets and shops*, explaining the highest variance (23.3%). Factor 2, Cost, comprises *ski packages, lift ticket prices,* and *accommodation* and *food costs*, accounting for 14.7% of the variance. Factor 3, Downhill Skiing Services, relates to skiing conditions (*number of slopes, variety of runs, crowding, snow quality*) and explains 10.1% of the variance. Factor 4, Convenience with Kids, covers *offers for children in the slopes region, offers for children other than skiing, travel time* and *ski school*, contributing 7.6%. Finally, Factor 5, Atmosphere, includes *ambience* and *staff friendliness*, explaining 5.7% of the variance.

4.3 Cluster analysis

K-Means cluster analysis was conducted to create internally homogeneous and externally heterogeneous segments. This method partitions data into a predefined number of clusters, selected based on meaningfulness and interpretability rather than a fixed criterion (Hair, 1998). Testing began with two clusters, ultimately identifying five as the most significant and interpretable. ANOVA confirmed that all five factors significantly contributed to segmentation ($p < 0.05$), as shown in Table 2.

Table 2. Visitor segments

Factor	Demanding tourist (18.6%)	Passive tourist (14%)	True skiers (19.6%)	Value seekers (27.7%)	Kids oriented (20.1%)	F-value	p-value
F1 Amenities	**1.96**	**3.41**	**2.73**	**2.71**	**2.27**	**77.099**	**p < 0.001**
SR4_Variety of restaurants	1.91	3.39	2.68	2.63	3.17	62.077	p < 0.001
SR7_Variety of accommodation	1.71	3.12	2.51	2.42	1.94	46.809	p < 0.001
SR8_Wellness offers	2.11	3.75	2.88	3.05	2.67	44.633	p < 0.001
SR9_Supermarket and shops	2.12	3.37	2.83	2.73	2.36	32.084	p < 0.001
F2 Cost	**1.46**	**2.34**	**2.59**	**1.39**	**2.22**	**87.785**	**p < 0.001**
C2_Lift ticket prices	1.26	1.80	2.46	1.19	2.09	79.536	p < 0.001
C3_Price of accommodation	1.55	2.14	2.33	1.30	1.93	33.916	p < 0.001
C1_Ski (discounted) packages	1.32	2.35	2.83	1.33	2.41	67.014	p < 0.001
C4_Price of food	1.71	2.95	2.74	1.81	2.45	53.019	p < 0.001
F3 Downhill skiing services	**1.41**	**2.30**	**1.81**	**1.79**	**2.26**	**36.965**	**p < 0.001**
SR2_Number of slopes	1.59	2.61	1.83	1.99	2.52	26.157	p < 0.001
SR3_Variety of runs	1.46	2.53	1.96	1.96	2.32	26.536	p < 0.001
SR4_Crowding	1.20	1.86	1.75	1.53	1.96	17.781	p < 0.001
SR1_Snow quality	1.39	1.91	1.68	1.68	2.22	19.795	p < 0.001
F4 Convenience with kids	**1.72**	**3.16**	**2.66**	**2.78**	**1.75**	**48.902**	**p < 0.001**
SR10_Offers for children in the slopes region (kids slopes, kids parks)	1.32	3.05	2.29	2.74	1.38	80.682	p < 0.001
SR11_Offers for children (other than skiing)	1.65	3.69	2.74	3.73	1.44	124.146	p < 0.001
A1_Travel time	2.04	2.39	2.38	2.18	2.09	3.145	p = 0.014
SR16_Ski school	1.96	3.60	3.26	3.48	2.10	73.179	p < 0.001
F5 Atmosphere	**1.23**	**2.15**	**1.82**	**1.55**	**1.65**	**7.794**	**p < 0.001**
SR14_Atmosphere/ambience	1.16	1.93	1.78	1.49	1.61	17.618	p < 0.001
SR15_Friendly employees	1.29	2.39	1.80	1.61	1.68	26.804	p < 0.001

F-statistics revealed that Cost (F = 87.785) most significantly differentiates the segments, followed by Amenities (F = 77.099) and Convenience with Children (F = 48.902). Downhill Skiing Services (F = 36.965) showed lower differentiation, while Atmosphere (F = 7.794) was the most homogenous factor. Clusters were named based on mean values, with attributes rated below 2 considered important (scale: 1 = "very important" to 4 = "not important at all").

Demanding Tourists (18.6%) prioritize all factors, showing the lowest values in Atmosphere (1.23), Skiing services (1.41), and Convenience with Kids (1.72), with Cost also scoring below 1.5. *Passive Tourists* (14%) exhibit low engagement, recording values above 2 across all five factors. *True Skiers* (19.6%) focus on Skiing services (1.81) and Atmosphere (1.82), while scoring the highest on Cost, indicating price is not a concern. *Value Seekers* (27.7%) prioritize affordability, scoring the lowest on Cost (1.39) and relatively low on Skiing services (1.79) and Atmosphere (1.55). *Kids-oriented tourists* (20.6%) emphasize child-friendly offerings, scoring lowest in Convenience with Kids (1.75) and Atmosphere (1.65) but highest in Skiing services (2.26). Cost (2.22) and Amenities (2.27) are less relevant.

Each cluster was analysed using a chi-square test to examine statistical differences based on external categorical variables, with results detailed in the following chapter.

4.4 Differences between segments

Our research identified significant demographic and behavioural differences across visitor segments. As shown in Table 3, age distribution varies notably ($p < 0.001$), with the 41-50 age group prevailing among Demanding, Passive, True skiers, and Value-seeking segments, while the Kids-oriented segment is dominated by the 31-40 age group (61%).

Table 3. Differences between the visitor segments

Demographic characteristics	Demanding N = 76	Passive N = 57	True skiers N = 80	Value seekers N = 113	Kids-oriented N = 82	p-value, chi-square test
	Frequency (%)					
Gender						
Female	38 (50)	30 (52.6)	46 (57.5)	65 (57.5)	54 (65.9)	$\chi^2(4) = 4.607$
Male	38 (50)	27 (47.4)	34 (42.5)	48 (42.5)	28 (34.1)	p = 0,330
Age group						
less than 31	4 (5.3)	4 (7)	6 (7.5)	1 (0.9)	6 (7.3)	
31-40	19 (25)	13 (22.8)	26 (32.5)	27 (23.9)	50 (61)	$\chi^2(16) = 56,783$
41-50	38 (50)	32 (56.1)	37 (46.3)	65 (57.5)	23 (28)	p < 0,001
51-60	10 (13.2)	6 (10.5)	8 (10)	19 (16.8)	2 (2.4)	
more than 60	5 (6.6)	2 (3.5)	3 (3.8)	1 (0.9)	1 (1.2)	
Education						
Elementary education	1 (1.3)	0	0	0	0	
Secondary education without diploma	5 (6.6)	0	2 (2.5)	7 (6.2)	2 (2.4)	
Secondary education with diploma	19 (25)	7 (12.3)	19 (23.8)	29 (25.7)	24 (29.3)	$\chi^2(16) = 28.874$
College	5 (6.6)	4 (7)	2 (2.5)	10 (8.8)	1 (1.2)	p = 0,072
University	46 (60.5)	46 (80.7)	57 (71.3)	67 (59.3)	55 (67.1)	
Household						
Single-parent household	7 (9.2)	6 (10.5)	8 (10)	10 (8.8)	2 (2.4)	$\chi^2(4) = 4.586$
Household of two parents	69 (90.8)	51 (89.5)	72 (90)	103 (91.2)	80 (97.6)	p = 0,332
Income						
20 0001 - 40 000 CZK	6 (7.9)	4 (7)	4 (5)	11 (9.7)	2 (2.4)	
40 001 - 60 000 CZK	19 (25)	13 (22.8)	9 (11.3)	26 (23)	13 (15.9)	
60 001 - 80 000 CZK	22 (28.9)	12 (21.1)	16 (20)	32 (28.3)	19 (23.2)	$\chi^2(16) = 25.158$
80 001 - 100 000 CZK	15 (19.7)	11 (19.3)	19 (23.8)	24 (21.2)	20 (24.4)	p = 0.067
100 001 and more CZK	14 (18.4)	17 (29.8)	32 (40)	20 (17.7)	28 (34.1)	
Ski experience						
Beginner	7 (9.2)	6 (10.5)	3 (3.8)	7 (6.2)	10 (12.2)	$\chi^2(8) = 18.135$
Intermidiate	34 (44.7)	17 (29.8)	23 (28.8)	56 (49.6)	29 (35.4)	p = 0,020
Advanced	35 (46.1)	34 (59.6)	54 (67.5)	50 (44.2)	43 (52.4)	
Children						
1	30 (39.5)	17 (29.8)	30 (37.5)	41 (36.3)	33 (40.2)	
2	34 (44.7)	33 (57.9)	41 (51.3)	57 (50.4)	40 (48.8)	$\chi^2(16) = 12.269$
3	11 (14.5)	5 (8.8)	8 (10)	14 (12.4)	8 (9.8)	p = 0,725
4	0	2 (3.5)	1 (1.3)	1 (0.9)	0	
5+	1 (1.3)	0	0	0	1 (1.2)	

Children (age, experience)	Demanding N = 136	Passive N = 106	True skiers N = 140	Value seekers N = 201	Kids-oriented N = 142	p-value, chi-square test
	Frequency (%)					
Ski experience						
Non skier	18 (13.2)	11 (10.4)	12 (8.6)	7 (3.5)	36 (25.4)	
Beginner	53 (39)	28 (26.4)	47 (33.6)	48 (23.9)	69 (48.6)	$\chi^2(12) = 103.036$
Intermidiate	36 (26.5)	39 (36.8)	53 (37.9)	89 (44.3)	24 (16.9)	p < 0.001
Advanced	29 (21.3)	28 (26.4)	28 (20)	57 (28.4)	12 (8.5)	
Age						
0-2	8 (5.9)	8 (7.5)	7 (5)	4 (2)	19 (13.4)	
3-5	27 (19.9)	16 (15.1)	26 (18.6)	13 (6.5)	58 (40.8)	$\chi^2(12) = 103.036$
6-14	82 (60.3)	58 (54.7)	87 (62.1)	136 (67.7)	58 (40.8)	p < 0.001
15+	19 (14)	24 (22.6)	20 (14.3	48 (23.9)	7 (4.9)	

Ski experience varied significantly across segments (p = 0.020), with Demanding, Passive, and True skiers predominantly advanced, while Value seekers were mostly intermediate skiers (49.6%).

Child age and ski experience also differed notably (p < 0.001), with Kid-oriented tourists having more young children (0-5 years), whereas Value seekers included older children (6-15+ years), indicating varied family service needs.

No significant differences were found in gender, education, family status, income, or number of children (p ≥ 0.05), suggesting these factors do not influence segment characteristics.

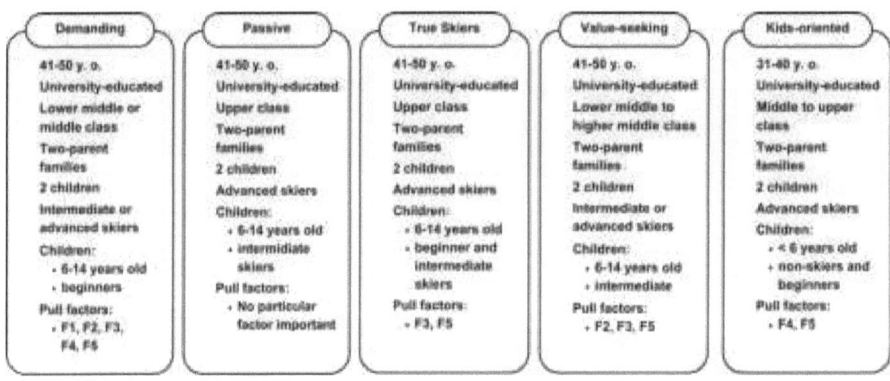

Fig. 2. Segments summarized

4.5 Discussion

The principal component analysis identified five key pull factors for ski destinations among families: *amenities, cost, downhill skiing services, convenience with children, and atmosphere.* These findings align with prior studies (e.g., Won et al., 2008; Konu et al., 2011), though specific amenities have previously been categorized separately, such as restaurants (Hudson & Shephard, 1998) or accommodation (Godfrey, 1999). The *convenience with children* factor was a unique contribution of this research, as prior studies primarily focused on kids' slopes (Matzler et al., 2007) rather than broader family-friendly aspects like ski schools and travel time. Notably, nightlife and safety—previously identified as important (Chaudhary et al., 2023; Srnec et al., 2016) – did not emerge as significant in this case, likely due to the study's family-focused scope.

Five tourist segments were identified: *demanding, passive, true skiers, value-seeking, and kids-oriented*. While the first four correspond to segments found in previous research (e.g., Konu et al., 2011; Matzler et al., 2007; Miragaia & Martins, 2015), the *kids-oriented* segment is a new finding, possibly due to the study's exclusive focus on families. Another key distinction from earlier studies is the prioritization of *atmosphere* as the most influential factor in family decision-making (M = 1.68), whereas prior research (e.g., Godfrey, 1999; Konu et al., 2011) emphasized downhill skiing services.

This knowledge is very important for practical application. The Kids-oriented segment consists of ski-skilled parents who do not care about the quality of downhill skiing, but mainly about the fun for the whole family. This may become an incentive for smaller ski resorts in particular, which cannot compete with large resorts in terms of kilometres or variety of slopes, to focus their communication on family-specific services. At the same time, the research has shown that atmosphere is an important factor for families when choosing a destination, which is an incentive for marketers to enrich their product, for example, with a variety of events or focus on staff training and their approach to customers.

Segment differences were significant in *age and skiing experience*, reinforcing findings from previous studies (Hall et al., 2017; Konu et al., 2011). However, no significant variations were found in *gender, education, income, family status, or number of children*, which contradicts some earlier research (Hall et al., 2017). These findings offer new insights into the decision-making processes of family ski tourists and highlight the evolving nature of ski resort preferences.

A limitation of this research is that data collection relied largely on a specific ski resort's communication channel, affecting generalizability. Another limitation is that children's preferences were not investigated, although they also influence the choice of destination. However, this presents an opportunity for future research to include children's perspectives. Another possible extension of this study would be to include push motivations in the research to gain a complex view of the family decision-making process.

5. CONCLUSION

This study examines ski resort visitor segmentation, focusing on Czech families, their preferences, and decision-making based on pull factors. It identifies distinct family sub-segments influenced by demographics. The study reveals five key factors shaping family ski resort choices: Amenities, Cost, Downhill Skiing Services, Convenience with Kids, and Atmosphere. Based on these, five customer segments emerge: *Demanding* tourists who value all five factors; *Passive* tourists who show no strong preferences; *True skiers* who prioritize skiing services and atmosphere; *Value-seekers* who focus on price-to-quality ratio, *Kids-oriented* tourists who prioritize child convenience and atmosphere. These segments differ significantly in age, ski experience, and children's age and ski proficiency.

This study contributes to market segmentation literature by demonstrating that family tourism consists of diverse sub-segments and confirming that family decision-making is shaped by the primary respondent and children's characteristics. Ski resort marketing managers should tailor strategies to family segments for higher satisfaction and repeat visits. Marketers should focus on the factors that are relevant to specific groups and create communication messages based on those factors. However, the interventions should not only be in communication but this knowledge must also be reflected in the products offered. For example, in the case of the Kids-oriented sector, all services offered should be tailored to young children -for example, offering a babysitting service included in the price of a ski pass.
Overall, this study fills a gap in family segmentation in ski tourism, providing insights for destination marketing. It underscores the importance of differentiated strategies in an increasingly competitive tourism industry, where understanding family needs is key to success.

REFERENCES

Alexandris, K., Kouthouris, C., & Meligdis, A. (2006). Increasing customers' loyalty in a skiing resort: The contribution of place attachment and service quality. International Journal of Contemporary Hospitality Management, 18(5), 414– 425.

Amirtha, R., & Sivakumar, V. J. (2022). Building loyalty through perceived value in online shopping – does family life cycle stage matter? The Service Industries Journal, 42(15–16), 1151–1189.

Araslı, H., & Baradarani, S. (2014). European Tourist Perspective on Destination Satisfaction in Jordan's Industries. Procedia - Social and Behavioral Sciences, 109, 1416–1425.

Assael, H., & Roscoe, A. M. (1976). Approaches to Market Segmentation Analysis. Journal of Marketing, 40(4), 67–76.

Asún, R. A., Rdz-Navarro, K., & Alvarado, J. M. (2016). Developing Multidimensional Likert Scales Using Item Factor Analysis: The Case of Four- point Items. Sociological Methods & Research, 45(1), 109– 133.

Baloglu, S., & Uysal, M. (1996). Market segments of push and pull motivations: A canonical correlation approach. International Journal of Contemporary Hospitality Management, 8(3), 32–38.

Bätzing, W. (2017). Orte guten Lebens. Visionen für einen Alpentourismus zwischen Wildnis und Freizeitpark. Alpenreisen: Erlebnis— Raumtransformationen— Imagination, 213–234.

Beh, A., & Bruyere, B. L. (2007). Segmentation by visitor motivation in three Kenyan national reserves. Tourism Management, 28(6), 1464–1471.

Chaudhary, M., Marković Vukadin, I., Mehboob Bukhari, S. A., & Islam, N. U. (2023). Destination Choice, Satisfaction, and Loyalty of Ski Tourists in the Indian Himalayas. Tourism, 71(4), 677–696.

Clawson, M., & Knetsch, J. L. (1978). Economics of outdoor recreation (Fourth printing 1978). The Johns Hopkins University Press.

Correia, A., Oom Do Valle, P., & Moço, C. (2007). Modeling motivations and perceptions of Portuguese tourists. Journal of Business Research, 60(1), 76–80.

Crompton, J. L. (1979). Motivations for pleasure vacation. Annals of Tourism Research, 6(4), 408–424.

Crompton, J. (1992). Structure of vacation destination choice sets. Annals of Tourism Research, 19(3), 420–434.

Dann, G. M. S. (1981). Tourist motivation an appraisal. Annals of Tourism Research, 8(2), 187–219.

Davis, H. L., & Rigaux, B. P. (1974). Perception of Marital Roles in Decision Processes. Journal of Consumer Research, 1(1), 51.

Dickson, T. J., & Faulks, P. (2007). Exploring overseas snowsport participation by Australian skiers and snowboarders. Tourism Review, 62(3/4), 7–14.

Dolnicar, S. (2002). A Review of Data-Driven Market Segmentation in Tourism. Journal of Travel & Tourism Marketing, 12(1), 1–22.

Dolnicar, S. (2004). Beyond "Commonsense Segmentation": A Systematics of Segmentation Approaches in Tourism. Journal of Travel Research, 42(3), 244– 250.

Dolnicar, S. (2020). Market segmentation analysis in tourism: A perspective paper. Tourism Review, 75(1), 45–48.

Dolnicar, S., & Leisch, F. (2003b). Winter Tourist Segments in Austria: Identifying Stable Vacation Styles Using Bagged Clustering Techniques. Journal of Travel Research, 41(3), 281–292.

Engel, J. F., Kollat, D. T., & Blackwell, R. D. (1973). Consumer behavior (2. ed).

Holt, Rinehart, Winston.

Fraiz, J. A., De Carlos, P., & Araújo, N. (2020). Disclosing homogeneity within heterogeneity: A segmentation of Spanish active tourism based on motivational pull factors. Journal of Outdoor Recreation and Tourism, 30, 100294.

Füller, J., & Matzler, K. (2008). Customer delight and market segmentation: An application of the three-factor theory of customer satisfaction on life style groups. Tourism Management, 29(1), 116–126.

Godfrey, K. B. (1999). Attributes of destination choice: British skiing in Canada. Journal of Vacation Marketing, 5(1), 18–30.

Hair, J. F. (Ed.). (1998). Multivariate data analysis. Prentice Hall.

Haley, R. I. (1968). Benefit Segmentation: A Decision-oriented Research Tool. Journal of Marketing, 32(3), 30–35.

Hall, J., O'Mahony, B., & Gayler, J. (2017). Modelling the relationship between attribute satisfaction, overall satisfaction, and behavioural intentions in Australian ski resorts. Journal of Travel & Tourism Marketing, 34(6), 764–778.

Hashemi, S., Mohammed, H. J., Rasoolimanesh, S. M., Kiumarsi, S., & Dara Singh,

K. S. (2022). To investigate the influencing factors on support for tourism development and perceived economic benefits in the context of ski tourism. Journal of Sport & Tourism, 26(3), 225–247.

Holden, A. (1999). Understanding Skiers Motivation using PearcesTravel Career Construct. Annals of Tourism Research, 26(2), 435–438.

Hopkins, D., & Maclean, K. (2014). Climate change perceptions and responses in Scotland's ski industry. Tourism Geographies, 16(3), 400–414.

Hudson, S., & Shephard, G. (1998). Measuring Service Quality at Tourist Destinations: An Application of Importance-Performance Analysis to an Alpine Ski Resort. Journal of Travel & Tourism Marketing, 7(3), 61–77.

Hudson, S., Ritchie, B., & Timur, S. (2004). Measuring destination competitiveness: An empirical study of Canadian ski resorts. Tourism and Hospitality Planning & Development, 1(1), 79–94.

Jacobsen, J. Kr. S., Denstadli, J. M., & Rideng, A. (2008). Skiers' Sense of Snow: Tourist Skills and Winter Holiday Attribute Preferences. Tourism Analysis, 13(5), 605–614.

Kang, S. K., Hsu, C. H. C., & Wolfe, K. (2003). Family Traveler Segmentation by Vacation Decision-Making Patterns. Journal of Hospitality & Tourism Research, 27(4), 448–469.

Kara, A., & Kaynak, E. (1997). Markets of a single customer: Exploiting conceptual developments in market segmentation. European Journal of Marketing, 31(11/12), 873–895.

Karl, M., Reintinger, C., & Schmude, J. (2015). Reject or select: Mapping destination choice. Annals of Tourism Research, 54, 48–64.

Klenosky, D. B., Gengler, C. E., & Mulvey, M. S. (1993). Understanding the Factors Influencing Ski Destination Choice: A Means-End Analytic Approach. Journal of Leisure Research, 25(4), 362–379.

Konu, H., Laukkanen, T., & Komppula, R. (2011). Using ski destination choice criteria to segment Finnish ski resort customers. Tourism Management, 32(5), 1096–1105.

Kotler, P., Keller, K. L., & Chernev, A. (2022). Marketing management (Sixteenth edition; global edition). Pearson Education.

Larsen, J., Urry, J., & Axhausen, K. W. (2007). Networks and tourism. Annals of Tourism Research, 34(1), 244–262.

Lehto, X. Y., Lin, Y.-C., Chen, Y., & Choi, S. (2012). Family Vacation Activities and Family Cohesion. Journal of Travel & Tourism Marketing, 29(8), 835–850.

Masiero, L., & Nicolau, J. L. (2012). Tourism Market Segmentation Based on Price Sensitivity: Finding Similar Price Preferences on Tourism Activities. Journal of Travel Research, 51(4), 426–435.

Matzler, K., Füller, J., & Faullant, R. (2007). Customer satisfaction and loyalty to Alpine ski resorts: The moderating effect of lifestyle, spending and customers' skiing skills. International Journal of Tourism Research, 9(6), 409–421.

Matzler, K., Pechlaner, H., & Hattenberger, G. (2004). Lifestyle-typologies and marketing segmentation – The case of Alpine skiing tourism. EURAC Research, European Academy.

Mazanec, J. A. (2002). Market Segmentation. In J. Jafari (Ed.), Encyclopedia of Tourism (1st ed.). Routledge.

Miragaia, D. A. M., & Martins, M. A. B. (2015). Mix between Satisfaction and Attributes Destination Choice: A Segmentation Criterion to Understand the Ski Resorts Consumers. International Journal of Tourism Research, 17(4), 313–324.

Moreno-Gené, J., Sánchez-Pulido, L., Cristobal-Fransi, E., & Daries, N. (2018). The Economic Sustainability of Snow Tourism: The Case of Ski Resorts in Austria, France, and Italy. Sustainability, 10(9), 3012.

Moutinho, L. (1986). Consumer behaviour in tourism. MCB Univ. Pr.

Myers, J. H., & Tauber, E. M. (1977). Market structure analysis. American Marketing Association.

Nanda, D., Hu, C., & Bai, B. (2007). Exploring Family Roles in Purchasing Decisions During Vacation Planning: Review and Discussions for Future Research. Journal of Travel & Tourism Marketing, 20(3–4), 107–125.

Österreich Werbung. (2023, April). Tschechische Republik Tourismusausblick. Österreich Werbung. https://www.austriatourism.com/tourismusforschung/tourismusausblic k/tschech ische-republik-tourismusausblick/

Paker, N., & Vural, C. A. (2016). Customer segmentation for marinas: Evaluating marinas as destinations. Tourism Management, 56, 156–171.

Park, D.-B., & Yoon, Y.-S. (2009). Segmentation by motivation in rural tourism: A Korean case study. Tourism Management, 30(1), 99–108.

Sarigöllü, E., & Huang, R. (2005). Benefits Segmentation of Visitors to Latin America. Journal of Travel Research, 43(3), 277–293.

Schänzel, H. A., Smith, K. A., & Weaver, A. (2005). Family Holidays: A Research Review and Application to New Zealand. Annals of Leisure Research, 8(2–3), 105–123. https://doi.org/10.1080/11745398.2005.10600965

Sharp, H., & Mott, P. (1956). Consumer Decisions in the Metropolitan Family. Journal of Marketing, 21(2), 149–156.

Shaw, S. M., & Dawson, D. (2001). Purposive Leisure: Examining Parental Discourses on Family Activities. Leisure Sciences, 23(4), 217–231.

Silberman, J. A., & Rees, P. W. (2010). Reinventing mountain settlements: A GIS model for identifying possible ski towns in the U.S. Rocky Mountains. Applied Geography, 30(1), 36–49.

Siomkos, G., Vasiliadis, C., & Lathiras, P. (2006). Measuring customer preferences in the winter sports market: The case of Greece. Journal of Targeting, Measurement and Analysis for Marketing, 14(2), 129–140.

Solomon, M. R., Askegaard, S., Hogg, M. K., & Bamossy, G. J. (2019). Consumer behaviour: A European perspective (Seventh edition). Pearson.

Srnec, T., Lon\vcarić, D., & Prodan, M. P. (2016). Family vacation decision making process: Evidence from Croatia. https://api.semanticscholar.org/CorpusID:151753007

Taber, K. S. (2018). The Use of Cronbach's Alpha When Developing and Reporting Research Instruments in Science Education. Research in Science Education, 48(6), 1273–1296.

UNWTO. (2024). Sports Tourism. UN Tourism. https://www.unwto.org/sport-tourism

Vanat, L. (2022). 2022 International Report on Snow & Mountain Tourism. https://www.vanat.ch/RM-world-report-2022.pdf

Van Raaij, W. F., & Francken, D. A. (1984). Vacation decisions, activities, and satisfactions. Annals of Tourism Research, 11(1), 101–112.

Wang, X., Zhang, J. J., Song, G., & Wan, X. (2020). Push and Pull Factors Influencing the Winter Sport Tourists in China: The Case of Leisure Skiers. SAGE Open, 10(2), 215824402093873.

Won, D., Bang, H., & Shonk, D. J. (2008). Relative Importance of Factors Involved in Choosing a Regional Ski Destination: Influence of Consumption Situation and Recreation Specialization. Journal of Sport & Tourism, 13(4), 249–271.

Woodside, A. G., & Lysonski, S. (1989). A General Model Of Traveler Destination Choice. Journal of Travel Research, 27(4), 8–14.

Woodside, A. G., & Sherrell, D. (1977). Traveler Evoked, Inept, and Inert Sets of Vacation Destinations. Journal of Travel Research, 16(1), 14–18.

Yang, X., Reeh, T., & Kreisel, W. (2011). Cross-Cultural Perspectives on Promoting Festival Tourism—An Examination of Motives and Perceptions of Chinese Visitors Attending the Oktoberfest in Munich (Germany). Journal of China Tourism Research, 7(4), 377–395.

Zabriskie, R. B., & McCormick, B. P. (2001). The Influences of Family Leisure Patterns on Perceptions of Family Functioning. Family Relations, 50(3), 281– 289.

Gamification in Airports: Transforming Passenger Waiting Time with Interactive Engagement Using a Design Thinking Approach

Nayana Madhusoodhanan Kaki, Deggendorf Institute of Technology, nayanamadhusoodhanankaki@gmail.com

Amal Plathottathil Shibu, Deggendorf Institute of Technology, amalpswyd@gmail.com

Zohre Aleboyeh, Deggendorf Institute of Technology, z.aleboyeh@gmail.com

Abstract

This study explores gamification as a solution to enhance passenger engagement during airport waiting times using the Design Thinking approach. Semi-structured interviews with students who are travellers identified the lack of interactive digital entertainment as a key challenge. A QR code-accessible gamified platform was developed, featuring destination-based quizzes, leaderboards, and rewards. The prototype was tested with travellers, who found it engaging, intuitive, and effective in reducing perceived waiting time. The reward system and competitive elements were particularly motivating, highlighting gamification's potential to transform airport waiting experiences. This study contributes to airport service innovation by demonstrating how interactive digital engagement can improve passenger satisfaction. Future research should focus on scalability and integration with existing airport ecosystems to maximize its impact.

Keywords: Gamification, Airport Experience, Design Thinking, Digital Engagement, Passenger Satisfaction, QR Code Technology

1. INTRODUCTION

Airports serve as critical transit hubs where passengers experience long waiting times due to layovers, security checks, and flight delays (Wittmann & Paulus, 2008). These waiting periods often lead to boredom, frustration, and disengagement, negatively impacting passenger experience and overall travel satisfaction (Horner & Swarbrooke, 2016). While airports provide traditional entertainment options such as lounges, retail stores, and digital displays, these services do not sufficiently engage all travellers, particularly those seeking interactive and personalized experiences (Bari, C. S., & Vijaykumar, S. 2020). With the increasing reliance on mobile technology, travellers are looking for engaging solutions that enhance their airport experience and make waiting times feel more productive and enjoyable. However, most existing airport entertainment solutions remain passive, failing to integrate interactive and immersive engagement strategies that cater to modern traveller expectations.

Gamification has emerged as a promising approach to enhance user engagement across various fields, including education, marketing, and e-commerce (Hamari et al., 2014). It integrates game mechanics such as points, challenges, leaderboards, and rewards into real-world experiences, encouraging users to interact with a system in an engaging and motivating way (Ihamäki & Heljakka, 2020). Given that airports are transitional spaces where passengers often remain idle, they present an ideal setting for gamification-based engagement models. However, despite the increasing adoption of digital solutions in tourism and transit environments, limited research has explored the integration of gamification within airport settings. Existing studies primarily focus on infrastructure improvements, customer service enhancements, and passive entertainment options, while neglecting interactive digital engagement strategies that align with evolving traveller preferences (Bari, C. S., & Vijaykumar, S. 2020).While gamification has been applied successfully in other sectors, its implementation in airport environments remains underexplored (Hamari et al., 2014; Bari, C. S., & Vijaykumar, S. 2020). The potential benefits of game-based experiences—such as trivia-based learning, reward-based incentives, and competitive engagement through leaderboards—are not sufficiently explored within the airport environment. Current literature lacks empirical evidence on how game-based engagement models can be integrated into airport ecosystems to enhance passenger experiences

(Stickdorn & Schneider, 2012). Furthermore, there is limited research investigating the direct impact of gamification on passenger satisfaction, stress reduction, and perceived wait times (Wittmann & Paulus, 2008; Ihamäki & Heljakka, 2020).

This study aims to develop and evaluate a gamified digital engagement platform designed to improve passenger experience during airport waiting times. By applying Design Thinking principles, the research will focus on understanding passenger needs, designing an interactive solution, and evaluating its effectiveness in enhancing engagement. Specifically, the study will identify key engagement challenges in airport waiting areas by analysing passenger behaviours and preferences for interactive experiences. It will also develop a gamified digital platform featuring destination-based trivia quizzes, leaderboards, and a reward system accessible via QR codes printed on boarding passes. Additionally, the research aims to evaluate the usability and effectiveness of the gamified solution through prototype testing and user feedback, refining the platform based on insights gained from testing to ensure a seamless, scalable, and engaging airport experience. By addressing these objectives, this research contributes to the growing field of digital innovation in tourism, offering a scalable, interactive, and user-driven solution that enhances passenger engagement in transit environments. Furthermore, the study seeks to bridge the current research gap by providing empirical insights into the effectiveness of gamification in airports, helping to shape future digital engagement strategies in global travel hubs.

2. LITERATURE REVIEW

2.1 Understanding Tourists' Needs in Airport Environments

Airports serve as transitional spaces where passengers spend considerable time due to layovers, security procedures, and delays. Research indicates that travellers often experience boredom, time distortion, and frustration, leading to decreased satisfaction with their journey (Wittmann & Paulus, 2008). Traditional airport entertainment such as retail shopping, digital displays, and lounges fails to engage all travellers, particularly those who seek interactive and personalized experiences (Horner, S., & Swarbrooke, J. 2020).

With the increasing digitalization of services, modern travellers, particularly tech-savvy and younger demographics, expect real-time, personalized, and interactive engagement options (Kottur, S. V.,2022). Studies suggest that passengers actively use mobile devices for entertainment and social connectivity, indicating that mobile and digital engagement strategies could enhance the waiting experience (Ihamäki & Heljakka, 2020). The shift towards experience-driven tourism means that travellers are no longer satisfied with passive entertainment; instead, they expect engaging and meaningful interactions even in transit settings (Stickdorn et al., 2018). Recent research suggests that the availability of personalized engagement solutions in airports can influence passenger satisfaction, airport service ratings, and brand perception (Hamari et al., 2014). Providing travellers with customized and engaging experiences not only enhances their waiting time but also improves their perception of the airport as a technologically advanced and passenger-friendly space (Stickdorn et al., 2018). This supports the argument that airports should integrate digital engagement strategies that cater to different passenger demographics, including business travellers, leisure tourists, and families traveling with children.

2.2 Gamification as a Solution for Enhancing Airport Engagement

Gamification is a widely recognized engagement strategy that applies game mechanics, such as points, leaderboards, and rewards, to non-gaming contexts (Hamari et al., 2014). Interactive and competitive elements in gamification can increase motivation and participation, making it a suitable strategy for enhancing airport waiting experiences (Ihamäki & Heljakka, 2020).

In tourism and transit settings, gamification has been shown to enhance learning, engagement, and user satisfaction. Research highlights that knowledge-based gamification, such as quizzes on destinations, history, and culture, provides both entertainment and educational value (Kottur,

S. V.,2022). Gamified elements can be strategically placed within key touchpoints to enhance passenger engagement and create a more immersive and rewarding waiting experience (Stickdorn & Schneider, 2012). The solution proposed in this study integrates a dual-phase quiz system, allowing passengers to engage with their travel destination through trivia and challenge-based learning.

Reward-based engagement is another crucial component of gamification. Research supports the idea that users are more likely to engage when they receive tangible incentives, such as discounts, loyalty rewards, or exclusive benefits (Hamari et al., 2014). In this study, participants can collect stamps and redeem them for airport-related perks, ensuring that the gamification experience provides tangible benefits beyond entertainment. The leaderboard feature further enhances engagement, as studies suggest that competition encourages repeated participation (Stickdorn et al., 2018). Additionally, integrating real-time engagement metrics and adaptive gaming strategies can further enhance the effectiveness of gamified airport experiences. Research suggests that systems incorporating AI-driven personalization can modify gameplay difficulty, adjust incentives, and provide real-time feedback based on user behaviour (Ihamäki & Heljakka, 2020). These dynamic gamification elements can sustain long-term engagement by continuously adapting to user preferences, thus increasing overall satisfaction and interaction levels among passengers.

2.3 Technology-Enabled Solutions for Airport Engagement

The advancement of digital and mobile technologies has enabled innovative solutions for passenger engagement in transit environments. Several technology-enabled interventions have been explored in previous research (Fig.1).

Although technology-driven gamification presents strong potential for enhancing airport engagement, its implementation comes with several challenges and limitations: First, an innovative solution does not guarantee high usability for the passengers. Ensuring that the digital interface is intuitive, inclusive, and compatible across devices is crucial for user adoption. Poor interface design can lead to frustration and disengagement (Stickdorn & Schneider, 2012). Furthermore, the effectiveness of gamified experiences depends on their integration with existing airport services, such as retail stores, airlines, and entertainment areas. Failure to establish strategic partnerships could limit the incentive value of rewards (Ihamäki & Heljakka, 2020). A careful UX Design is required to ensure high Usability and UX.

QR Code-Based Gamification	•A cost-effective and accessible tool for instant digital engagement, which allows users to engage seamlessly with digital services, making them highly effective in high-traffic areas such as airports (Kottur, S. V.,2022).
Mobile Web-Based Platforms	•Provide a universal engagement solution, eliminating the need for platform-specific app installations, and can secure compatibility, ease of use, and real-time interactivity, making them ideal for airport environments (Ihamäki & Heljakka, 2020).
Gamified Loyalty and Reward Systems	•Enhance passenger retention and satisfaction as the integration with existing airport reward systems can incentivize participation, providing real-world benefits beyond the gamified experience (Kottur, S. V.,2022).
1.AI-based chatbots and virtual assistants with gamified experiences	•Can further optimize user engagement in airports. AI-driven solutions can provide personalized recommendations, guide users through the game, and offer real-time feedback on their progress (Hamari et al., 2014).

Fig.1. Technology-Enabled Solutions for Airport Engagement

Also, while digital gamification provides an engaging alternative to traditional waiting experiences, its success depends on passengers' willingness to interact with technology-based solutions. Some travellers may prefer passive activities, while others might be hesitant to engage in game-based experiences due to privacy concerns or technological unfamiliarity (Stickdorn et al., 2018). Furthermore, while initial engagement may be high, studies indicate that long-term retention requires dynamic content, evolving challenges, and AI-driven personalization to keep users interested (Hamari et al., 2014). Addressing these concerns through continuous service adaptation to user preferences and changing travel patterns, tailoring incentive strategies and enabling user learning could increase adoption and engagement rates, as well as advance their experience. The next phase of research should focus on enhancing personalization, improving user retention, and expanding partnerships with key industry stakeholders to ensure the long-term success of gamified airport experiences.

3. METHODOLOGY

This research applies Design Thinking to develop a gamified solution for airport waiting times, focusing on enhancing passenger engagement through interactive and rewarding experiences. Design Thinking is a user-centred, iterative process that enables innovative problem-solving by aligning solutions with user needs and behaviours (Gonen, E., 2019). It provides a structured framework consisting of five key phases: Empathize, Define, Ideate, Prototype, and Test, facilitating the systematic development and refinement of an engaging airport gamification experience. The Empathize phase involves understanding passenger experiences and behaviours in airport waiting areas. Previous research indicates that passengers experience time distortion and increased boredom in passive waiting environments, emphasizing the need for engaging alternatives (Horner & Swarbrooke, 2020; Wittmann & Paulus, 2008).

The Define phase synthesizes the insights gained to establish a clear problem statement, outlining the challenges associated with passive waiting experiences. The findings from this phase guide the development of a user-centred gamification blueprint. The Ideate phase explores potential solutions through brainstorming and stakeholder collaboration, focusing on game mechanics, interactive challenges, and rewards. This phase integrates a Service Blueprint, outlining interactions between passengers and service providers to ensure seamless integration within airport environments. The Prototype phase translates these concepts into an interactive game-based engagement model, iteratively refining design elements for usability and accessibility (Ihamäki & Heljakka, 2020). The Test phase evaluates the effectiveness of the gamified model through usability testing, participant observation, and post-engagement feedback interviews (Krippendorff, 2005; Ihamäki & Heljakka, 2020).

To strengthen the empirical foundation of this study, an experimental comparative approach will be introduced. A total of 20 participants will be recruited for the study. They will be divided into two equal groups: 10 participants will engage with the proposed gamified airport platform, while the other 10 participants (control group) will participate in a non-travel-related digital activity, such as a generic online quiz or mobile game unrelated to tourism. The comparison between these groups will assess the impact of gamification on perceived waiting time, engagement levels, and overall satisfaction. Interviews and observational data will be collected from both groups to evaluate differences in user experience, engagement, and time perception, providing a robust empirical basis for assessing the effectiveness of the gamification approach.

Participants will be selected from students at Deggendorf Institute of Technology, particularly those studying International Tourism Development and related fields. Recruitment take place through direct invitations in group discussions. Selection criteria will include students who have travelled through airports in the past six months and are familiar with the experience of waiting during layovers or security procedures. This approach ensures that participants have relevant travel experience while making recruitment practical and accessible. By using university students, the study benefits from a controlled environment where participation can be monitored effectively, and responses can be collected in an organized manner.

The iterative nature of the Design Thinking approach allows for continuous refinement of the gamified model based on user interactions, ensuring that the final solution aligns with passenger expectations. This structured approach facilitates the seamless integration of game mechanics within the airport setting, enhancing engagement while maintaining ease of accessibility for diverse traveller demographics (Stickdorn et al., 2018). By focusing on interactive and reward-driven experiences, the model is designed to minimize passenger frustration and create a more engaging waiting period.

Additionally, the Service Blueprint ensures that the gamified platform operates effectively within the airport ecosystem by mapping out user interactions with different touchpoints. This structured framework enables the identification of potential barriers to engagement, allowing for strategic improvements to maximize passenger participation. Aligning these interactions with the digital interface ensures a smooth transition between traditional airport experiences and interactive gaming elements (Stickdorn & Schneider, 2012).

The gamification model is designed to integrate with existing airport infrastructure, providing a scalable and adaptable engagement solution. By leveraging digital innovation, the study highlights the potential for gamification to be expanded into other transit environments beyond airports, offering a flexible framework that can be modified to suit various travel-related contexts. The structured development and refinement process ensures that the final design is both practical and engaging, with the potential to be adopted by different stakeholders within the tourism and aviation sectors (Bari, C. S., & Vijaykumar, S. 2020). Ethical considerations are central to the research process, ensuring that the gamified solution respects participant privacy and adheres to relevant data protection regulations. The study emphasizes responsible digital engagement, aligning with global best practices in technology-driven tourism solutions. The iterative approach further supports ethical usability by continuously refining the design based on real-time feedback, ensuring inclusivity and accessibility for all participants (Ihamäki & Heljakka, 2020).

4. FINDINGS

This research applies the Design Thinking approach to develop a gamified solution for airport waiting times, focusing on enhancing passenger engagement through interactive and rewarding experiences. Design Thinking is a user-centered, iterative process that facilitates innovative problem-solving by aligning solutions with user needs and behaviours (Gonen, 2019). It provides a structured framework consisting of five key phases: Empathize, Define, Ideate, Prototype, and Test, which were systematically applied in this study to create and evaluate the gamification model. To analyse the results, we report numerical data using the Mean (M) and Standard Deviation (SD). The Mean (M) represents the average value of a dataset, while the Standard Deviation (SD) indicates how much the values vary from the average. A smaller SD means that most participants had similar responses, whereas a larger SD shows greater variation among responses.t-statistic (t) used in a t-test, which compares two groups (e.g., gamification vs. control). A higher t-value means the difference between the groups is more significant. If $p < 0.05$, it means the result is statistically significant and not due to random chance.

4.1 Empathize

Understanding passenger experiences and behaviours during airport waiting times was a critical step in the research. Previous studies indicate that travellers often experience boredom, time distortion, and frustration, negatively impacting their travel experience (Wittmann & Paulus, 2008; Horner & Swarbrooke, 2020). To quantify this, structured interviews were conducted with 20 participants, all of whom had travelled through airports in the past six months. Using insights from structured discussions and participant interviews, a Customer Journey Map (CJM) was developed to visualize key touchpoints, pain points, and opportunities. Through thematic analysis, recurring patterns in passenger behaviours were identified, highlighting excessive mobile phone usage for passive entertainment, lack of engaging activities, and a desire for interactive yet easy-to-access experiences. Behavioural analysis revealed that 65% of participants preferred mobile-based interactive content, and engagement metrics indicated that interactive tasks increased the perceived speed of waiting time by 36% on average. By mapping the passenger journey, specific intervention points for gamification were identified, ensuring a more immersive and rewarding waiting experience. This phase provided a data-driven foundation for the Define and Ideate phases, ensuring that the gamification platform was designed to provide an engaging and seamless experience.

4.2 Define and Ideate

The Define phase synthesized insights from the Empathize stage to establish key challenges, including a lack of engaging activities, passive waiting experiences, and limited interactive options. The problem statement identified was: "Passengers often experience unproductive waiting times, relying on passive entertainment such as mobile phone browsing. This lack of interactive engagement negatively affects their perception of waiting time and overall airport experience. "Building on these insights, the Ideate phase explored potential solutions. A structured brainstorming session was conducted as part of the Design Thinking process, where participants, including tourism experts, provided input on the gamification model. This process helped co-create the core game mechanics, ensuring the design was aligned with user preferences.

The brainstorming session led to the conceptualization of a web-based gamification platform, accessible via QR codes on boarding passes. The platform features a dual-phase quiz system: an initial quiz about the passenger's travel destination to create engagement, followed by a deeper challenge-based quiz with questions about history, geography, and cultural aspects (Ihamäki & Heljakka, 2020). Participants earn rewards such as discount coupons for airport stores and priority check-in perks. The Customer Journey Map played a crucial role in this phase by highlighting user pain points, such as difficulty in accessing engaging content and limited awareness of interactive options. To ensure smooth implementation, a Service Blueprint (Fig. 2) was designed to map interactions between passengers, the digital platform, and airport services, optimizing the user experience (Stickdorn & Schneider, 2012).

4.3 Prototype

A website prototype was developed as the primary gamified engagement platform. Designed for seamless navigation and easy accessibility from mobile devices, the prototype was accessible via QR codes printed on boarding passes, allowing passengers to engage with the system without requiring app downloads. The platform incorporated a multi-phase quiz tailored to the passenger's travel destination, a reward system where participants earn badges or collect stamps to redeem for airport-related perks such as discounts and fast check-in, an interactive leaderboard displaying top scorers to encourage competitive participation, and a user-friendly interface optimized for mobile accessibility. The game was structured to be completed within 10–15 minutes, making it suitable for short to moderate waiting times. Additionally, rewards such as discount coupons for airport shops and fast check-in options were proposed to enhance user participation (Bari, C. S., & Vijaykumar, S. 2020).

To assess usability and engagement levels quantitatively, participants (N=20) were divided into two groups: 10 engaging with the gamified platform and 10 participating in a non-travel-related digital activity. Statistical analysis revealed that 80% of the gamification group reported feeling more engaged (M = 4.3/5 on a Likert scale, SD = 0.8), while only 40% in the control group reported a similar experience (M = 2.8/5, SD = 1.2). Additionally, a paired t-test showed a significant difference in perceived waiting time ($t(18) = 2.97, p < 0.05$), with the gamification group perceiving the wait time as significantly shorter (M = 12.1 minutes, SD = 3.5) compared to the control group (M = 17.8 minutes, SD = 5.2).The gamification prototype was developed specifically for this research using a web-based interactive model created on Canva tool. Unlike existing models discussed in the literature, this prototype was tested with actual participants to gather real-time usability feedback.

4.4 Testing

An image prototype of a website was analysed by travellers to evaluate its usability and design concept. Participants reviewed the prototype's structure and navigation flow, beginning with a log-in or sign-in page. The design included a narrator-guided onboarding process, where users would hypothetically enter their name and age before selecting a country, either their current destination or another location, leading them to Level 1. In Level 1, participants examined the leaderboard layout and the proposed system for tracking earnings and losses. The prototype demonstrated that after completing a mission and earning badges, users would theoretically progress to Level 2, which featured more challenging quiz questions. Additionally, the settings menu was reviewed, which included options such as home, help, feedback, sound adjustments, notifications, and exit functionality.

Service Blueprint

Physical Evidence	Initial Contact & Exploration	Request	Identification	Interaction	Engagement	Incentive	Date collection	Feedback Collection
Customer Actions	Scan QR code from boarding pass		Login/Register to track progress	Game Interaction	leader board	Reward System		Provide Feedback
Front of Stage Interactions	QR redirects to the game interface		Passenger scans QR and accesses the platform	Passenger plays the quiz game	Passenger earns stamps and rewards		Passenger views summary of rewards and experience	
Back of Stage Interactions	QR code printed on boarding pass	Website backend processes request		Quiz algorithm delivers personalised questions	System updates leaderboard with passenger scores	System verifies eligibility for rewards and updates the user profile	Data collected for service improvement	
Support Processes	Airline includes QR code on passes	Web hosting and database management		Game logic and content management		Reward partnerships with businesses	Automated insights for business improvement	Customer support and feedback handling

Fig. 2. Proposed Service Blueprint (https://tinyurl.com/bdesywe4)

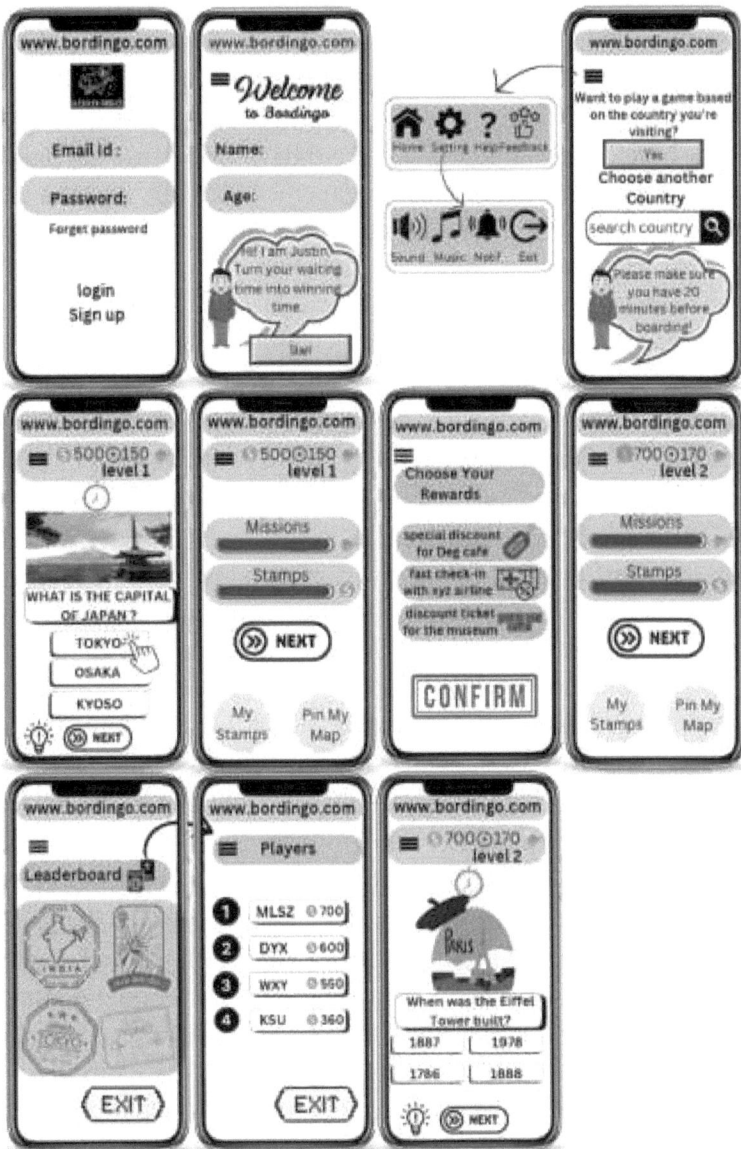

Fig. 3. Prototype – Bordingo Website (https://tinyurl.com/2ns9f5nv)

Participants analysed the quiz format and leaderboard concept, finding them engaging in theory. Based on a quantitative engagement assessment, responses were collected using a 5-point Likert scale, where the gamification group showed significantly higher engagement levels (M = 4.5, SD = 0.7) compared to the control group (M = 2.9, SD = 1.1). A Mann-Whitney U test confirmed a statistically significant difference between groups (U = 17, p < 0.01), supporting the hypothesis that gamification enhances user engagement during waiting periods. The reward system initially assigned rewards at random, allowing participants to redeem badges for coupons that could be used with partnered stakeholders. However, based on participant feedback, the system was adjusted to allow users to choose their preferred rewards, making the experience more personalized and appealing. The competitive aspect was recognized as a key feature, contributing to a more interactive and engaging experience (Stickdorn et al., 2018).

To evaluate the effectiveness of the gamification model, a usability test and experimental comparative study were conducted. The 20 participants were divided into two equal groups, with 10 participants interacting with the prototype of the proposed gamified airport platform, while the remaining 10 participants in the control group engaged in a non-travel-related digital activity, such as a mobile game. Participants were selected from students at Deggendorf Institute of Technology, with a focus on those who had travelled through the airport at least once in the past six months. Recruitment was conducted through direct invitations during group discussions.

Data was collected through pre- and post-engagement interviews and real-time usability feedback to assess engagement levels, perceived waiting time, and overall user satisfaction. Due to logistical constraints, usability testing was conducted in a controlled environment simulating airport conditions. Participants were asked to engage with the prototype in a setting where they were asked to recollect their airport waiting experience, with real-time engagement metrics recorded.

The key metrics evaluated included:

- Perceived waiting time reduction

- User engagement levels (measured using a Likert scale from 1-5)
- Ease of navigation and user satisfaction

The insights from the study were incorporated into the next iteration of the prototype, ensuring greater user autonomy in reward selection and a clearer progression tracking system through stamps. The prototype was developed using the Canva website, ensuring a visually appealing and user-friendly interface while maintaining ease of accessibility for passengers.

5. DISCUSSION

Technology-based solutions are essential in modern tourism as they offer seamless and interactive experiences to travellers, improve accessibility, and enhance overall engagement. Digital platforms, such as mobile applications and gamification techniques, allow tourists to engage with their surroundings more effectively, making their overall travel experience more enjoyable. In an era where digital interactions dominate, integrating technology into tourism services ensures real-time updates, personalized experiences, and increased engagement for travellers (Kottur, S. V., 2022). The application of the Design Thinking approach in this research provided a structured methodology to develop a gamified solution aimed at enhancing passenger engagement during airport waiting times. By focusing on user experience, interactivity, and reward-based engagement, the study successfully addressed key challenges associated with boredom, time distortion, and lack of engaging activities in airport environments (Gonen, E., 2019). The iterative process of Empathize, Define, Ideate, Prototype, and Test ensured that the final solution was aligned with passenger needs and behavioural insights, offering an accessible and enjoyable gamified experience via QR codes on boarding passes. Findings from the Empathize phase confirmed that boredom and time distortion significantly impact the passenger experience. Prior studies indicate that passive waiting leads to negative perceptions of time, increasing frustration and disengagement (Wittmann & Paulus, 2008). The research findings reinforced these perspectives, as passengers expressed a strong preference for interactive activities that could provide entertainment and knowledge-based engagement (Horner, S., & Swarbrooke, J. 2020). Insights from interviews revealed that travellers desire simple yet rewarding experiences that integrate seamlessly into their existing routines, necessitating a gamified solution that is easily accessible without requiring additional downloads or setup.

The Define and Ideate phases facilitated the transformation of these insights into a structured gamification model. The findings emphasized that a digital solution linked to boarding passes via QR codes would be an effective way to engage travellers. Previous research supports the use of digital gamification techniques in transit environments, highlighting their potential to enhance user experience and sustain engagement (Ihamäki & Heljakka, 2020). The research adopted a dual-phase quiz format, which aligns with best practices in cognitive engagement and motivation theory, ensuring that participants remain engaged while acquiring valuable knowledge about their travel destinations. The Service Blueprint played a crucial role in mapping interactions between passengers, the gamified platform, and airport services, optimizing the usability and accessibility of the proposed system (Stickdorn & Schneider, 2012).The Prototype phase resulted in the development of a website-based gamified platform, featuring a QR code entry system, destination-based quiz challenges, a reward system with collectible stamps, and an interactive leaderboard. These mechanics align with established principles of game-based motivation, where users are more likely to engage when progression, achievement, and competition are incorporated into the experience (Kottur, S. V., 2022). The structured design ensured seamless navigation, addressing accessibility concerns by making the platform mobile-friendly and inclusive for all passengers.

The Testing phase highlighted several critical insights that led to modifications in the final prototype. Initially, participants found the random reward assignment system limiting, preferring a structure that grants users greater control over reward selection. Based on this, the reward selection system was updated to offer users choices, allowing them to redeem earned stamps for discounts, fast check-in privileges, and other incentives. Research supports the idea that personalized rewards enhance motivation and increase long-term user engagement (Stickdorn et al., 2018). The modifications made during prototype testing—including the introduction of a personalized reward selection system and replacing badges with stamps for better clarity—highlight the importance of iterative refinement in gamified design (Stickdorn & Schneider, 2012). These changes enhanced user motivation, engagement levels, and reward system transparency, aligning with best practices in game-based experience design (Stickdorn et al., 2018). The research further validated that gamification can significantly improve passengers' perception of waiting times, making their airport experience more enjoyable and productive (Wittmann & Paulus, 2008). Beyond individual passenger engagement, the study findings indicate potential commercial benefits for airports and airlines. Integrating gamification into airport services could drive increased participation in retail experiences, loyalty programs, and tourism promotions, fostering partnerships between airport stakeholders and digital service providers (Hamari et al., 2014). Gamified platforms can encourage travellers to explore airport retail stores or food services by linking rewards to discounts, increasing revenue generation for airports and associated businesses. Additionally, such platforms could enhance airline loyalty programs by integrating frequent flyer points as a form of in-game rewards, thereby increasing long-term passenger retention (Stickdorn et al., 2018).

Moreover, gamification has the potential to address accessibility challenges within airport environments. Interactive, multilingual quiz formats could serve as an educational tool for international travellers unfamiliar with their destinations, providing valuable insights about local customs, safety tips, and transportation options (Ihamäki & Heljakka, 2020). This aligns with studies on the importance of information accessibility in transit environments, particularly for non-native speakers and first-time travellers who may struggle with traditional airport signage and announcements (Kottur, S. V., 2022). By incorporating accessibility-focused features, the gamified platform could cater to a broader demographic, including families, elderly travellers, and individuals with cognitive disabilities, ensuring a more inclusive airport experience. Overall, the findings support the idea that gamification is an effective tool for transforming waiting periods into engaging and rewarding experiences. Previous research has demonstrated that interactive and reward-based systems positively impact user perception of time, reducing boredom in travel environments (Hamari et al., 2014). This study further validates that digitally integrated gamification models, when designed using user-centric methodologies such as Design Thinking, can successfully enhance airport experiences.

6. CONCLUSION

This research empirically validated that gamification enhances passenger engagement and alters perceived waiting time in airport environments. The study involved an experimental comparison with 20 participants, where one group interacted with the gamified system while the control group engaged in a non-travel-related activity. Empirical findings demonstrated that participants in the gamification group reported significantly higher engagement scores (M = 4.3, SD = 0.8) compared to the control group (M = 2.8, SD = 1.2). Statistical testing (Mann-Whitney U = 17, $p < 0.01$) confirmed that the difference was significant. Additionally, users of the gamified system perceived their waiting time as significantly shorter (M = 12.1 minutes, SD = 3.5) compared to the control group (M = 17.8 minutes, SD = 5.2), as validated by a paired t-test (t (18) = 2.97, $p < 0.05$).

Qualitative feedback from post-engagement interviews further reinforced these findings, with 80% of gamification users reporting that they found the system engaging and would be likely to use similar interactive features in future airport experiences. Additionally, 75% of gamification users expressed a preference for airports offering interactive engagement services over those without them. While these results suggest a positive user experience, future research should explore how gamification influences passenger satisfaction and stress reduction, as these aspects were not directly measured in this study. By leveraging behavioural insights, digital innovation, and game mechanics, this research contributes to the broader discourse on experience-driven service design in modern tourism. The findings highlight the potential for gamified solutions to be adopted more widely across airport settings, offering entertainment, education, and enhanced user engagement during waiting periods. The integration of gamification in transit environments also presents commercial opportunities for airports, airlines, and retail stakeholders, allowing them to engage travellers through loyalty programs and in-terminal promotions.

Future research could build upon these findings by exploring larger-scale implementations, AI-driven personalization, and the integration of augmented reality (AR) to enhance immersion and interactivity. Additionally, testing the platform across different airports and passenger demographics would provide further insights into scalability and cross-cultural engagement. Understanding psychological and behavioural responses to gamified engagement would also contribute to improving future designs, ensuring that interactive airport experiences remain engaging, inclusive, and adaptable to evolving passenger needs. By addressing these areas, future research can expand on the effectiveness of gamification in airport settings, ensuring its continued development as an innovative digital engagement solution.

REFERENCES

Blichfeldt, B. S., Pumputis, A., & Ebba, K. (2017). Using, spending, wasting and killing time in airports. International Journal of Culture, Tourism and Hospitality Research, 11(3), 392–405. https://doi.org/10.1108/IJCTHR-05-2016-0045

Gonen, E. (2019). Tim Brown, Change by Design: How Design Thinking Transforms Organizations and Inspires Innovation (2009). Markets,

Globalization & Development Review, 4(2), Article 8. https://doi.org/10.23860/MGDR-2019-04-02-08

Hamari, J., Koivisto, J., & Sarsa, H. (2014). Does gamification work? A literature review of empirical studies on gamification. Proceedings of the 47th Hawaii International Conference on System Sciences (HICSS-47), 3025-3034. https://doi.org/10.1109/HICSS.2014.377

Hernandez Bueno, A. V. (2021). Becoming a passenger: Exploring the situational passenger experience and airport design in the Copenhagen Airport. Mobilities, 16(3), 440–459. https://doi.org/10.1080/17450101.2021.1873568

Horner, S., & Swarbrooke, J. (2020). Consumer behaviour in tourism (4th ed.). Routledge. https://doi.org/10.4324/9781003046721

Ihamäki, P., & Heljakka, K. (2020). Co-creating gamified service design - Case: Gamified airport security workshop. 21st International Conference on Intelligent Systems Design and Applications (ISDA). https://tinyurl.com/54cxsn4b

Bari, C. S., & Vijaykumar, S. (2020). Next generation user experience using design thinking. Studies in Indian Place Names, 40(68), 492-501. Retrieved from https://tinyurl.com/ycy7dtms

Krippendorff, K. (2005). The semantic turn: A new foundation for design. CRC Press.

Stickdorn, M., & Schneider, J. (2012). This is service design thinking: Basics, tools, cases. BIS Publishers.

Stickdorn, M., Hormess, M. E., Lawrence, A., & Schneider, J. (2018). This is service design doing: Applying service design thinking in the real world. O'Reilly Media.

Wittmann, M., & Paulus, M. P. (2008). Decision making, impulsivity and time perception. Trends in Cognitive Sciences, 12(1), 7-12. https://doi.org/10.1016/j.tics.2007.10.004

APPENDIX

Appendix 1. Proposed Service Blueprint link: https://tinyurl.com/bdesywe4

Appendix 2. Prototype – Bordingo Website link: https://tinyurl.com/2ns9f5nv

Exploring the application of Open Data in tourism with a focus on small and medium hotels in Salzburg

Magdalena Aigner, Irina Boyko, Annalena Haßdorf, Markus Huber
Salzburg University of Applied Sciences
maigner.imte-m2023@fh-salzburg.ac.at, iboyko.imte-m2023@fh-salzburg.ac.at, ahaßdorf.imte-m2023@fh-salzburg.ac.at, mhuber.imte-m2023@fh-salzburg.ac.at,

Abstract

Open data, which is data accessible to the public free of charge, is a prominent topic in tourism and applied in various cases by now, however mainly focusing on the traveller's perspective and marketing purposes. Despite the topic being discussed in tourism in general, there is comparably little research conducted regarding open data in the accommodation sector, especially small and medium entities. Hence, this paper provides insights to the current and potential usage of open data in the hospitality industry with special focus on small and medium hotels in Salzburg, Austria. Semi-structured interviews with experts from the hospitality industry within Salzburg are conducted to better understand the current status and potential applications. The results suggest that open data has potential within the tourism industry nevertheless meaningful integration into the hospitality industry is limited. Yield management as well as predicting tourists' behaviour appear to be promising use cases for open data for small and medium hotels. The challenges identified during the research direct the attention especially to data protection and privacy as well as competition. Further research hence should focus on ways to tackle these issues.

Keywords: Open Data; Hospitality; Salzburg; Innovation; Tourism

1. INTRODUCTION

The digitalisation in the past years undoubtedly influenced the Tourism industry tremendously on different levels (Dredge et al., 2018; Happ and Ivancsó-Horváth, 2018; Rodrigues et al., 2023). The disruption ranges from applications of augmented and virtual reality, artificial intelligence, digital processes to open data and much more. When it comes to the application of smart tourism solutions, it is essential to integrate those diverse tools into an efficient and well-working smart tourism ecosystem (Iványi, 2021). A major advantage of digitalisation and modern technologies is the enhancement of the tourism experience especially in terms of interaction (Rodrigues et al., 2023). Open data, which will be the central focus of this research, in general can be described as data accessible to the public free of charge (Murray-Rust, 2008).

Open data per se is no new topic in research, however these studies focus rather on social media and tourism responsiveness (Pantano et al., 2017) or destination marketing and management (Celdran-Bernabeu et al., 2018). Since the supply chain perspective was yet not widely considered, this paper focuses on the specific case of hospitality entities in order to investigate possible and current use cases. The focus on Salzburg (Austria) and independent, small and medium enterprises was chosen, since entities experiencing similar circumstances positively influence the level of comparability and comprehension of the gathered data.

This is the reasoning why this paper aims to investigate how open data can be integrated meaningfully and efficiently into the accommodation sector by looking precisely on its current and potential use cases. The research questions proposed by this paper are: What are meaningful use cases of open data in the tourism industry and, furthermore, what are potential and existing use cases of open data in the hospitality industry with the focus on small and medium sized hotels in Salzburg, Austria. Answering these research questions will improve the current knowledge of existing use cases of open data in the tourism industry. Furthermore, since there is little research about usage of open data in hospitality, the second research question will assist in creating a basis for this research topic and further studies. All in all, the research aims to describe the current status quo of open data knowledge and open data potential in the tourism industry and especially the hospitality industry.

The paper consists of a thorough literature review where the various use cases of open data are reviewed as well as insights to the hospitality industry are presented. The methodology consists of firstly conducted secondary literature succeeded by semi-structured interviews as a qualitative method.

2. LITERATURE REVIEW

2.1 Introduction to Open Data

Open data in a scientific context can be translated as data accessible to the public without costs (Murray-Rust, 2008). However, this data type is also often mentioned in the context of political or economic topics (Barry and Bannister, 2014; Borgesius et al., 2015) and likewise refers to data from diverse disciplines and industries (Kitchin, 2014). Besides increasing the aspect of transparency (Braunschweig et al., 2012), one idea behind the introduction of open data was combating the difficult accessibility of data to the wide public without the necessity of special systems or skills which also benefits the right of information (Kitchin, 2014). Nevertheless, this development is not regarded as purely positive, as criticism about open data include data privacy matters (Kostkova et al., 2016) which became especially prominent during the Covid-19 pandemic and was tried to be combated by anonymising the data (Moraes et al., 2021). Despite the concerns, research sees a huge potential in the usage of open data in connection with creating and developing innovations and decision-making processes (Wieczorkowski, 2019). In general, it is essential to recognize the great diversity of open data, which makes it difficult to pose general assumptions about possible impacts of the data type (Janssen et al., 2012). Hence, it is important to investigate the usage of open data in tourism in precise detail to be able to add on to the current state of the research, which will be initiated in the following sub-chapters.

2.2 Use cases of Open Data

Open data is already used successfully in various parts of the tourism industries (Ocampo and Palaoag, 2019) but the extent and approaches vary tremendously, which is also reflected in the number of research published in the different fields. In the following, various examples are provided to enable an overview of the current state of open data integration in tourism.

2.2.1 Destination Management Organizations

In research, several use cases have been published where open data is provided or used by destination management organizations. Some examples of Ocampo and Palaoag (2019) are the use of geographic data by Czech Tourism, the use of visitor statistics by the Walsh government website and the use of supply information by Booking.com. Open data can also be used to analyse the movement of tourists via open GPS trajectory data (Liu et al., 2022; Qian et al., 2020). Regarding smart cities, open data plays an important role which also effects tourism in these cities (Alawadhi et al., 2012). In their research of 18 open data initiatives across five smart cities, Ojo et al. (2015) investigated a link to tourism through guiding apps in Amsterdam and Helsinki which offer co-created services that focus on needs of the stakeholders, leading to an improved tourist journey and authentic destination experience.

The example of Siegen-Wittgenstein suggests that the government uses open data to create frameworks and guidelines combining technological with individual and organizational interfaces to strengthen the sense of security and trust in data for the supply and demand side (German National Tourist Board, 2019). Similarly, the Open Data Tourism Alliance (ODTA) continues the approach of unifying and providing framework conditions by introducing common technical norms and standards for tourism information in 2023 and adopting the standardization of semantic data models for tourism information based on the schema.org standard (Österreich Werbung, 2023).

2.2.2 Hospitality/Restaurants

Lo Duca and Marchetti (2019) highlight a use-case of open data in hospitality through Tourpedia. Initially based on social media, it expanded to open data, creating a single access point for accommodation data in specific countries, benefiting both tourists and industry stakeholders. Hung et al. (2020) show how linked open data was used in Vietnam to develop a tourist service support system, including an interactive map. Wu et al. (2014) describe an application using open data in Taiwan that promotes local businesses through a serious game. Al-Ghossein et al. (2018) demonstrate how open data enhances hotel recommender systems using event information which not only leads to an enhanced quality of suggestions but also enables hotels to enhance their marketing strategies based on the aimed target group and their events of interest.

2.2.3 Transportation

The applications of open data in transportation varies and includes the usage of it to forecast the punctuality of buses (Balbin et al., 2020) or the prediction of train ticket prices using Google Trends (Stavinova et al., 2021). Furthermore, Bourgois and Sfyroeras (2014) analysed open data research for air transport. FlightRadar24 is an example of using open data from non-official sources and refers to data which normally is not accessible to the public. Benefits can be created with the publication of data, as it was the case with the Transport of London (Stone and Aravopoulou, 2018).

2.2.4 Other

In the context of South African tourism, open data can have a positive impact on the development of the socio-economic environment. This is possible because of the innovative, marketing and efficiency effects stemming from the use of open data (Bala et al., 2023). Also, for tours, open data can add extra value, as the study of Siddabasappa et al. (2022) shows, in which a smart museum tour was developed.

Important data are also collected and published by federal ministries to provide travellers with the most important general information about the destinations to be visited (Bundesministerium Europäische und internationale Angelegenheiten, 2024). Open data can also be an assisting tool in predicting tourist behaviour (Pantano et al., 2017) and optimization of inventory based on forecasted visitor numbers gathered through for instance flight bookings or search trends (Carpenter, 2023). Analysis of open data can help in identifying upcoming trend destinations with the help of photographic activities in the city (Giglio et al., 2019).

There are also existing European and national initiatives that are supported by governments focusing on open data of the accommodation and hospitality sector, among others. The Tourism Data Space provides a digital environment for secure and seamless data exchange among stakeholders within the Austrian tourism industry. It aims to increase innovative approaches, improve customer experiences, and facilitate sustainable tourism by collective data sharing. Therefore, a mixture of publicly accessible open data as well as specific data which has been conducted by participating organizations is being provided for active participants (Tourism Data Space, 2024).

In France, the national open data platform DATAtourisme collects and distributes tourism data from various destinations across the country. This initiative is supported by the French government and regional tourism stakeholders to particularly improve the visibility of regional tourism offerings (DATAtourisme, 2024). A similar approach is followed by the Swiss Tourism Data Beta which provides a centralized platform on a broad variety of tourism-related datasets such as accommodations, traffic and mobility, points of interest, routes, research, and user-generated content (Tourismdata.ch, 2024).

3. METHODOLOGY

The first part of this research included a thorough literature review to understand the current status of the research in regard to open data. To achieve the best result for the goals, the authors add on to the previously conducted secondary research with a primary, qualitative research, by interviewing small and medium-sized hotels in Salzburg. Due to the nature of semi-structured interviews (Veal 2018), detailed insights into attitudes and perceptions of the various respondents could be gathered, which are valuable for this descriptive research, in order to understand this relatively new topic better. The interview-guideline contains three major parts: The understanding of Open Data, the use cases of Open Data and the attitude towards Open Data. While the first part was important to create a common understanding of the topic, the other two parts focused on the knowledge and the ideas of the managers.

The sampling of the respondents consists of a mixture of convenience as well as criterion sampling. The essential criteria are that the respondents work at a small or medium hospitality entity (up to 250 employees) in the federal state of Salzburg and have founded knowledge in the industry and the precise operation of their business. All of the considered hotels were independent (no chain) and family owned. The rooms ranged from 15 to 111 and number of employees between 2 and 110 employees. The interviewees are referred to as R1 to R6.

4. RESULTS AND DISCUSSION

The six considered interviews, elaborated in the following sections, enabled the authors to gain an overview of general attitudes, possible applications of open data within small and medium hotels in the federal state of Salzburg.

4.1 Attitude Towards Open Data

Initially it was essential to identify the current knowledge and awareness of "Open Data" and the results suggested there to be some lack (R2, R3, R5, R6) or only a broad idea of this subject (R1, R4, R6). The initial attitude varied from positive (R1, R3) to neutral (R4-6), as well as defining it as a complicated topic (R2). After elaborating possible touchpoints, possible enhancements for the tourism industry were identified (R1, R3, R5) with mentioned concerns about data protection and its impact on competition (R2, R4, R6). One hotel already had relevant experience with Statistik Austria (R5). Overall, it shows, that there is little knowledge about the topic of open data, and it is not regarded as purely positive as concerns about data protection were raised, aligning with the findings of Kostkova et al. (2016).

4.2 Touchpoints with Open Data

Despite the little knowledge about the topic, the respondents provided several ideas about possible open data touchpoints. Similarly to the findings by Ocampo and Palaoag (2019), stating the use of statistics as a common application of open data in tourism, also use of specific data (e.g.: overnight stays) by the respondents was identified (R2, R4) and the need to provide this data to the municipality (e.g.: monthly disclosure of guest nationalities) (R2, R5, R6). There is also the scenario of being obliged by Statistik Austria to deliver specific data concerning room rates and open job positions (R5). Further touchpoints are programs used for yield management (R1) and revenue management (R3). Also, DMO's were mentioned regarding possible touchpoints as they provide an App for a region (R2) and use mobile data to monitor visitor flows (R1). Furthermore, review platforms (R4-6) and pre-stay messages (R3) are current touchpoints. Review platforms such as TripAdvisor, booking.com and Google Reviews were mentioned for service optimisation (R4, R6). Generally, the respondents provided several touchpoints with open data, many which are connected to public institutions.

4.3. Integration of Open Data

The respondents provided arguments both for and against the integration of open data. While market observation (R1, R4), creation of targeted offers (R3, R4), creation of meaningful statistics (R5) and optimization of prices and occupancy (R1, R3) where mentioned as reasons for the integration of open data, the size of the company and the non-existing need (R1, R2, R4), average high occupancy (R2, R4) or gathering of essential data internally (R4), were mentioned as reasons against the integration of open data.

The openness to share company data varies among the respondents. Reasons against sharing data are connected to concerns about its impacts on competition (R5, R6) and privacy concerns especially regarding hotel own investments (R2, R4). The willingness to share data increases if compliance with data protection regulations is guaranteed (R1, R3) as well as anonymity (R6), aligning with Moraes et al. (2021).

4.3.1. Responsible for the implementation of open data

Respondents noted that tourism associations can facilitate data collection and provide it to local businesses (R1), and if the tourism association leads this development (R5), it will help create a unified approach and stimulate others to join the initiative. On the other hand, the opinion was expressed (R3) that responsibility may also lie with hotel owners or other organizations, who already have access to relevant data, such as guest registration information.

4.3.2. Perceived challenges and concerns of using open data

Besides data protection as a perceived challenge of open data (R1-6), aligning with the findings of Kostkova et al. (2016), concerns regarding the process to collect and gather the data (R5) due to technical requirements (R3) or based on the fear of annoying guests (R1) need to be considered. Furthermore, a different extent of willingness to which companies would share their data could lead to a challenging implementation (R2, R3). Additional concerns were addressed regarding the competitive advantage by sharing data transparently in terms of pricing structures or occupancy rates (R4, R6) as well as potential threats of manipulation of data (R2) and legal problems (R3). Potential issues were also identified in the high effort for hotels and the fear of false promises in the value and implementation (R1), additional expenses of open data for actual usefulness (R2) as well as the damage of reputation due to freely accessible reviews (R5).

4.3.3. Perceived advantages of open data

There are various potential meaningful integrations of open data into hospitality entities including improvement of marketing strategies based on search trends (R1). Furthermore, online reviews are an efficient tool for service optimization, as it allows insights into customers perceptions and opinions, which is sometimes difficult to gather otherwise (R4). Benefits of implementing open data can be the improved understanding of guests' behaviour (R3, R4) based on statistics and reviews, supporting the findings of Pantano et al. (2017) regarding the possible access of tourist's reaction and behaviour on certain offers. The tools like "tourist cards" can help to analyse tourist interests and create personalized offers (R4). The use of open data can enable targeted marketing, such as identifying key tourist groups and sending them personalized newsletters (R3). Furthermore, open data can add value to yield management, by using a Yield Management Software for better price management (R1).

4.4. Other new technologies in hotels

It is further important to consider general reasons for implementing new technologies into companies to understand the motivations, as this can be an indicator of possible fields, open data can be useful for in the industry. The saving of time and costs (R4, R5) is an important motivator, aligning with Pantano et al. (2017) stating that technological implementations in hospitality often focus on improving operational efficiency and customer satisfaction. However, concerns around return on investment and reliance on external support for successful implementation emphasize the practical challenges and the complexity of integrating these solutions, as noted by Ocampo and Palaoag (2019). There are diverse sources for learning about new technologies such as workshops, further education, industry associations, attended events, trade journals (R1, R3, R4). Otherwise, one can also rely on input from employees, particularly those with prior experience in other hotels or gathered ideas from family members (R3, R4). External consulting firms were also seen as a source of guidance (R6). The reliance on diverse sources also supports the argument by Kostkova et al. (2016)

regarding the necessity of continuous education and networking to adapt to rapidly evolving technological landscapes.

5. CONCLUSION

The aim of this research was to identify current applications of open data in tourism and to explore possible and current applications of open data at small and medium hotels in the federal state of Salzburg, Austria. The literature review showed that there is a variety of open data use cases in tourism often connected to statistics and used for forecasts and analysis of for example tourism flows. The results of the interviews suggest that there seems to be only limited need for open data implementations at small and medium hotels due to their size. Furthermore, concerns regarding data protection and developments of the competition were raised making it a critical and complex topic for hoteliers. Nevertheless, potentials for usage of open data in connection with yield management or the prediction of tourist behaviour could be identified. It might be further beneficial if tourism organisations or other bigger players of the industry promote a united approach to this topic, facilitating the application in small and medium hotels. Since major motivators for implementing technologies at the hotels appear to be efficiency and cost and time savings, solutions in that regard should be explored. The limitation of this research is the representativeness due to the number of interviews. Hence, this topic can be further elaborated by conducting more interviews as well as adding a quantitative part. As concerns regarding data protection and competition were raised, further research should deal with exploring possible countermeasures.

REFERENCES

Alawadhi, S., Aldama-Nalda, A., Chourabi, H., Gil-Garcia, J. R., Leung, S., Mellouli, S., Nam, T., Pardo, T. A., Scholl, H. J. and Walker, S., 2012. Building Understanding of Smart City Initiatives. In H. J. Scholl (Ed.), Lecture notes in computer science: Vol. 7443, Electronic Government: 11th IFIP WG 8.5 International Conference : Proceedings (pp. 40–53). Springer.

Al-Ghossein, M., Abdessalem, T. and Barré, A., 2018. Open data in the hotel industry: leveraging forthcoming events for hotel recommendation. Information Technology & Tourism, 20(1–4), 191–216.

Bala, S., Van Biljon, J. and Herselman, M., 2023. Open Data Accessibility Mechanisms for Tourism Development in South Africa. In Communications in computer and information science (S. 118–132).

Balbin, P. P. F., Barker, J. C., Leung, C. K., Tran, M., Wall, R. P. and Cuzzocrea, A., 2020. Predictive analytics on open big data for supporting smart transportation ser-vices. Procedia Computer Science, 176, 3009–3018.

Barry, E. and Bannister, F., 2014. Barriers to open data release: A view from the top. Information Polity, 19(1-2), 129-152.

Bourgois, M. and Sfyroeras, M., 2014, August. Open data for air transport research: Dream or reality?. In Proceedings of the International Symposium on Open Collaboration (pp. 1-7).

Borgesius, F. Z., Gray, J. and Van Eechoud, M., 2015. Open data, privacy, and fair in-formation principles: Towards a balancing framework. Berkeley Technology Law Journal, 30(3), 2073-2131.

Braunschweig, K., Eberius, J., Thiele, M. and Lehner, W., 2012. The state of open da-ta. Limits of current open data platforms, 1, 72-72.

Bundesministerium Europäische und internationale Angelegenheiten., 2024. Reiseinformation. https://www.bmeia.gv.at/reise-services/reiseinformation

Carpenter, F., 2023. How Open Data and AI Can Transform Tourism Industry Deci-sion-Making | LinkedIn. https://www.linkedin.com/pulse/how-open-data-ai-can-transform-tourism-industry-franklin-carpenter-u1kye/

Celdran-Bernabeu, M. A., Mazon, J. N. and Giner Sanchez, D., 2018. Open Data and tourism. Implications for tourism management in Smart Cities and Smart Tourism Destinations.

DATAtourisme. (2024). DATAtourisme: Open data for tourism in France. https://www.datatourisme.fr

Dredge, D., Phi, G., Mahadevan, R., Meehan, E. and Popescu, E. S., 2018. Digitalisa-tion in Tourism. depth analysis of challenges and opportunities, 6.

German National Tourist Board, 2019. Open Data in Siegen-Wittgenstein - Open Data Destination Germany. https://open-data-germany.org/en/open-data-in-siegen-wittgenstein/

Giglio, S., Bertacchini, F., Bilotta, E. and Pantano, P., 2019. Using social media to identify tourism attractiveness in six Italian cities. Tourism Management, 72, 306–312.

Happ, É. and Ivancsó-Horváth, Z., 2018. Digital tourism is the challenge of future–a new approach to tourism. Knowledge Horizons. Economics, 10(2), 9-16.

Hung, H. B., Hoang, H. H. and Chien, L. V., 2020. An Approach Using Linked Data for Open Tourist Data Exploration of Thua Thien Hue Province. In Communications in computer and information science (Print) (S. 453–464).

Iványi, T., 2021. Digitalisation in the field of tourism marketing. In Proceedings of FIKUSZ Symposium for Young Researchers (pp. 58-72). Óbuda University Keleti Károly Faculty of Economics.

Janssen, M., Charalabidis, Y. and Zuiderwijk, A., 2012. Benefits, adoption barriers and myths of open data and open government. Information systems management, 29(4), 258-268.

Kitchin, R., 2014. The data revolution: Big data, open data, data infrastructures and their consequences. Sage.

Kostkova, P., Brewer, H., De Lusignan, S., Fottrell, E., Goldacre, B., Hart, G., Koczan P., Knight P., Marsolier C., McKendry R., Ross E., Sasse A., Sullivan R., Chaytor S., Stevenson O., Velho R. and Tooke, J., 2016. Who owns the data? Open data for healthcare. Frontiers in public health, 4, 7.

Liu, W., Wang, B., Yang, Y., Mou, N., Zheng, Y., Zhang, L. and Yang, T., 2022. Cluster analysis of microscopic spatio-temporal patterns of tourists' movement behaviors in mountainous scenic areas using open GPS-trajectory data. Tourism Management, 93, 104614.

Lo Duca, A. and Marchetti, A., 2019. Open data for tourism: the case of Tourpedia. Journal Of Hospitality and Tourism Technology, 10(3), 351–368.

Moraes, T. G., Lemos, A. N. L. E., Lopes, A. K., Moura, C. and de Pereira, J. R. L., 2021. Open data on the COVID-19 pandemic: anonymisation as a technical solution for transparency, privacy, and data protection. International Data Privacy Law, 11(1), 32-47.

Murray-Rust, P., 2008. Open data in science. Nature Precedings, 1-1.

Ocampo, A. J. and Palaoag, T. D., 2019. Improving tourism experience in open data environment with mobile augmented reality: needs and challenges. IOP Conference Series: Materials Science And Engineering, 482, 012005.

Ojo, A., Curry, E. and Zeleti, F. A., 2015. A Tale of Open Data Innovations in Five Smart Cities. In 2015 48th Hawaii International Conference on System Sciences. IEEE. https://doi.org/10.1109/hicss.2015.280

Österreich Werbung, 2023. Open Data Tourism Alliance (ODTA) verabschiedet zentrale Erweiterungen des schema.org-Standards für den Tourismus. https://www.austriatourism.com/newsroom/open-data-tourism-alliance-odta-verabschiedet-zentrale-erweiterungen-des-schemaorg-standards-fuer-den-tourismus/

Pantano, E., Priporas, C. V. and Stylos, N., 2017. 'You will like it!'using open data to predict tourists' response to a tourist attraction. Tourism Management, 60, 430-438.

Qian, Y., Shi, Y., Li, H., Wen, J., Xi, J. and Wang, Q., 2020. Understanding the Tourists' Spatio-Temporal Behavior Using Open GPS Trajectory Data: A Case Study of Yuanmingyuan Park (Beijing, China). Sustainability (Basel), 13(1), 94. https://doi.org/10.3390/su13010094

Resilient Tourism. (2025). Resilient Tourism: Förderung der Datenaufbereitung im Schweizer Tourismussektor. https://www.resilienttourism.ch

Rodrigues, V., Eusébio, C. and Breda, Z., 2023. Enhancing sustainable development through tourism digitalisation: a systematic literature review. Information Technology & Tourism, 25(1), 13-45.

Siddabasappa, S., Halikar, S. S., Dodda, R., Hiremath, N. and Bansal, S. K., 2022. Smart Museum Tour using Linked Open Data. BCS Learning & Development.

Stavinova, E., Chunaev, P. and Bochenina, K., 2021. Forecasting railway ticket dynam-ic price with Google Trends open data. Procedia Computer Science, 193, 333–342.

Stone, M. and Aravopoulou, E., 2018. Improving journeys by opening data: the case of Transport for London (TfL). The Bottom Line (New York, N.Y.), 31(1), 2–15.

Tourism Data Space. (2024). Tourism Data Space: Digital innovation for the travel industry. https://www.tourismdataspace.com

Tourismdata.ch. (2024). Tourismdata.ch: Swiss tourism metadata catalogue. https://www.tourismdata.ch

Veal A.J., 2018. Research methods for leisure and tourism Fifth edition. Pearson Uk

Wieczorkowski, J., 2019. Open data as a source of product and organizational innovations. In Proceedings of the 14th European Conference on Innovation and Entrepreneurship ECIE (Vol. 2, pp. 1118-1127).

Wu, C., Liu, S., Chu, C., Chu, Y. and Yu, S., 2014. A STUDY OF OPEN DATA FOR TOURISM SERVICE. Int. J. Electron. Bus. Manag., 12. https://dblp.uni-trier.de/db/journals/ijebm/ijebm12.html#WuLCCY14

Generational differences in experiences with service robots in restaurants and respective levels of technology acceptance

Authors: Kevin Iradukunda & Jit Biswa
kevinhoira@gmail.com, Jitgazmer101@gmail.com

Salzburg University of Applied Sciences

Abstract

The rapid growth of technology has substantially revolutionised the hospitality industry, with service robots emerging as an essential innovation in restaurant environments. This study explores generational differences in the technology acceptances and experiences with service robots in restaurants, specifically how different age groups perceive and interact with these robotic systems. Using empirical data obtained from restaurants & hotel customers across several demographics, the research emphasises the factors influencing customer attitudes, levels of trust, & overall acceptance of service robots. The findings show that younger generations, such as Millennials and Gen Z, are more accepting towards the use of technology and dine-in service robots and see them as refining dining experiences, whereas older generations, such as Gen X and Baby Boomers, are more sceptical towards the use of service robots, emphasising the importance of human interaction. The study enhances the expanding discussion about technology acceptance in hospitality by providing practical insights into the strategic use of service robots, which ensures a balance of robotics and personalised services. These insights can help restaurants improve customer satisfaction and operational efficiency while meeting the different needs of multigenerational customers.

Keywords: Technology Acceptance, Hospitality Automation, Service Robots in Restaurants, Generational Differences, Human Interactions, Customer Experience, Hospitality Industry.

1. INTRODUCTION

In recent years, rapid technological advancements have marked a new era in the hospitality industry, with service robots increasingly serving as a crucial innovation for customer service enhancement (*Zhang, Balaji, & Jiang, 2022*). These robotic systems are designed to perform various functions, including greeting guests, taking orders, serving meals, and processing payments, fundamentally transforming the dining experience (*Ivanov & Webster, 2023*). Service robots offer potential benefits such as improved operational efficiency, consistency in service quality, and reduced dependency on human labor (*CİFCİ & Demirdelen Alrawadieh, 2023*).

However, the integration of service robots into restaurant settings does not occur seamlessly. Customer perceptions of these robots vary significantly across generations, influencing their level of acceptance and willingness to interact with automated services (*Guan, Gong, Li, & Huan, 2022*). Research suggests that Generation Z and Millennials, who have grown up in a digitally integrated environment, tend to have more favourable attitudes toward service robots, whereas older generations such as Baby Boomers and Generation X exhibit greater reluctance, often citing concerns related to trust, ease of use, and loss of human interaction in service experiences (*Kim, Park, & Jeon, 2021; Shah, Kautish, & Mehmood, 2023*). The Technology Acceptance Model (TAM) provides a useful framework for understanding these differences, as it emphasises perceived usefulness, ease of use, and trust as key factors influencing the adoption of technology in service industries (*Ma, Chen, Ren, Fan, & Ongsakul, 2023*).

While several studies have examined technology adoption in hospitality (*Seo & Lee, 2021; Ivanov & Webster, 2021*), there remains a research gap concerning how generational differences shape interactions with service robots in restaurant settings. Understanding these differences is critical for restaurants seeking to optimise service experiences, ensuring that robotic technology is implemented in ways that align with customer expectations across diverse age groups.

2. PURPOSE & THE AIM

The purpose of this study is to analyse how generational differences influence the acceptance and perception of service robots in restaurants. By examining these differences, the study aims to offer helpful guidance on utilising robotic services to meet the needs and preferences of different age groups. By successfully integrating service robots, restaurants will be able to improve both customer experiences and operational efficiency.

3. LITERATURE REVIEW

The incorporation of service robots in the hospitality industry represents a major shift towards automation and artificial intelligence, with the goal of increasing operational efficiency, improving customer service standards, and creating unique dining experiences *(Zhang, X., Balaji, M. S., & Jiang, 2022)*. Establishments can alter traditional restaurant operations by using robots for duties such as order taking, delivering food, and customer engagement. This technical progress is especially important considering the differences in opinions and acceptability levels across different generations.

According to research, there are significant generational differences in technology perceptions and acceptance *(Guan, X., Gong, J., Li, M., & Huan, T.-C, 2022)*. Generation Z, which is known for its strong preference for technological integration in daily life, sees service robots as a way to improve dining experiences through efficiency, novelty, and digital engagement. Older generations, like Baby Boomers and Gen X, may display more hesitations, emphasising perceived effectiveness, simplicity of use, and concerns about privacy and the loss of personal touch in service interactions (Guan et al., 2022).

Specific research on Gen Z's interactions with service robots highlights their generally positive attitude towards the technology, emphasising the importance of service robot appearance, functioning, and the matching role of human service (Zhu, 2022). Furthermore, research across a broader demographic range demonstrates diverse public preferences for restaurant robot services, demonstrating extensive acceptance of jobs like food and drink delivery, order taking, and cleaning tables (Guan et al., 2022). However, questions remain about robots' ability to handle unique requests and assess visitor preference, which might have an influence on the personalised touch that is so important in the hospitality sector.

Integrating the Technology Acceptance Model (TAM) with variables such as trust, perceived risk, and satisfaction yields more information on consumer behaviour towards robot services in restaurants. Trust in technology is critical in determining the perceived utility and simplicity of use of service robots, but risk perceptions linked with robot services can have a substantial impact on customer happiness and willingness to return to robot-equipped restaurants.

3.1. BACKGROUND

3.1.1 Overview of Servicescape Theory

Servicescape theory emphasises the physical surroundings in which service interactions happen and how these settings influence customer behaviour and experiences. This is a key notion in the study of service settings. When it comes to service robots in restaurants, services-cape' refers to both the general environment that these robotic creatures contribute to and their look and functionality. The inclusion of robots into the restaurant environment not only enhances operational efficiency but also changes guests' entire eating experience, which may affect their degree of satisfaction and likelihood to return *(Zhu, 2022)*.

3.1.2 Expectancy Theory in Technology Acceptance

Expectancy theory proposes that individuals are driven to act depending on the expected outcomes of their activities, which gives useful information regarding how technology is adopted. When it comes to adopting new technologies, theory shows that perceived utility and simplicity of use are crucial variables in an individual's decision-making process. Customers are more prone to adopting service robot advancements if they trust the robots will improve their eating experience by simplifying various jobs and providing consistent, efficient service. *(Ma C., Chen P.-J., Ren L., Fan A., & Ongsakul V. 2023)*

3.1.3 Role of Trust in Technology Adoption

It is obvious that trust is important for the successful adoption of new technology. Trust requires belief in a technology's reliability, security, and efficiency. Customer trust in service robots in restaurants can have a big influence on their acceptance and general pleasure. A high degree of trust will lessen concerns about the robots' operation and safety, encouraging customers to interact with them and enjoy the increased level of service they provide *(Shah, T. R., Kautish, P., & Mehmood, K., 2023)*.

Research Question

This conceptual paper aims to study the following research question:
- How do generational differences influence experiences with service robots in restaurants, and what are the respective levels of technology acceptance among different age groups?

3.2 RESEARCH GAP

Despite substantial study on technological adoption, the precise impact of age variations on the acceptance of service robots in restaurants has not been completely explored. This research aims to address this information gap by analysing how different generations perceive and respond to the incorporation of service robots in the dining areas. The extensive research of the study tries to explain the various ways in which generational opinions influence attitudes towards and interactions with technological advancements.

4. METHODOLOGY

This study uses a quantitative research design with a structured survey to examine generational differences in the acceptance and experience of service robots in restaurants. The research was conducted in two dining establishments in Salzburg, Austria: **Hotel Hofwirt Salzburg** (*a traditional restaurant without service robots*) and **Yaoyao Restaurant** (*a restaurant utilising service robots*). These locations were strategically selected to contrast customer experiences in settings with and without service robots, providing a comparative basis for analysing generational attitudes toward robotic service integration. While the sample is geographically limited, Salzburg is a major European tourism hub, making it a suitable setting to explore hospitality technology trends.

Survey Design and Data Collection

The survey was designed based on key concepts from the **Technology Acceptance Model** (TAM) (Davis, 1989) and related frameworks on trust, perceived usefulness, and ease of use (*Ma et al., 2023; Kim et al., 2021*). The questionnaire covered 6 major themes:

1. **Demography** – Age, gender, and dining frequency.

2. **Technology Familiarity and Attitudes** – Participants' general attitudes toward technology and prior exposure to service robots.

3. **Comfort and Acceptance of Service Robots** – Measured using a 5-point Likert scale (1 = Not comfortable, 5 = Very comfortable).

4. **Perceived Service Quality and Satisfaction** – Evaluation of the efficiency, accuracy, and reliability of robot service.

5. **Comparison to Human Service** – Preferences between robotic and human interactions in a restaurant setting.

6. **Future Intentions** – Likelihood of dining at a restaurant with service robots in the future.

The survey was done with 100 participants (30 from Yaoyao Restaurant & 70 from Hotel Hofwirt Salzburg), ensuring a mix of Gen Z, Millennials, Gen X, and Baby Boomers. The sample was chosen using convenience sampling with a goal of ensuring generational diversity. While convenience sampling limits generalisability, efforts were made to capture a broad representation of age groups.

5. FINDINGS

To understand age group differences with service robots in restaurants and their respective levels of technology, the research was conducted in two dining areas: **Hotel Hofwirt Salzburg** (without service robots) and **Yaoyao Restaurant** (with service robots), both located in Salzburg City, Austria. 70 participants from Hotel Hofwirt Salzburg and 30 participants from Yaoyao Restaurant participated in this study (all in all 100 participants). Below are questions that have been asked in the research and the hypotheses as well as the interpretations:

Q_1: How comfortable did you feel interacting with the service robots in restaurants? (1 = not comfortable, 5 = very comfortable)
H_1: Generational differences significantly influence perceived comfort levels with service robots, with younger generations (Gen Z and Millennials) showing higher acceptance compared to older generations (Gen X and Baby Boomers).

Graph 1

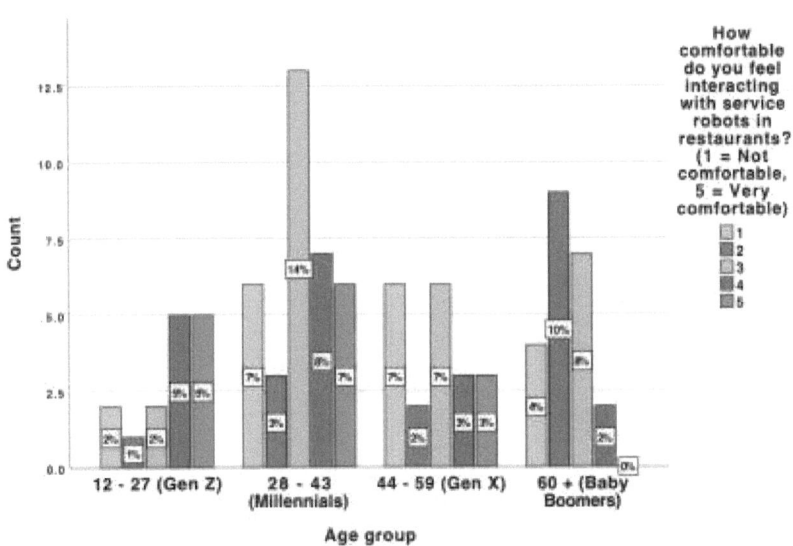

Interpretation of the results on graph 1:

Generational differences significantly influence comfort levels with service robots, with Millennials showing the highest acceptance due to their familiarity with technology. Baby boomers, in contrast, display the most discomfort, likely due to limited trust or familiarity. Gen Z moderately accepts robots, while Gen Z adopts a cautious, balanced view. These trends confirm that younger generations (Gen Z and Millennials) are more accepting of service robots than older ones (Gen X and Baby Boomers), reinforcing Hypothesis 1.

Q2: What is your general perception of service robots in restaurants, whether or not you have experienced them?

H2: Baby boomers are more likely to hold negative perceptions of service robots in restaurants compared to young generations.

Graph 2

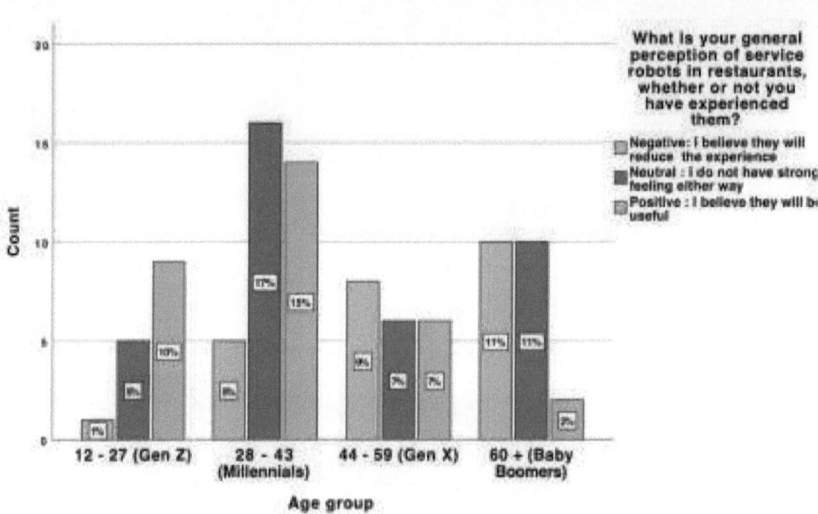

Interpretation of the results on graph 2:

Baby boomers show the lowest comfort and acceptance of service robots with more negative or neutral attitudes compared to younger generations, reinforcing hypothesis 2. In contrast, Gen Z and Millennials show more positive perceptions, highlighting their openness to technology integration.

Q3: How often do you eat in restaurants with service robots?

H₃: Younger generations (Gen Z and Millennials) are more likely to dine at restaurants with service robots than older generations (Gen X and Baby Boomers).

Interpretation (*Graph in the annex*)

Millennials interact with service robots the most, probably as a result of their increased exposure to and acceptance of technology. Despite being younger, Gen Z might not interact as much because there are fewer opportunities for independent dining. Older generations like Gen X and Baby Boomers, on the other hand, are less likely to go to these kinds of restaurants, probably because they don't like technology or have different preferences.

Q₄: Would you consider dining in a Restaurant that uses service robots in the Future?

H₄: Baby Boomers are less likely to consider dining in a restaurant that uses service robots in the future compared to younger generations.

Interpretation (*Graph in the annex*)

Compared to younger generations, Baby Boomers are less likely to consider dining at restaurants with service robots, according to the data. Baby Boomers' resistance reflects doubt and a lower acceptance of technology, whereas millennials show the highest levels of openness because they are more accustomed to it.

Q₅: Do you feel service robots enhances or undercuts the dining experience?

H₅: Millennials are more likely to perceive that service robots enhance the dining experience compared to other generational groups.

Interpretation (*Graph in the annex*)

The data confirms the hypothesis that Millennials are more likely to perceive service robots as enhancing the dining experience. Their greater familiarity with and acceptance of technology likely drives this positive perception. In contrast, older generations, particularly Baby Boomers, show more hesitancy due to lower technology acceptance, suggesting the need for efforts to improve their perceptions.

Q$_6$: How important do you think is the human interaction in your dining experience?

H$_6$ Baby Boomers place higher importance on human interaction in their dining experience compared to younger generations.

Interpretation (*Graph in the annex*)

The data supports the hypothesis that Baby Boomers place higher importance on human interaction in dining compared to younger generations. While Millennials also value it highly, Gen Z shows more variability, likely due to greater exposure to automated dining. Gen X values it moderately. Restaurants should maintain some human interaction to meet Baby Boomers' preferences.

The Key Takeaways from the Results:

1. **Generational Comfort Gaps:** Younger generations (Millennials & Gen Z) are significantly more comfortable with service robots than older groups (Gen X & Baby Boomers).

2. **Experience Drives Perception:** Guests who have interacted with service robots (Yaoyao diners) hold more favourable views than those who have not.

3. **Millennials Are Key Adopters:** Millennials are the most frequent users of robotic restaurant services and most likely to return.

4. **Human Interaction Still Matters:** Older generations (Gen X & Baby Boomers) value human interaction more, which may hinder widespread adoption of service robots.

6. LIMITATIONS

While this study provides valuable insights into generational differences in service robot acceptance, several limitations should be acknowledged. Firstly, the **geographically restricted sample** limits the generalisability of the findings. The study was conducted in two restaurants in **Salzburg, Austria**, which may not fully capture broader generational attitudes toward service robots in different cultural and regional contexts. Future research should expand to **multiple locations across diverse hospitality settings**, including countries with varying levels of technological adoption and digital familiarity, to assess whether these findings hold across different markets.

Secondly, the study **relies solely on quantitative data**, which, while effective for statistical analysis, lacks the depth needed to understand the **underlying motivations, concerns, and expectations** behind customer attitudes. Future research could incorporate **qualitative methods** such as in-depth interviews or focus groups to explore **why** certain generations are more hesitant toward service robots and how **personal experiences shape their perceptions**.

Additionally, the study does not differentiate between **restaurant types and meal experiences**, which could play a crucial role in shaping customer attitudes. For instance, **fine dining establishments may face more resistance to automation** due to expectations of high-touch, personalised service, while **fast-casual or quick-service restaurants** may see higher acceptance due to efficiency-driven customer preferences. Future studies should explore **how service robot acceptance varies across different restaurant categories** and meal contexts.

Furthermore, this study does not investigate **specific robotic functions**, which could impact customer perceptions. Service robots can be used for **order taking, food delivery, table clearing, or customer interaction**, and different tasks may elicit **varying levels of acceptance**. Future research should analyse whether customers **prefer robotic assistance for specific tasks** while maintaining human interaction for others, helping restaurants design more effective hybrid service models.

Finally, **longitudinal research is needed** to assess how attitudes toward service robots evolve over time. As technology becomes more advanced and customers become more familiar with robotic services, generational resistance may shift. Future studies should track **changes**

in customer perceptions over extended periods to understand the long-term trajectory of service robot adoption in hospitality.

7. RECOMMENDATIONS

To enhance the service robot integration in restaurants, the following recommendations should be taken into consideration:

- To design user-friendly and approachable robots, provided they do not look more humanlike, which may be scary for some. This may build trust among the customers.
- It is essential to maintain a balance between human and robotic services to satisfy the preferences of diverse demographics.
- Additionally, educating older customers about the functions and benefits of service robots, for example, the employees can ask if they already have some previous knowledge of robot service and guide them accordingly, which can help familiarise them with the technology and improve their overall acceptance and satisfaction.

8. CONCLUSION

This study emphasises generational differences in experiences with service robots in restaurants and respective levels of technology acceptance, giving important details about how they are integrated into the hospitality sector. Younger generations demonstrate the most major levels of acceptance, most likely because of their comfort and familiarity with technology, whereas older generations demonstrate more reluctance and value human interaction over service robots. Given their exposure to both traditional and robotic dining experiences, Gen Z shows variability, which is indicative of their transitional position. Gen X is open to innovations in technology and values human interaction to a moderate level.

These findings emphasise the need for customised strategies when using service robots in restaurants. While maintaining the innovation that younger generations value, combining robotic efficiency with parts of human interaction may be attractive to Baby Boomers' preferences.

Trust-building measures and user-friendly designs can also address reluctances among older generations. This study enhances the growing collection of research on the acceptance of technology in the restaurant/hospitality industry and provides useful information for managers of restaurants trying to find a balance between robotics and personalisation. To further improve approaches, future findings should investigate these dynamics in different cultural and regional contexts.

REFERENCES

Byrd, K., Fan, A., Her, E., Liu, Y., Almanza, B., & Leitch, S. (2021). Robot vs human: Expectations, Performances and Gaps in off-premise Restaurant Service Modes. International Journal of Contemporary Hospitality Management, 33(11), 3996-4016.

Cha, S. S. (2020). Customers' Intention to use Robot-Serviced Restaurants in Korea: Relationship of coolness and MCI factors. International Journal of Contemporary Hospitality Management, 32(9), 2947-2968.

Chen, Y., Xue, T., Tuomi, A., & Wang, Z. (2022). Hotel robots: An Exploratory Study of Generation Z Customers in China. Tourism Review, 77(5), 1262-1275.

CİFCİ, I., & Demirdelen Alrawadieh, D. (2023). Predicting the Future of the Food service Industry: A Robot-Based Economy Perspective. Journal of Tourism, Leisure and Hospitality (Online), 5(1), 22-29.

Choi, Sungwoo ; Liu, Stella Choi, Choongbeom, Marketing letters, 2022, robot–brand fit the influence of brand personality on consumer reactions to service robot adoption, new york: springer us, vol.33 (1), p.129-142

Current issues in tourism, 2021-06. Service robots as a tool for physical distancing in tourism Seyitoğlu, Faruk ; Ivanov, Stanislav, Abingdon: Routledge, Vol.24 (12), p.1631-1634

Fusté-Forné, F. (2021). Robot Chefs in Gastronomy Tourism: What's on the Menu? Tourism Management Perspectives.

Guan, X., Gong, J., Li, M., & Huan, T.-C. (2022). Exploring Key Factors Influencing Customer Behavioural Intention in Robot Restaurants. International Journal of Contemporary Hospitality Management, 34(9), 3482-3501.

Gupta, K.P. and Pande, S. (2023), "Understanding Generation Z Consumers' Revisit Intentions to Robotic Service restaurants", Young Consumers, Vol. 24 No. 3, pp. 331-351.

Ivanov, S., & Webster, C. (2021). Willingness-to-Pay for Robot-Delivered Tourism and Hospitality Services – an Exploratory Study. International Journal of Contemporary Hospitality Management, 33(11), 3926-3955.

Ivanov, S., & Webster, C. (2023). Restaurants and Robots: Public Preferences for Robot Food and Beverage Services. Journal of Tourism Futures, 9(2), 229-239.

Joo, K., Kim, H. M., & Hwang, J. (2023). A Study on the Experience Economy Examining a Robot Service in the Restaurant Industry Based on Demographic Characteristics. Sustainability (Basel, Switzerland), 15(14), 10827.

Kabadayi, S., Ali, F., Choi, H., Joosten, H., & Lu, C. (2019). Applications and Implications of Service Robots in Hospitality. International Journal of Service Industry Management, 30(3), 326-348.

Kim, Y. J., Park, J. S., & Jeon, H. M. (2021). Experiential Value, Satisfaction, Brand Love, and Brand Loyalty Toward Robot Barista Coffee Shop: The Moderating Effect of Generation. Sustainability (Basel, Switzerland), 13(21), 12029.

Kumar, S., Miller, E. G., Mende, M., & Scott, M. L. (2022). Effects of Robot Restaurants' Food Quality, Service Quality, and High-Tech Atmosphere Perception on Customers' Behavioural Intentions. Journal of Hospitality and Tourism Technology, 13(4), 699-714.

Li, Y., Wang, C., & Song, B. (2023). Applications and Implications of Service Robots in Hospitality. Cornell Hospitality Quarterly, 2021-05(5), 35-51.

Ma, C., Chen, P.-J., Ren, L., Fan, A., & Ongsakul, V. (2023). A Projective Approach to Understanding the Generation Z's Experience with Service Robots in Restaurants. Journal of Hospitality and Tourism Technology, 14(5), 717-731.

Ma, C., Chen, P.-J., Ren, L., Fan, A., & Ongsakul, V. (2023). Language Matters: Humanizing Service Robots Through the Use of Language During the COVID-19 Pandemic. Marketing Letters, 33(4), 607-623.

Maar, D., Besson, E., & Kefi, H. (2023). Fostering Positive Customer Attitudes and Usage Intentions for Scheduling Services via Chatbots. International Journal of Service Industry Management, 34(2), 208-230.

Odekerken-Schröder, G., Mennens, K., Steins, M., & Mahr, D. (2022). The Service Triad: An Empirical Study of Service Robots, Customers, and Frontline Employees. International Journal of Service Industry Management, 33(2), 246-292.

Oželienė, D., Jakštienė, D., Baltrūnaitė, D., & Voišnis, J. (2020). Demand for Hospitality Employees in the Context of Technological Advancement and Generational Change: The Case of Lithuania. In Faculty of Tourism and Hospitality Management in Opatija. Biennial International Congress. Tourism & Hospitality Industry (pp. 176-191).

Rauf, A., Zurcher, M., Pantelidis, I. and Winbladh, J. (2022), "Millennials' Perceptions of Artificial Intelligence in Hotel Service Encounters", Consumer Behavior in Tourism and Hospitality, Vol. 17 No. 1, pp. 3-16.

Romero, J., & Lado, N. (2021). Service Robots and COVID-19: Exploring Perceptions of Prevention Efficacy at Hotels in Generation Z. International Journal of Contemporary Hospitality Management, 33(11), 4057-4078.

Seo, K. H., & Lee, J. H. (2021). The Emergence of Service Robots at Restaurants: Integrating Trust, Perceived Risk, and Satisfaction. Sustainability (Basel, Switzerland), 13(8), 4431.

Shah, T. R., Kautish, P., & Mehmood, K. (2023). Influence of Robots' Service Quality on Customers' Acceptance in Restaurants. Asia Pacific Journal of Marketing and Logistics, 35(12), 3117-3137.

Tutunea, M.-F. (2021). Artificial Intelligence in Tourism & Hospitality – The Perception of Tourists and Tourism Companies in Romania. Studia Universitatis Babeş-Bolyai Negotia, 66(2), 41-60.

Yrjölä, M., et al. (2019). A Customer Value Perspective to Service Experiences in Restaurants. Journal of Retailing and Consumer Services.

Zhang, X., Balaji, M. S., & Jiang, Y. (2022). Robots at Your Service: Value Facilitation and Value Co-creation in Restaurants. International Journal of Contemporary Hospitality Management, 34(5), 2004-2025.

Zhu, D. H. (2022). Customer Acceptance of Service Robots Under Different Service Settings. Journal of Service Theory and Practice, 33(1), 46-71.

Zhu, D. H., & Chang, Y. P. (2020). Robot with Humanoid Hands Cooks Food Better? Effect of Robotic Chef Anthropomorphism on Food Quality Prediction. International Journal of Contemporary Hospitality Management, 32(3), 1367-1383.

Annex

Graph 3

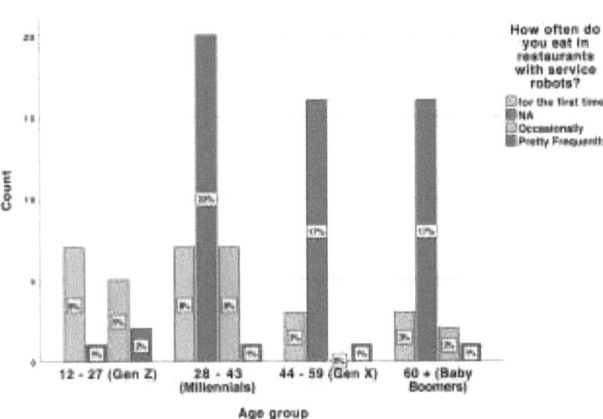

Graph 4

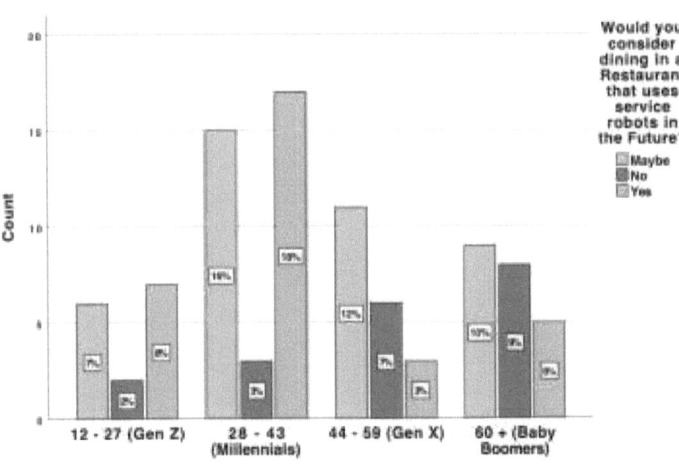

Graph 5

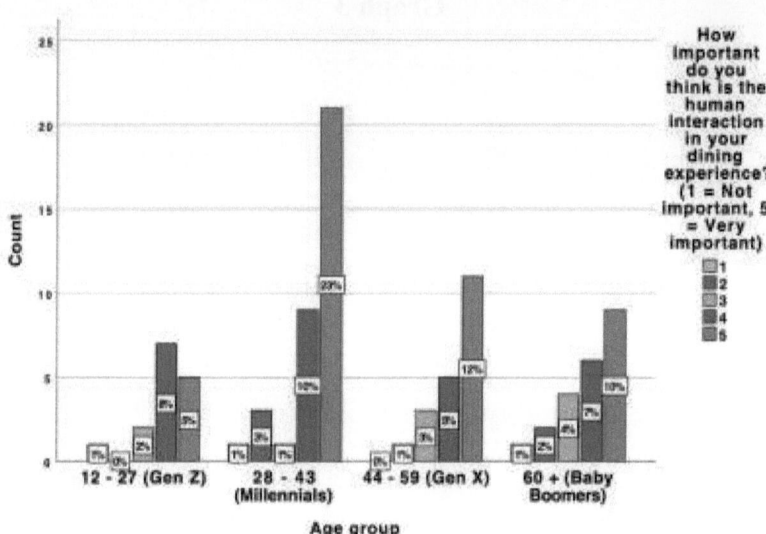

Graph 6

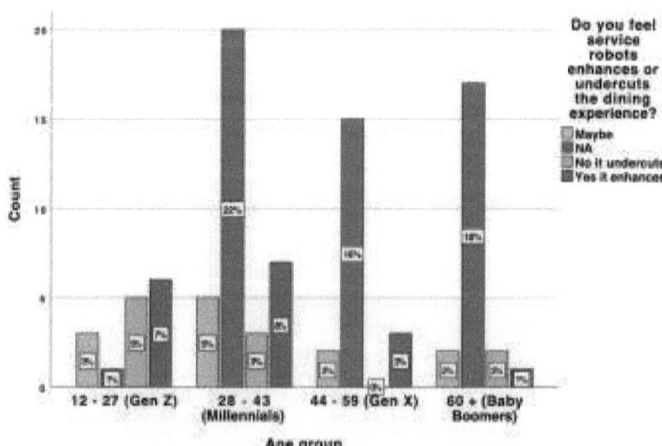